The Pain of Knowledge

Holocaust and
Genocide Issues
in Education

The
Pain
of
Knowledge

Yair Auron
Translated by Ruth Ruzga

Transaction Publishers
New Brunswick (U.S.A.) and London (U.K.)

Translation copyright © 2005 by Transaction Publishers, New Brunswick, New Jersey. Originally published in Hebrew. Copyright © 2003. All rights reserved. Published by arrangement with the original publisher, The Open University of Israel.

All rights reserved under International and Pan-American Copyright Conventions. No part of this book may be reproduced or transmitted in any form or by any means, electronic or mechanical, including photocopy, recording, or any information storage and retrieval system, without prior permission in writing from the publisher. All inquiries should be addressed to Transaction Publishers, Rutgers—The State University, 35 Berrue Circle, Piscataway, New Jersey 08854-8042. www.transactionpub.com

This book is printed on acid-free paper that meets the American National Standard for Permanence of Paper for Printed Library Materials.

Library of Congress Catalog Number: 2004058029
ISBN: 0-7658-0276-7
Printed in the United States of America

Library of Congress Cataloging-in-Publication Data

Auron, Yair.
   [Makh'ov ha-da'at. English]
   The pain of knowledge : Holocaust and genocide issues in education / Yair Auron ; translated by Ruth Ruzga.
      p. cm.
   Includes bibliographical references and index.
   ISBN 0-7658-0276-7 (cloth : alk. paper)
    1. Holocaust, Jewish (1939-1945)—Study and teaching—Israel.
  2. Holocaust, Jewish (1939-1945)—Moral and ethical aspects. 3. Holocaust, Jewish (1939-1945)—Study and teaching. I. Title.

D804.33.A9713 2005
940.53'18'07105694—dc22
                                                2004058029

"[T]he entire history of the brief "millennial Reich" can be reread as a war against memory, an Orwellian falsification of memory, falsification of reality, negation of reality."—Primo Levi, "The Memory of the Offense," *The Drowned and the Saved*

"Verses for Memorial Day, a psalm of remembering for the war dead. The generation of memory-veterans is dying out. Half at a ripe old age, half at a rotten old age. And who will remember the rememberers?"—Yehuda Amichai, "And Who Will Remember the Rememberers?" *Open Closed Open—Poems*

Contents

Preface to the English Edition — ix
Acknowledgments — x
Introduction — xi

1. On the Construction of Memory — 1
2. Philosophical Reflections on the Holocaust — 7
3. Constructing the Memory of the Holocaust in Israel — 13
4. The Teaching of the Holocaust in Israel: Historical Processes — 31
5. On Teaching the Holocaust: Didactic Aspects — 41
6. Learning Programs in Israel — 51
7. Holocaust Martyrs' and Heroes' Remembrance Day — 59
8. Journeys of Youth to Poland — 65
9. About the Attitudes of Israeli Adolescents towards the Holocaust — 73
10. About the Attitudes of Israeli Arabs towards the Holocaust — 79
11. To Remember or to Forget? — 85
12. On the Teaching of the Holocaust Around the World — 91
13. On the Teaching of Genocide — 153

Afterword — 173
Bibliography — 175
Index — 183

Preface to the English Edition

The Pain of Knowledge: Holocaust and Genocide Issues in Education appeared in Hebrew as part of the study materials for a course offered by the Open University of Israel within the framework of studies for a master's degree in democracy studies. Due to the special importance and relevance of this topic, and because of its universal interest, the Open University published it as a separate book, in Hebrew. For the same reasons, it now appears in English and Russian as well, and is being translated into German.

The book deals with a broad range of sensitive issues—some of them controversial in both Israeli and world society and academia—that in our opinion have as yet not been given the in-depth attention they deserve. We hope that this book will arouse in its readers both questions and thoughts that we sometimes refrain from dealing with even amongst ourselves.

To make the English version of the book more accessible to readers who may not be familiar with the minutiae of Israeli society and the issues with which it and its education system are concerned, minor changes have been made and some explanations added. In addition, the English version of many of the books referred to originally in their Hebrew form or translation replace the Hebrew references.

I want to thank Professor Benny Neuberger, Professor David Zissenvine, Dr. Ilan Gur-Ze'ev, and Dr. Ariel Hurwitz, who read early versions of the manuscript, for their comments and suggestions.

Many thanks also to the staff of the Open University of Israel who were so helpful in the preparation of the book, and especially to its Hebrew editor Ruth Ramot, who contributed to the character and the quality of the book. Ruth Ruzga translated the Hebrew version of the book into English with great dedication and competence.

Yair Auron
Tel Aviv
February 2005

Acknowledgments

Grateful acknowledgment is made for permission to reprint the following copyright material:

Cover photograph: Anselm Kiefer, Bruch der Gefässe (Breaking the Vessels), 1990. By kind permission of the artist.

Pages v, 2-3, 59: Excerpts, "And Who Will Remember the Rememberers?" from *Open Closed Open—Poems*, copyright © 2000 by Yehuda Amichai, English translation copyright © 2000 by Chana Bloch and Chana Kronfeld. Reprinted by permission of Harcourt, Inc.

Page 8: From Yosef Gorny, *Between Auschwitz and Jerusalem* (London and Portland: Vallentine Mitchell, 2003). By kind permission of the publisher.

Pages 51-53: From Yisrael Gutman and Haim Schatzker, *The Holocaust and its Significance: Teacher's Guide* (Jerusalem: Zalman Shazar Center, 1983) (Hebrew).

Pages 53-5: A. Carmon. "Teaching the Holocaust as a Means of Fostering Values," *Curriculum Inquiry* 9, 3, 1979, pp. 209-228. By permission of Blackwell Publishing

Pages 56-7: Iakovos Kambanelis, "Song of Songs," translated from Greek by Gail Holst-Warhaft, poet and translator. She directs the Mediterranean Institute at Cornell University.

Pages 62-3: From Tamar Barkay and Gal Levy, "Holocaust Remembrance Day in Progressive Eyes: Ethnicity, Class and Education in Israel," *Politika* 1, 1999, pp. 27-46 (Hebrew). By kind permission of the Leonard Davis Institute for International Relations.

Pages 66-8: From Jackie Feldman, "Delegations of Israeli Youth to Poland in the Wake of the Holocaust and their Object," *Yalkut Moreshet* 66, 1998 (Hebrew). All rights reserved to Moreshet Publishing. For further details see J. Feldman, *Above the Death Pits, Below the Flag* (New York: Berghahn Press, forthcoming).

Pages 87-8: Yehuda Elkana, "On the Right to Forget," *Haaretz*, March 2, 1988. By kind permission of the author.

Pages 88-9: Boaz Evron, "Education towards Fascism and Escape," *Yediot Ahronoth*, March 4, 1988. By kind permission of the publisher.

Page 90: Yisrael Eldad, "The so-called Forgetting of the Holocaust," *Haaretz*, April 14, 1988. By kind permission of Professor Arie Eldad.

Pages 94-99: From *Le Débat* 96, September-October, 1997. By kind permission of Editions Gallimard.

Pages 124-8: Courtesy of the United States Holocaust Memorial Museum, Washington, D.C.

Pages 145-50 (tables): From *Knowledge and Remembrance of the Holocaust in Different Countries* (New York: American Jewish Committee, September 1999). By kind permission of the American Jewish Committee.

We have endeavored to trace the copyright owners of all the external material. We sincerely apologize for any omission or error and, upon notification, will be pleased to rectify it in future editions.

Introduction:
"...and he that increases knowledge increases pain..." (Ecclesiastes 1:18)

Violation of the rights of a human being and indifference in the face of suffering jeopardize the very existence of human society. The Holocaust is almost certainly the most extreme case of such a violation, and thus the greatest moral failure mankind has known. Contending with the general as well as the specifically Jewish aspects of this subject may contribute to an understanding of the importance of humanistic and democratic values, and may also be helpful in the construction of tools for making moral judgments.

Different peoples, as well as ideological streams and movements, try to retain historical events, especially the most central ones, in their collective memories, and to derive from them various different lessons. Such is also the subject of this book, which deals with moral lessons rather than the historical events, and with how to use these events as learning material for teaching the Holocaust and for teaching genocide (terms that, along with others, will be defined below). Put differently, our purpose in this book is to describe how the moral messages of the Holocaust can be transmitted to future generations, to those living in the world in which horrific acts of genocide were carried out in the past, and are still being carried out to this day.

Thus, as noted above, this book focuses on the ethical issues the subject engenders, and the lessons that can be derived from it. The first question to be asked, therefore, is whether it is possible at all to speak of any one "lesson" of the Holocaust. The answer to this question is clear: There is no one and only "lesson" of the Holocaust; there are, rather, various different lessons, implications, messages and interpretations. Different people and groups in Israeli society, in the Jewish world, and in the international community are divided on these matters. The Jewish public, as a group, deals with them also in connection with the link between the Holocaust and the definition of its national identity, about which there is no general agreement.

It appears, in any case, that three major categories of lessons can be delineated. Two of these are "particularistic"; the third is "universal":

- "Zionist lessons"—as they pertain to Israel and Zionism.
- "Jewish lessons"—as they pertain to Jewish existence in general, not only to Israel.
- "Universal lessons"—as they pertain to human societies in general, and not to the Jewish, Israeli, or Zionist reality alone.

In relating to this division of categories, the many socialization factors that affect the processes connected with the formation of individual and collective attitudes, in different ways and to different extents, must be taken into account. In every discussion connected with these aspects, various different elements must be considered, such as the family unit, peer group, close and distant social circles, the education system and its various components, the diverse media (whose power have been expanding greatly in the last few decades), and so on.

In extracting the lessons from an historical event the question that naturally arises is that of the differences between historical research, historical memory, historical consciousness, and historical truth, and the relationships between them. Historical research, using the accepted tools and methodology of the discipline, provides a critical analysis of the past that attempts to explain the characteristics of the historical events and processes, their roots, the causal relationships between them, and the called-for conclusions. As a discipline, history needs both a critical distance from the topic being studied and rational explanations. Borrowing an adage from another field it is possible to say that historical research is "sworn to [discover] the truth, the whole truth, and nothing but the truth," although it is undoubtedly impossible to fulfill that ideal objective. "History," says Pierre Nora, ". . . is the reconstruction, always problematic and incomplete, of what is no longer."[1] The knowledge provided by historical research is also used (or is supposed to be used) for teaching history, whose purpose is to formulate historical memory and historical consciousness.

These two concepts—memory and consciousness—are related to each other, but it is important to keep in mind the difference between them, because we are not always aware of what we remember. Thus, while one's historical consciousness may be created out of historical memory, historical memory may not be created out of historical consciousness. Historical, or collective, memory, unlike historical consciousness, may to a large extent be guided and even formed, depending in many ways on what the society wants to know of the historical truth—and what it is capable of comprehending of this truth. Put differently, the collective historical memory is dependent on what the society chooses to remember and what it chooses to forget. A society or a state may give form to its historical memory in such ways as, for example, memorial days and ceremonies, but the goals of such forms are, obviously and naturally, different from those of historical research and study, and may even be antithetically different. It has even been claimed that the planned objective of various collective memorial ceremonies is to envelop the collective's sorrow and suffering in a shared sense of warmth through a metaphysical experience that is somewhat removed in time, and to thus create a relieving catharsis. The collective may thus be better able to deal with some poorly defined and completely inexplicable "hand of fate," before which the individual human being and society as a whole stand helpless.

This basic perception underlies the arguments of those who are critical of the intentional nurturing of the culture of collective remembering, and of those who negate it completely for other reasons. They claim that the nurturing of memory through annually repeated rituals, or by erecting memorial sites such as museums and monuments, is intended to mythologize the past and, thus, replace religion. The intention of the state, according to these critics, is to invent new rituals and ceremonies for a society that has lost or given up its old ones, to bestow a new identity on a society that has repudiated its old one, and, in many cases, to legitimize the ideologies that serve the needs of the state, such as Zionism in the Israeli case.

The scholars and teachers of history are supposedly the ones who formulate the collective historical consciousness, and there is, undoubtedly, a reciprocal relationship between the teaching and the research of this and any other specific subject. Thus, the comprehensive research of the Holocaust during the past several decades has undoubtedly affected the ways in which it is taught, and we can assume that the extensive study of this topic, in Israel and throughout the world, influences and will continue to influence Holocaust research.

In addition to the dialectic between the research and the teaching of the Holocaust (in Israel and elsewhere), there is also a continually growing tension in the process of the formulation of the memory of the Holocaust between the competing "agents of memory": the education systems, literary and artistic creations, myths (which include ceremonies, symbols, and monuments), the media, various propaganda methods, institutions representing the different trends of the society or the subgroups within them, and so on. Many of these agents of memory use the past, at times, for their own purposes, manipulating and even creating memories as the means for setting the national—and even the world—agenda, and to serve different ideological and political interests and opposing causes.

Be that as it may, it is clear that in the world and especially in Israel a central component of the messages related to genocidal events, and in particular to the Holocaust, is transmitted to society through its education systems. By their very nature these systems are characterized by their conscious intention of influencing the subjects that constitute their target audience, over whose consciousness they have considerable influence, depending on the time, the situation, and the place. The power wielded by the education system is expressed through laws, rulings, and teaching programs, but the educational messages are also transmitted to the pupils in their schools through what is ostensibly neutral factual information in lessons scheduled for that purpose within the framework of the curriculum, as well as in civics lessons and informal school-related activities. For example, schools in Israel hold Holocaust Martyrs' and Heroes' Remembrance Day ceremonies and, since the late 1980s, organized visits of high school students to death camps in Poland. The term "teaching of the Holocaust and of genocide" thus refers not only to textbooks on that subject, or to the official learning programs. Moreover, the teaching of these subjects is always affected, at any given time, both in Israel and elsewhere in the world, by the vast range of local and world political, ideological, economic, and social factors. The end of the Cold War, for example, almost surely led to greater openness in various countries and made it easier for them to contend with issues connected to the Holocaust and to the question of their own involvement in it, for as long as the Cold War continued, all of the countries, on both sides of the conflict, were taken up in their own struggles.

One of the main questions that concerns us in this book centers on which of the gamut of issues connected with the Holocaust and other genocides, and of the remorse and distress that these events awaken, should be raised, discussed, and studied in the Israeli education system, and what significance and which moral lessons should be emphasized. We also address these same questions—although to a much lesser degree—to the education systems in other countries in the world, of which very little is known in Israel. Exposing Israeli students to this information can not only broaden their own general worldview; it can also help them to understand the ways in which Israeli society can cope with the Holocaust itself, and with how to teach it.

The main difficulty in teaching about the Holocaust led to this subject being taught in Israel, until recently, only within the framework of Jewish history and not as part of general history. This categorization itself has significant implications for the entire field of education. Only in the past few years (since 1999) has the Holocaust, like other topics in Jewish history, been taught as part of a program that integrates general and Jewish history.

In some parts of the world—and to a lesser degree in Israel—the Holocaust is now studied within the framework of such disciplines as literature, art, cinema, philosophy, or even foreign languages. But, as noted above, the teaching of the Holocaust and of genocide—in the broadest meaning of the term "teaching"—is realized through many factors, other than the official educational ones, which thus become educational agents in practice if not in name. For example, four well-received films produced and screened in the past couple of decades have served such a purpose: *Shoah* (Claude Lanzmann, 1985), *Schindler's List* (Steven Spielberg, 1993), *Life Is Beautiful* (Roberto Benigni, 1997), and *The Pianist* (Roman Polanski, 2002). These films were seen by many millions of people, including adolescents and young adults, in Israel and all over the world and, along with other artistic creations of different types, have influenced, and continue to influence, their audiences in various ways. All of these creations are what the American Jewish historian Yosef Hayim Yerushalmi (who we shall quote more broadly below) refers to as part of the "crucible" that shapes the image of the Holocaust.[2] To these must be added the monuments and museums dedicated to this subject, of which the United States Holocaust Memorial Museum in Washington D.C. is one of the most prominent examples. This museum clearly has far-reaching educational influence on its millions of visitors, and above and beyond that through the activities it initiates both directly and indirectly. In an entirely different way the controversy surrounding the erection of a central monument in memory of the victims of the Holocaust in Berlin has exerted great educational influence. The arguments surrounding this memorial site and about how the memory of the Holocaust should be marked in Germany did not end even with the decision of the Bundestag, the German parliament, in June 1999 that adopted the plan for a complex devoted only to the Jewish victims of the Nazi rule, to be built on a site next to the Brandenburg Gate. The complex will include an historical documentation center surrounded by an "area," the size of a football field, on which 2,700 gravestone-like columns will be placed. The storm that arose around the question of whether the memorial should represent all of the victims of Nazism, or only the Jewish ones (as voted on by the Bundestag), did not end after the decision, and in its wake a suggestion was made to establish a watch-dog institute to deal with the prevention of genocide.

The questions that citizens of different countries in the world, and especially those of present-day Germany, the "murderers' heirs," must contend with are very different from those that we, the "the victims heirs," have to face. We must nonetheless ask ourselves whether or not we, too, must contend with and discuss some of those questions. These issues are of course far from simple, and they arise again and again in both historical research and in the field of education. Yerushalmi claims that:

> . . . although Judaism throughout the ages was absorbed with the meaning of history, historiography itself played at best an ancillary role among the Jews, and often no role at all; and, concomitantly, that while memory of the past was always a central component of Jewish experience, the historian was not its primary custodian.[3]

The beginning of the modern era saw the rapid development of secular-Jewish historiography, which led to increased Jewish historical research, and following that, the teaching of history: "[T]he Jews of the diaspora, bound in daily devotion to the rituals of tradition, who as 'peoples of memory' found little use for historians until their forced exposure to the modern world," wrote Pierre Nora.[4]

By the beginning of the 1980s the study of the Holocaust had already become, according to Yerushalmi, the main impetus for the development of more extensive historical research than any other event in Jewish history:

> The Holocaust has already engendered more historical research than any single event in Jewish history, but I have no doubt whatever that its image is being shaped, not at the historian's anvil, but in the novelist's crucible. Much has changed since the sixteenth century; one thing, curiously, remains. Now, as then, it would appear than even where Jews do not reject history out of hand, they are not prepared to confront it directly, but seem to await a new, metahistorical myth, for which the novel provides at least a temporary modern surrogate.[5]

"The choice for Jews as for non-Jews," according to Yerushalmi, "is not whether to have a past, but rather—what kind of past shall one have."[6] After the Holocaust the Jewish people were poised at a fork in the road, one not much different from that of the generations that followed the Spanish Expulsion in 1492. The generation of the expulsion favored myth over history; the question today is which of these the present generation will choose. Be that as it may, there is in any case a considerable amount of reciprocal give-and-take between the myth and the memory. The questions of what will happen in the future to the Jewish (and the universal) history of the Holocaust, and what will happen to its Jewish (and its universal) memory are still open.

In this matter the education system has a two-fold role that, as suggested above, is liable to generate tension, and sometimes even contradiction and dissension. On the one hand this system is responsible for the teaching itself, which is supposed to be carried out according to objective criteria and in line with rational learning processes. On the other hand this same system is also the one that fills a central role in directing and organizing the commemoration of remembrance days, including memorial ceremonies, as well as for forging the content of the collective memory, with all of the emotional aspects this encompasses. The result is that the schools are using two different languages: "the language of the memory" and "the language of the classroom." By their very nature memory and commemoration emphasize the totality of the event and, in doing so, blur the meaning of time and obscure the details. The "language of the memory" creates an emotional connection with the subject that encourages overall identification with the loss, and a feeling of sharing in it. The "language of the classroom," on the other hand, is structured on exactly those elements that are either blurred or even not dealt with at all in the "language of memory"; the language of the classroom asks the "small questions," while the language of the memory seeks to provide the "large answers." The schools are thus enjoined to teach the Holocaust cognitively and to commemorate its memory emotively. It is eminently clear that the bodies involved in this have to take into consideration that an uncontrolled combination of the two, as well as of the didactic methods used to achieve them, may undermine the success of both.

Beyond the distinctive factors that affect the ways in which each country and each society deals with the Holocaust and with how it is taught, there are others that are common, in whole or in part, to all of them, and affect them in similar ways. For example, there were countries that found it difficult to deal with and to teach about the Holocaust, at least during the first twenty-five years following it. It appears that the Eichmann trial, which was held in Israel in 1961, had a strong affect on all of them, bringing them to deal with memories of the Holocaust. In some countries this led to refraining, even after the trial ended, from facing the sensitive and complex questions that the trial brought to the fore concerning the guilt of the German people, collaboration in the murder of Jews of countries that fell under German rule, indifference in the face of such acts, the failure of non-Jewish citizens to try to save their Jewish neighbors, the limited efforts of the world in general to save Jews, and other similar issues.

In the time that has passed since the Holocaust, the conditions for dealing with the past have undoubtedly become more "comfortable" and, perhaps, less painful. The influence of the generation that was active during the Second World War lessened and continues to lessen, and those that had no part in the war became more and more dominant. Nonetheless, it is clear that dealing with the subject of the Holocaust is, in any place and at any time, a painful and traumatic experience, as well as a complex and tension-filled one. And there is no doubt that one of the significant factors that affects the way each country and society confronts the subject is its attitude towards the Jews, not only during the Holocaust, but before it as well.

Thus, for example, following the war both France and in Holland fostered myths about their widespread opposition to the Nazi conquest, the "Resistance." Holland has claimed, ever since the end of the war, that it had made great efforts to help the Jews. These myths began to be undermined in the 1970s, and the question of the fate of the Jews who lived in Holland during the war became a significant element in the Dutch people's new perception of their history. In France, on the other hand, the myth of widespread opposition to the conquest was broadly accepted almost to the end of the twentieth century (although this diminished somewhat during the last decades of the century). The issue of the direct responsibility of the French for the fate of its Jews, including the phenomenon of collaboration with the Nazi conquerors, which began to appear on the public agenda during the seventies, reached a (painful) confrontation with the reality only during the nineties.

Another example, unlike that of France and Holland in its character, concerns the difference in the reactions of Great Britain and the United States, which share a close cultural heritage. The two countries were similar in that both refrained from trying to save Jews during the Holocaust: Great Britain did nothing at all, and the United States did very little, and then only from 1944 on. But after the war their reactions to the subject of the Holocaust were very different. In the United States, beginning in the 1970s, a widespread public debate developed. (Some observers believe that one of the factors that led to this debate was the Jewish-Christian dialogue that took place after the war, and that dealt with such sensitive questions as the link between the Holocaust and Christian anti-Semitism. This subject is discussed in chapter 2.) In Great Britain, on the other hand, the reactions to the Holocaust were very minimal prior to the 1990s, and until the 1980s even the Jews of Great Britain dealt with it only to a very limited degree. Even in the second half of the 1990s it was still not clear if, when, and how Great Britain would adopt an official response to the Holocaust, and only in October 1999 did the government do so, with its declaration that it planned to table a law establishing an official memorial day commemorating the Holocaust and the Nazi atrocities, as well as the memories of all victims of genocidal actions throughout the world. Indeed, in 2001, January 27 was designated Holocaust Memorial Day in Great Britain.

To sum up the above description, it can be said that from the 1970s on there has been a growing interest in the Holocaust, along with an increased amount of public debate about it, in many countries of the West, and that from the end of the seventies to the middle of the eighties there was an additional increase of interest in the subject in countries outside the "Iron Curtain." Some of the things that affected this growing interest were the screening of the American television series *Holocaust* and several memorial events that were held in the 1980s to mark forty years since the Holocaust. During those years the subject became increasingly important in literature and the cinema, in scholarly research and, to a lesser degree, in the education systems of several countries. The governments of these, and other, countries have also recognized the importance of raising and dealing with the questions inherent in the Holocaust.

In the countries of Eastern Europe significant changes in attitudes to the Holocaust occurred only after the fall of the Communist bloc, at the end of the eighties and the beginning of the nineties. Before that their approach was dictated by the Soviet position, which universalized the Holocaust by turning it into part of its communist ideology: the destruction of the Jews was viewed as part and parcel of the fascist, racial murder of millions of Eastern Europe's citizens. And since fascism was perceived to be the final stage of capitalism, it was capitalism that was presented as the seed from which this mass murder sprang. It thus followed that there was neither any difference nor anything special about the murder of the Jews by the Nazis and the murder of any other peoples or social groups. The governments, the historians, and the masses of the people in these countries thus completely ignored the Holocaust, and it was, of course, completely absent from school textbooks, and rarely appeared even in literary works. Furthermore, since the Holocaust was non-existent in the public consciousness, there was no need to face various sensitive issues, such as the cases of collaboration of local populations in the murder of Jews, which accompanied the subject.

Moreover, the communist ideology considered the areas under East Germany's control to have been territories "conquered" by the Nazis during the Second World War. The East Germans were therefore perceived as victims of the Nazis and were thus not expected to take any responsibility for what had happened to the Jews nor, unlike the West Germans, were any demands made on them to confront the issue of the Holocaust. Some changes in East Germany's attitude to this subject began to appear, however, even before the fall of the Berlin Wall in 1989, possibly because the government wanted to improve its ties with the countries of the West, and among them Israel.

Of the countries discussed above we have chosen to focus on Germany and the United States (and on Great Britain and France to a lesser degree). Germany was chosen because of the special significance of its confrontation with the memory of its Nazi past, including the Holocaust; the United States was chosen because of the enormous influence that the processes occurring there have on the entire world.

The chapter in which Germany and the United States are dealt with is based mainly on the book *The World Reacts to the Holocaust*, edited by David S. Wyman and published by Johns Hopkins University Press (Baltimore, 1996), which contains comprehensive background articles that deal with the reactions to the Holocaust of twenty-one countries, and one that deals with that of the United Nations. (The reader desiring to broaden his or her knowledge is advised to peruse these articles, which were written by different researchers, each in his or her particular field of interest. The articles include sections dealing with the history of the Jews before the Holocaust and brief reviews of the period of the Holocaust in each of the countries discussed. Various questions are dealt with, such as the extent of the destruction of a country's Jewry, the degree to which its citizens collaborated with the Nazis, the reactions of the country's Jewish citizens, and the efforts made or not made to save them. Also examined, among other things, are the official and non-official responses of the different governments to the Holocaust, as well as the reactions of the local religious communities, the different voluntary organizations, the education system, the media, science, literature, cinema, and the broad public.) Another source used extensively for the writing of this chapter is *The Treatment of the Holocaust in Textbooks*, edited by Randolph L. Braham,[7] which contains a broad survey of textbooks about the Holocaust in Israel, the United States, and Western Germany.

The comprehensive dimension and comparative perspective that characterizes both of these books can, in our opinion, contribute to a deeper understanding of the broad range of topics with which we shall deal. Another comparative perspective is provided by several comprehensive public surveys probing issues related to knowledge and remembrance of the Holocaust that were carried out in the last few years in different countries, among them a series of public opinion surveys by the American Jewish Committee that explored questions related to public knowledge and remembrance of the Holocaust in various countries.

* * *

The Hebrew version of the present book comprises the first of two parts of the study materials for the Open University of Israel course "The Pain of Knowledge: Holocaust and Genocide Issues in Education." The first chapters of the book deal with theoretical questions connected with the formulation of collective memory, followed by chapters dealing with the teaching of the Holocaust in Israel and in other countries, and, finally, with the teaching of genocide in the world and in Israel. The second part of the course materials is an extensive source book containing a broad range of articles on the subjects dealt with in the course. The articles appear in the same topical order as the chapters of the book and relate to the subject dealt with in the chapter. A list of these articles, in the order in which they appear in the source book, is provided in an appendix at the end of this book.

So much has been written on the broad range of these topics in the last few decades that including even most of them would have resulted in the publication of several very thick volumes. Because of this abundance of material, one of the most difficult problems we faced was to select the texts to be discussed in the present book. The selection of reading material is an issue of utmost importance in the teaching and educational process; the use of other texts is, of course, possible, as are changes in the emphases in the structure of the book and the source materials.

The reader of this book will no doubt notice a certain imbalance in the range of materials discussed in the different sections. The decision about where to expand and where to reduce was the result of considerations about the level of knowledge of the target readership in regard to the different topics. The sections of the book and the source materials, and their order, were determined by the premise that the reader should be allowed to examine the different aspects connected with teaching about the Holocaust and genocide, in Israel and elsewhere in the world, gradually, step-by-step, with each discourse comprising the preparation for the one that follows.

In preparing this book we were guided by the desire to present to the reader the different viewpoints connected with the teaching of this topic in Israel and elsewhere in the world, views that sometimes appear to be completely opposed to each other, and at other times confront and complement each other. Our main interest here is, naturally, the teaching of the Holocaust and matters related to this field of study in Israel (where an especially broad range of literature exists) and elsewhere; readers are well advised to refer to this material, some of which is listed in the bibliography of the present book.[8]

We hope that this book will contribute to the knowledge and understanding of the readers, especially those who are educators and teachers of Holocaust studies, as well as of the large and growing general public that is interested in Holocaust and genocide, and that it will encourage them to examine these issues from the broadest possible perspective.

Notes

1. Pierre Nora, "Between Memory and History: *Les Lieux de Mémoire*" ("Sites of Memory"), *Representations*, 26, Special Issue: Memory and Counter-Memory (Spring 1989), p. 8.
2. Yosef Hayim Yerushalmi, *Zakhor: Jewish History and Jewish Memory* (Seattle and London: University of Washington Press, 1982).
3. Ibid., p. xiv.
4. Nora, "Between Memory and History," p. 8.
5. Yerushalmi, *Zakhor*, p. 98.
6. Ibid., p. 99.
7. Randolph L. Braham (ed.), *The Treatment of the Holocaust in Textbooks* (New York: Boulder Institute for Holocaust Studies of the City University of New York, 1987).
8. For example, the Open University of Israel course *In Days of Holocaust and Reckoning* (Main writers: Dan Michman and Yechiam Weitz), (Tel Aviv: Open University of Israel, 1983) (Hebrew). A course dealing with the phenomenon of genocide, prepared by Yair Auron, will appear shortly.

1

On the Construction of Memory

In the preface of his book *The Drowned and the Saved*, Primo Levi, the Italian Jewish writer who was sent to Auschwitz in 1944, describes how the S.S. soldiers would amuse themselves by cynically taunting the camp inmates, telling them that even if any of them survived their cruelties and abasement no one would believe them if they recounted what had happened in the camps. He adds that almost all of the survivors described, orally or in writing, a constantly recurring dream they had during their internment. Although the details varied from one survivor to another, the essence was identical: They are returning to their homes, and with fervor and relief they tell a person dear to them about the suffering they had endured, but no one will believe them; and not only that—no one will even listen. In the dream's most characteristic, and most typical and cruel version, Levi writes, the interlocutor simply turns around and silently walks away.[1]

Among other things, Levi's description illustrates the significance and importance of the collective memory for the individual and the way it is created, as well as the power with which it can reflect the historical truth (if such a thing is possible at all) or deny it. In the first chapter of the same book, entitled "The Memory of the Offense," Levi discusses the deceptive character of human memory in general:

> The memories which lie within us are not carved in stone; not only do they tend to become erased as the years go by, but often they change or even grow, by incorporating extraneous features. Judges know this very well: almost never do two eyewitnesses of the same event describe it in the same way and with the same words, even if the event is recent, and if neither of them has a personal interest in distorting it.[2]

2   The Pain of Knowledge

In terms of the ability of memory to distort (willfully or unintentionally), there are few differences between personal and collective memory. However, while a personal memory may mislead one individual and his surroundings, the collective memory may lead astray entire societies, states, and cultures—and in extreme cases it may do this in a particular, and sometimes harmful, direction. There are situations in which "leading astray" does not literally mean just that but, rather, the reconfiguration of a narrative on the basis of collective associations. Thus, for example, in the collective memory of Israeli society an almost automatic link has been formed between the memory of the national rebirth and the memory of the Holocaust.

Another example, one of many, is Yehuda Amichai's poem "And Who Will Remember the Rememberers?" four of whose stanzas are presented here to illustrate this point.[3] The poet, reflecting on the memory of Israel's War of Independence, intentionally brings in the memory of the Holocaust, including "Seeking roots in the Warsaw cemetery." (Amichai also asks questions about the essence of the nation's "rebirth" and about what it has left in our collective memory).[4]

2

How does a monument come into being? A car goes up in a red blaze
   at Sha'ar HaGay. A car burnt black. The skeleton of a car.
And next to it, the skeleton of some other car, charred in a traffic accident
   on some other road. The skeletons are painted with anti-rust paint, red
   like the red of that flame. Near one skeleton, a wreath of flowers,
   now dry. From dry flowers you make a memorial wreath,
   and from dry bones, a vision of resurrected bones.
And somewhere else, far away, hidden among the bushes,
   a cracked marble plaque with names on it. An oleander branch,
   like a shock of hair on a beloved face, hides most of them.
But once a year the branch is cut back and the names are read,
   while up above, a flag at half-mast waves as cheerfully,
   as a flag at the top of the flagpole, light and easy,
   happy with its colors and breezes.
And who will remember the rememberers?

7

And who will remember? And what do you do to preserve memory?
How do you preserve anything in this world?

You preserve it with salt and with sugar, high heat and deep freeze,
> vacuum sealers, dehydrators, mummifiers.
But the best way to preserve memory is to conserve it inside forgetting
> so not even a single act of remembering will seep in
> and disturb memory's eternal rest.

8

Seeking roots in the Warsaw cemetery.
Here it is the roots that are seeking. They burst
> from the ground, overturn gravestones,
> and clasp the broken fragments in search
> of names and dates, in search
> of what was and will never be again.
The roots are seeking their trees that were burned to the ground.

9

Forgotten, remembered, forgotten
Open, closed, open.

The theoretical literature dealing with collective memory attempts to explain the problematic connections between "memory" and "history." The question of what societies—and among them national societies—remember, and how they transmit this memory to later generations, became a research topic in the second decade of the twentieth century. The work of the French scholar Maurice Halbwachs, still considered an important breakthrough in the study of collective memory, contributed greatly in this research. Halbwachs's basic postulation was that each group develops a picture of its past by highlighting its unique identity in comparison with that of other groups. These reconstituted images of its past provide the group with evidence about its origin and development, thus allowing it to identify itself throughout history. The collective memory, since it is bound together with the tendentious transmission of information from generation to generation, is broader than an individual's autobiographical memory, and it is meant to prevent the "forgetting," the "selective amnesia," that is always present alongside memory.

Halbwachs ascribed the utmost importance to the social context of the collective memory, as well as to the role of forgetting, and to the role of both in history. He asserted that memory and history were antithetical, and to a great extent even inimical.[5] Memory, he claimed, is a product of the social dynamic and changes constantly in accord with society's challenges; history is a scientific product unaffected (or supposedly unaffected) by current social and political pressures. Hence, forgetting can be a product of the collective memory, at times even deliberately so, but not of history. Halbwachs further asserts that the vast amount of documentation and historical research in our present era precludes modern societies from formulating collective memories for themselves.

Pierre Nora bases his assertions on Halbwachs's claims but disagrees with him on some points. In Nora's view, memory is a living entity maintained by an existing group of people:

> Memory and history, far from being synonymous, appear now to be in fundamental opposition. Memory is life, borne by living societies founded in its name. It remains in permanent evolution, open to the dialectic of remembering and forgetting, unconscious of its successive deformations, vulnerable to manipulation and appropriation, susceptible to being long dormant and periodically revived.... Memory, insofar as it is affective and magical, only accommodates those facts that suit it....[6]

According to Nora, "At the heart of history is a critical discourse that is antithetical to spontaneous memory."[7] Moreover, the development of historiographical consciousness, that is, the history or the philosophy of history, exposes history's ability to affect memory. In this way history efficiently improves the ways in which it cuts itself away from memory and "reconstitutes" itself.

It is on the background of this distinction that Nora coined the term "les lieux de mémoire"—"the sites of memory"—those that are subordinate to both remembrance and history. What regulates the sites of memory is the tension between memory and history, each of which is trying to break through the boundary of the other. According to Nora, this is especially true for France, where modern historiography tends to explode myths and to shake up the foundations of issues that have long been anchored in tradition (and does so with considerable hubris, again according to Nora).

Nora claims that, in effect, everything that today is termed memory is actually history. What Nora is referring to is not "true memory," which is primary and subjective, but "memory transformed by its passage through history . . . voluntary and deliberate, experienced as a duty, no longer spontaneous; psychological, individual and subjective; but never social, collective or all encompassing."[8]

In her book *Recovered Roots*, the American-Israeli researcher Yael Zerubavel reviews various different theories that deal with collective memory.[9] Zerubavel, too, relates to Halbwachs's postulation of an antithesis between collective memory and historical memory, although she doesn't completely accept it. She asserts that collective memory and historical memory do not work on separate and disconnected planes but are mutually affected by the ongoing and constantly changing conditions of the tension between them. Thus, in her opinion, there is no basis for Halbwachs's claim that modern societies have stopped creating collective memories. In her discussion of the collective memory of Israeli society, Zerubavel analyzes, among others, Josephus's account of the fall of Masada and the Holocaust, events considered symbolic historical milestones that, after being selectively shaped into historical stories, have become inseparable components of the Israeli-Jewish collective memory.

* * *

In view of all the above, it is obvious that the issues inherent in the connection between collective memory and history have important implications for the teaching of the Holocaust and genocide. When we discuss these topics within an educational framework we therefore have to ask ourselves several important questions: To what extent is our teaching dependent on collective memory and to what extent on history? Are we sufficiently aware of the educational significance of the interaction between the two? Are we aware of the complexity of this interaction? Is Pierre Nora's definition of the "sites of memory" as the interplay between memory and history-the reciprocal give-and-take that allows them to define one another-applicable and meaningful for the teaching of these subjects? And for the teaching of the Holocaust in Israel in particular? Is there sufficient room in the Israeli-Jewish collective memory and in Israeli-Jewish history for the "other" victims of the Holocaust? And is it not, in any case, the right thing to do to include them, too, within the framework of the teaching of the Holocaust in Israel?

6   The Pain of Knowledge

We also cannot ignore some particularly difficult and often very complex questions that arise when teaching about the Holocaust within the context of the collective memory: What is the place in the collective memory of Jewish speculators and profiteers who also lived in the ghettos? Of members of the Judenraat who differentiated between suffering and suffering and between blood and blood? Of those Jewish policemen in the ghettos who helped the Germans carry out the destruction? Of some of the *kapos* and block leaders who helped to enforce the rule of terror in the camps? And of all of these, what do we want our children to remember, and what do we want them to forget? Put differently, what do we prefer to keep in the collective memory and what do we choose to erase from it?

Notes

1. Primo Levi, *The Drowned and the Saved* (translated from the Italian by Raymond Rosenthal) (New York: Vintage International/Random House, 1989), p. 12.
2. Ibid., p. 23.
3. Yehuda Amichai, *Open Closed Open: Poems* (translated from the Hebrew by Chana Block and Chana Kronfeld) (New York, San Diego, London: Harcourt, 2000).
4. Ibid., pp. 170–171, Stanzas 2, 7, 8, 9.
5. Quoted in Pierre Nora, "Between Memory and History: *Les Lieux de Mémoire*," ("The Sites of Memory"), *Representations*, 26, Special Issue: Memory and Counter-Memory (Spring 1989), pp. 7–24.
6. Ibid., p. 8.
7. Ibid., p. 9.
8. Ibid., p. 13.
9. Yael Zerubavel, "The Dynamics of Collective Remembering," in *Recovered Roots: The Making of Israeli National Tradition* (Chicago: The University of Chicago Press, 1994), pp. 3–12.

2

Philosophical Reflections on the Holocaust

By its very nature the Holocaust raises fundamental questions about the essence of mankind, of human society, and of morality, and about belief and religion as well. The way in which the Holocaust is contemplated influences the way it is taught, both directly and indirectly, and may even constitute a significant part of the learning material itself.

A vast amount of secular and theological books, papers, and articles have been written about the Holocaust, only a few of which will be considered here. It is important to remember that in all activities connected with teaching and learning there is an element of sorting and selection, usually of only a small part of the available material. Since this selection undoubtedly strongly influences the entire process of learning, we will discuss the important questions of what is taught and what isn't, and where we should broaden and where we reduce. In this chapter we have chosen to discuss three texts that present, analyze, and summarize certain aspects of some of the important domains of thought—religious and secular—that are connected with the Holocaust.

The first is the book *Between Auschwitz and Jerusalem*, by Yosef Gorny,[1] which deals with different streams of thought connected to the Holocaust. The author doesn't deal with the general moral, theological, or philosophical questions that emanate from the Holocaust, but with various implications inherent in the connection between the Holocaust and "public thought," especially within the broad range of Jewish public thought in Israel and in the United States.

In Gorny's view, three approaches can be recognized, all of which deal with the tension between two tendencies: a centrifugal force that pushes the Jews out of the community and a centripetal force that pulls them inward, and draws them to concentrate in a separate community.

The centripetal force characterizes Jewish life in modern times in general, and in the period that followed the Holocaust and the establishment of the State of Israel in particular.

> The first approach attempts to ascribe absolute universal significance to the Holocaust. According to this view, the Jews' suffering and catastrophe are no different from the genocide of the Armenians during World War I, the slaughter of the Biafrans, the devastation caused by the atomic bomb in Japan, and even the massacres of Indians by European settlers in various periods of time in South America. This approach may be defined as markedly centrifugal; its ideational and political significance is expressed in the concept of Americanization of the Holocaust in the United States and in a neo-Canaanism of sorts in Israel.
> At the opposite extreme is a clearly centripetal approach, which deliberately attempts to transform the Holocaust into a collective experience that unites the Jewish people and a worldview that consolidates it as a national entity. Some attempt to endow the Holocaust with religious significance. This mindset, typical of Israeli and American right-wing groups, fosters a mentality of national siege in a world that, from its standpoint, is socioculturally open. It believes, for example, that the impending holocaust will emanate not only from the Arabs who encircle Israel but also from the Western world, which is as willing today as it was in the past to abandon the Jews to their fate. The practical inference arising from this is to seek power. This, a cornerstone in the Jewish normalization perception, takes on two forms: military power in Israel and political power for Jews in the United States and elsewhere in the Diaspora.
> The third approach, which lies between the first two, is favored by moderate liberals and conservatives and by the Zionists who espouse liberal and social-democratic values in Israel. Both camps note the inherent historical error that the radical liberals make by attempting to cast the Holocaust in a purely universal light, but they warn against the opposite approach, the ultranationalist attitude that tries, theoretically and practically, to erect a barrier of consciousness between Jews and their surrounding society. As stated, they disregard neither the Jewish uniqueness of the Holocaust nor several of its implications, such as the need for a politically and militarily strong Jewish state, but they express concern about the growing tendency to replace the drive to foster Jewish intellectual endeavor with an effort, which is also growing, to put the Jews' suffering and fate on public display. They have a further concern: that the Jewish collective persona may be transformed from People of the Book to People of the Crematorium. This attitude corresponds to what we have defined as singular normalization.[2]

And, indeed, the question that should be asked is whether, after the Holocaust, but also after the establishment of the State of Israel and the achievement of its sovereignty, the self-image of the Jewish people—and not always only the image—that throughout history has been that of the "People of the Book" will turn into an image of the "People of Martyrdom."

The other two texts we have chosen to present here appear in *Major Changes Within the Jewish People in the Wake of the Holocaust: Proceedings of the Ninth Yad Vashem International Historical Conference*, a conference that took place in Jerusalem in 1993.[3] The subject of the paper "The Influence of the Holocaust on Religious Judaism," by the Holocaust researcher Dan Michman, is Jewish religious thought connected with the Holocaust. Michman discusses mainly the adaptations of mourning rituals to cope with the loss and the "lessons" of the Holocaust, and with the formation of an independent identity amongst religious Jews in Israel and in the Diaspora after the Holocaust.

Michman emphasizes the fact that despite the many studies dealing with the different elements of religious Judaism's reactions to the Holocaust that have appeared recently, no scientific research examination of the Holocaust's influence on religious Judaism, on its thinking and on its beliefs, has yet been carried out—despite the fact that a great number of texts have raised the questions of whether and how it is possible to retain one's faith after Auschwitz. Michman believes that only since the early 1990s, after of a delay of almost a generation, can a more serious trend be seen in the readiness and the ability of religious Judaism to seek answers and ways of coping with this question and with all that it entails. According to Michman, the directions of this way of thinking were classified by the Israeli philosopher Eliezer Schweid according to three types of response, which through prayers and lamentations, ethical discussion, leaflets on the weekly Torah portion, and philosophical treatises that demand more time and intellectual effort, offer religious Jewry coping mechanisms:

> (1) the staunchly Orthodox response, which asserts that the Holocaust does not present believers with any new problem of principle that the Torah has not dealt with in the past and answered in several ways (this argument is proffered more forcefully today than in the past, because now—in view of the Holocaust—one can point to the failure of the secular alternative); (2) the revolutionary Zionist response, which forces the believer who accepts it to change his or her outlook; and (3) a compromise response that began to coalesce years after the Holocaust, arguing that the changes that occurred are not as radical or sweeping as they appeared at the time (e.g., during the Holocaust and immediately afterward), and that the Holocaust is essentially a salient example of processes that have been unfolding since the Emancipation.[4]

Michman accepts the broad outline of this division, but believes that is should be defined somewhat more radically. He wonders if, as far as the Holocaust is concerned, there is really a substantive difference between the third and the first responses, both of which claim, in effect, that the Holocaust is not within the realm of what can be defined as an intrinsic calamity. He maintains that:

> If this is the case, as Yerushalmi alluded with reference to previous disasters in Jewish history, there is a widening chasm between the intellectual characterizations and myths of the Holocaust that pervade all corners of the secular camp—which rejects even the most moderate manifestations of the ritual attitude—and the paradigms of remembrance that prevail among the various shades of religious Jewry. This is evidently more than a mere difference of opinion; it seems as though a real struggle is developing among segments of Jewry on the question of who owns the "true interpretation" of the Holocaust.[5]

If this is indeed the picture of the present situation, then the question that has to be asked is: How does this affect the Israeli education system in general, especially in regard to how the Holocaust is taught in its various different sectors, religious and secular?

As indicated by its title, the article "Inventing the Holocaust: A Christian's Retrospect," by Franklin H. Littell, deals with the same question, but from a Christian perspective.[6] It focuses on the various aspects of how the Christian world and the different denominations within it cope with the trenchant question of the role played by the Christian churches in the Nazi genocide of the Jews. The author also discusses different attitudes related to a profound question that has been raised many times: Would the Holocaust have happened if the Christian world had not paved the way for it during hundreds of years of theological and cultural anti-Semitism? It is important to note that the moral connection, and even the practical one, between religion and various acts of genocide in the twentieth century is an issue that has recently drawn the attention of researchers in the field.[7] (It is well known that Christian nuns participated in the genocide in Rwanda in 1994, and that in 2001 two of them were even convicted by a panel of jurors in Belgium.)

Littell asserts that it is precisely because of the need to face the question of how the Christian churches reacted to Nazism and the destruction of the Jews, and not to dismiss it out of hand, that both the research and the teaching of the Holocaust must not revolve only around an Israeli-centered framework. Learning about the Holocaust must be interdenominational, interdisciplinary, and international: "No discussion of the Holocaust should allow the topic to be sequestered as 'a

Jewish affair.'"[8] The Holocaust, according to Littell, is a past, present, and future historical event—in the history of the Jews, of the Christian world, of Western cultures, and of all mankind. These are concentric circles around a single focal point, each of which has its own distinctive mode of reference and background. Littell emphasized that:

> I deliberately end here with controversial and unresolved questions and concepts, to emphasize again that the study and articulation of the lessons of the Holocaust must avoid premature closure. Presentation of the story and the lessons must be left open to work upon us and upon generations to come. The Holocaust cuts across every academic discipline and involves the life and liberty of every free citizen. It should be so programmed as to avoid *both* emasculating its thrust by bracketing it within some theoretical category on which we already have answers *and* by denying its accessibility to scholars of other than Jewish lineage.[9]

He is troubled by the apprehension that in Israel there is insufficient awareness of the importance of this matter:

> Telling the story of the Holocaust, researching the facts, and communicating the truth of the event to unbelieving and skeptical observers of this and future generations, can only be accomplished through a genuinely caring collegiality between Jewish, Christian, and other gentile scholars. By such collegiality—in itself only possible through *chesed* [grace/loving-kindness]—the brute facts of the Nazi genocide of the Jews may enter the continuum of history as "*the* Holocaust"; recognized as a historical watershed, an "epoch-making event" (Emile Fackenheim), a "true myth," rooted deep in the consciousness of all persons of feeling and conscience.[10]

In this matter Littell emphasizes the importance of cooperation between researchers and thinkers in regard to the questions connected with the Holocaust and how it is taught:

> Littell's thoughtful questions can, of course, have direct and indirect implications on the way in which we deal with the teaching of the Holocaust in Israel. But are we sufficiently open to listen to—and really hear—opinions such as these, and are we doing anything to apply them?[11]

It appears that the importance of the question of whether religious faith—of any religious denomination—as a guarantee for moral human behavior cannot be exaggerated. Has the religious world become open enough to ask itself the full range of questions that a "world-changing event" such as the Holocaust summons up?

However, the question of the full significance and the lessons of the Holocaust are equally important in the context of secular thought, and especially of the world outlook of the large number of non-religious Jewish Israelis: What should be our moral reaction to an unprecedented event so iniquitous that it cannot be comprehended—an event in which the Jews were the main victims? Are we to deal with its particularistic implications for Zionism and Judaism, or can we succeed and relate as well to the universal ramifications of the Holocaust that link it to our very essence as human beings, to our moral ethic, and to our perception of our path in the socio-political frameworks within which we live? These and similar questions of supreme importance, not only questions that have philosophical ramifications on our lives here and now but pragmatic and concrete ones as well, must be asked again and again—and it is our obligation to at least try to answer them to the best of our ability and understanding.

Notes

1. Yosef Gorny, *Between Auschwitz and Jerusalem* (London and Portland: Vallentine Mitchell, 2003).
2. Ibid, pp. 231-232.
3. Dan Michman, "The Impact of the Holocaust on Religious Jewry," in Yisrael Gutman (ed.), *Major Changes Within the Jewish People in the Wake of the Holocaust: Proceedings of the Ninth Yad Vashem International Historical Conference (Jerusalem, June 1993)* (Jerusalem: Yad Vashem, 1996), pp. 659-707.
4. Ibid., pp. 705-706, as per Eliezer Schweid, "The Significance of the Holocaust in Jewish History," *Et La'asot*, 1, Summer 1988, pp. 28-31 (Hebrew) and recently republished in Eliezer Schweid, *Wrestling Until Daybreak*, (Tel Aviv: Hakibbutz Hameuchad, 1991) (Hebrew), pp. 166-169.
5. Michman, "The Impact of the Holocaust on Religious Jewry," p. 707.
6. Franklin H. Littell, "Inventing the Holocaust: A Christian's Retrospect," in Gutman, op. cit., pp. 613-634.
7. And see, for example, Omer Bartov and Phyllis Mack (eds.), *In God's Name: Genocide and Religion in the Twentieth Century* (New York and Oxford: Berghahn Books, 2001).
8. Littell, "Inventing the Holocaust," p. 633.
9. Ibid., p. 633.
10. Ibid., p. 634.
11. Ibid.

3

Constructing the Memory of the Holocaust in Israel

In his book *Imagined Communities*,[1] Benedict Anderson claims that, as a rule, a national narrative appropriates from its graveyards "exemplary suicides, poignant martyrdoms, assassinations, executions, wars and holocausts," and reconstructs them as paragons of bravery and heroism. Anderson claims that the nation's establishment makes certain that these violent deaths will be "remembered [or] forgotten as 'our own'." He asserts that it is in this spirit that "the ancestor of the Warsaw Uprising is the state of Israel."[2] In other words, although the Warsaw ghetto revolt is an actual, recorded historic event, in Anderson's opinion the meaning and the central place that it has been given in Israeli, Jewish, and even the world's historical memory were created by the State of Israel.

Whether we accept or reject Anderson's argument, there is undoubtedly a significant connection between the memory of the Holocaust and the ideological basis on which Israel was established and on the values on which it is—at least to some degree—still based. The direct and significant relationship between the formulation of the memory of the Holocaust in Israel and in its education system derives from this connection and, especially during the first years of the state's existence, the Holocaust was perceived as a tool for instilling the desired values. The ideological approaches as perceived by the leadership of the country and its different streams of education that dictated the State Education Law 5713–1953 were "bestowed" at that time, directly and exactly, upon the student body. Instilling the memory and the lessons of the Holocaust in the pupils' consciousness was viewed by the Israeli education and socialization systems to be of extreme importance, even during a period when the Holocaust itself was not officially an important subject for study in the country's schools. There is no doubt in any case that, from the very beginning of the state's existence, the (politically directed) education establishment in Israel tried to influence the affective and the cognitive positions of young Israelis towards the Holocaust, and to do so in accordance with a Zionist worldview, mainly to emphasize the connection between Holocaust and Heroism and Holocaust and Rebirth, which will be discussed below.

The significant changes and transformations that took place in Israeli society and in the country in the decades following the Holocaust had interesting effects on how it was taught in the country's schools. The short period between the end of the Second World War and the establishment of Israel in 1948 were years of changes fraught with meaning for the country's existential reality. Throughout the height of the war years the people in the Yishuv (the pre-state Jewish population of Palestine) had gone from a struggle to save European Jews to a struggle to establish the state, a country that would soon have to absorb the Jewish survivors of that same war. The Zionist Yishuv was unflagging in its efforts to bring the refugee survivors into the country, both in clandestine operations (against the British Mandate, which limited Jewish immigration to a very small quota) and by sending emissaries who reached and operated in the main displaced persons camps in Europe. During these few years, with the country struggling for its very existence, with the costly fighting in the War of Independence (in which upwards of six thousand of the country's 600,000 Jews were killed, this in a state that had yet to be established), and with the absorption of a very large number of immigrants, the population doubled—and the majority of this population, at least during the first years following the state's establishment, were survivors of the Holocaust.

As is well known, in the last few years a great amount of polemic arose insofar as the research of Israel's history is concerned. One of the controversies revolves around such questions as: Did the Yishuv do "enough" to save European Jews? Was "everything" possible done to absorb the survivors? Was the attitude towards them "proper"? Were newly-arrived immigrants sent to fight in the war (of Independence) with insufficient training"? There were other penetrating questions, but even the fact that they were raised undoubtedly has and will continue to have a long-range affect on Israeli society in general, and on its attitude towards the Holocaust in particular.

Holocaust Remembrance Day

In the second-half of the 1940s in Israel, the memory of the Holocaust was repressed, at least to a certain degree, and without any collective awareness that this was occurring. The effects of this repression may be discerned and discussed by following the vicissitudes of the official decisions regarding the designation of a Holocaust remembrance day, which was established only at the beginning of the 1950s.

During the first few years after the Holocaust ended it was marked on two different days: the first, secular commemoration, on April 19, the second, religious one, on the tenth of Tevet, a day of fasting on which the mourners' *Kaddish* (memorial prayer for the dead) is recited for all who have died and whose place of burial is unknown. In this way two different ideologies and two different ways of life were expressed. The first date was that on which the uprising in the Warsaw ghetto broke out (April 19, 1943) and emphasized displays of Jewish heroism during the Holocaust; the second embodied the continuity of the Jewish tradition, as it is a day of fasting and mourning according to established Jewish religious practice (*Halakha*) and thus, in the opinion of its proponents, expresses the "authentic" Jewish response to the Holocaust. However, because it sometimes happens that according to the Jewish lunar calendar the 19th of April falls during the week of Passover, and also because the country's legislators wanted to choose a date that would be meaningful for all elements of Israeli society, a general trend developed to find an official day of remembrance on a Hebrew date close to the 19th of April in 1943. But in that very year this date fell on the 14th of Nisan, the day before Passover, and would create problems of *Halakha*. It was therefore decided to appoint another day in the same month, the 27th of Nisan, which is seven days (*shiv'a*, the traditional number of days of mourning in Judaism) before Israeli Independence Day. This date, according to the legislators, also symbolically strengthens the conceptual links among "Holocaust," "Heroism," and "Re-birth." Thus, in 1951 the Holocaust Remembrance Day Law was passed, marking the first step in the process of official commemoration that determined, once and for all, the date of Israel's official memorial of the Holocaust. At this stage, the legislators refrained from defining the character of this day of remembrance.

The "Yad Vashem Law"

Only two years later, the Holocaust Martyrs' and Heroes' Remembrance Authority—Yad Vashem Law, 5713–1953 (8 Ellul 5713, August 19, 1953) was passed. The law, which was passed more than ten years after a proposal to establish a project to memorialize the victims of the Holocaust was first made (in 1942), determined that Yad Vashem is the "State Remembrance Authority for the Holocaust and Heroism." The connection between Holocaust and Heroism, which was fostered by Israeli society, was thus given official expression; moreover, this was done within the framework of one of the important laws passed by the Knesset for creating the memory of the Holocaust. Insofar as the purpose of Yad Vashem is concerned, one of its functions and responsibilities, according to Article 12 of the law, is "to collect, examine and publish testimony of the disaster and the heroism of the Jewish People during the Holocaust and to bring home its lesson to the nation." The law does not say, apparently not due to an accidental omission, what the "lesson" of the Holocaust is—and it specifies the singular "lesson," and not the plural "lessons"—but the intention is undoubtedly the "Zionist lesson."

The law also defines the manifold duties of the institution, which include: to outline ways of commemoration; to initiate activities and other projects; to collect and publish the evidence of survivors and to promote further historical and social research on the Holocaust; to help the young generation contend with the subject of the Holocaust, while emphasizing the heroism and courage of its Jewish victims; to create frameworks whose task is to maintain contact with Jewish communities in the Diaspora, in order to provide them, too, with forms for the collective commemoration of Holocaust Remembrance Day; to cooperate with organizations or institutions dealing with the commemoration of the Holocaust on an international level; and to bestow "Israeli memorial citizenship" upon the Jewish Holocaust victims (a symbolic act meant to tie the memory of the victims to the State of Israel).

Yad Vashem is a complex of buildings, gardens, and paths built on the "Mount of Remembrance" in Jerusalem, adjacent to the Mount Herzl cemetery, where Theodor Herzl, the "Prophet of the State" and many of the nation's leaders are interred, and to the national military cemetery. In addition to the proximity of the three separate remembrance days—for the Holocaust, for those who fell defending Israel, and Independence Day—this geographical juxtaposition emphasizes the ideological trends of the new nation, which tried to embrace within one overarching emotive experience the notions of "Holocaust and Rebirth" and of "Holocaust and Heroism."

The Holocaust Martyrs' and Heroes' Remembrance Day

Only several years later, in 1959, was the Holocaust Martyrs' and Heroes' Remembrance Day Law—whose title defines the spirit of the memorial day for the Holocaust—passed. The law determined that this would be a day of national mourning, with all of the customs this entails: the lowering of flags to half-mast, a siren marking two minutes of nationwide silence and the cessation of all activity, the closure of all places of entertainment, the organization of cultural activities connected with the Holocaust, as well as radio and, later, television programs devoted to the subject. In accordance with this law and the Yad Vashem Law, it was established that an official ceremony, inaugurated by the president of the State of Israel, would be held on the eve of Holocaust Memorial Day, and that it would be held at Yad Vashem itself.

More than twenty years passed before another dimension was added to Holocaust Memorial Day with the initiation of a project entitled "Every Person Has a Name" (which had already been suggested in the 1940s). Within the framework of this project, in different places in Israel and throughout the world, the names of those who died in the Holocaust are read aloud. The names are sometimes those of relatives of the people reading them, or they may have some connection to a specific place or with the victims' country of origin. In this unique way a solemn ritual was originated to personalize the meaning of this special day, along with its general significance. The recitation of each individual name impresses upon the hearers the fact that behind each of the unimaginable number of "six million" there was a person, and like each and every one of us, that person was a world unto himself or herself, and that despite not having a known burial site and headstone, that person is remembered.

Israeli Society's Attitude to the Holocaust in Israel's Second Decade

Although during the 1950s more than half of the country's Jewish population had a direct or indirect link to the Holocaust, the processes for formalizing the memory of the Holocaust, described in the brief overview above, bear witness to the general atmosphere at that time. This atmosphere did not encourage discussion of the calamities of the past, including the Holocaust, perhaps because of the extremely difficult social, economic, and security situation in the country. It is therefore interesting to note that in spite of the fact that amongst the survivors there were some who initiated the establishment of the first memorial sites, the symbolic reburial in Israel of ashes of some of the victims, and the publication of "Yizkor" (memorial) books, most of the survivors refrained from devoting their time to activities that focused on turning the Holocaust into a central topic in Israel's daily life.

A sign of impending change began to appear following three events, two that took place in that same decade, and another in the early 1960s. The first of these events was the Reparations Agreement that was signed with Germany in 1952; the second was the Kasztner Trial, in 1954; and the third was the Eichmann trial in the early sixties (he was apprehended in Argentina in May 1960, tried, and executed in May 1962). Among their other results, these events, which became milestones in the life of Israeli society and its attitude to the Holocaust, made it possible for the survivors to express their feelings and thoughts more freely.

The Reparations Agreement

This agreement, which was signed with West Germany, touched off stormy altercations crossing all political lines; those opposing it called for the resignation of the government, some of them protesting with fierce violence. The most important element in the controversy was the moral issue: Was the meaning of acceptance of restitution from Germany the same as a pardon or forgiveness? Does it contain any element of profanation of the memory of the Jewish victims and the Jewish suffering? These and other questions were raised in connection with the education of future generations as well. In addition, questions with a political coloring were also raised, such as the extent to which the agreement would contribute to Germany's return to the family of nations. The Israeli government, in this case, used pragmatic arguments in support of receiving the reparations, claiming the need of assistance in the survivors' rehabilitation, and made it clear that the agreement was neither an expression of forgiveness of the Germany of the past, nor legitimization of the new Germany.

The Kasztner Affair

This very complex affair raised a storm in Israel that lasted from 1954 to 1958. Israel Kasztner, a Hungarian Jew, was accused of collaboration with the Nazis by helping in the preparations that led to the murder of Hungarian Jews, and with giving evidence in favor of Nazi criminals tried in the Nuremberg Trials (1945–46). Rezso (Rudolf) Israel Kasztner (1906–1957), a newspaperman, lawyer, and Zionist leader, was the central figure in the Zionist rescue movement in Budapest during the period of the Holocaust. Kasztner believed that at that time, and in the conditions that existed in Hungary under the Nazi occupation, the only possibility of saving Jews was by negotiating with the Germans, including in the matter of the bitter fates of the Jewish parachutists, among them Hannah Senesh, who were dropped over Hungary in order to establish contact with the Jews there. The Jerusalem district court found him guilty of collaborating with the Nazis; in the harsh wording of the verdict delivered by the judge who presided over the trial, Kasztner had "sold his soul to the devil." The government, for its part, appealed this verdict, and in January 1958 Kasztner was acquitted of all guilt except for that of giving evidence in the defense of a Nazi criminal in the Nuremberg trials. This acquittal came, however, ten months after Kasztner had been murdered by three Jewish nationalist extremists who had taken the court judge's words literally. The tragic figure of Kasztner has been the subject of several books and plays, and is a matter of controversy to this day. The affair and the trial opened the door for the discussion of many complex and controversial issues, such as: the response of the Jews to the "Final Solution"; the behavior of the Jewish leadership under the Nazi occupation; the response of the Yishuv in Palestine to the fate of the Jews of Europe; and the conflict between the image of the "free and fighting" Israeli and the "subjugated and passive" Jew of the ghetto.

The Eichmann Trial

On May 23, 1960 Israel's then Prime Minister David Ben-Gurion announced that Adolph Eichmann, the chief architect of the "Final Solution," had been captured in Argentina and brought to Israel, where he would be placed on trial under the 1950 Law for the Punishment of Nazis and Nazi Collaborators. The trial began in 1961 and ended with a death sentence and Eichmann's hanging in May 1962. In addition to its many political, social, and educational goals, achieved through what was a very public trial (broadcast in full on what was Israel's only radio station at that time), some of the Holocaust survivors who wanted to see as many war criminals punished as possible derived a certain amount of consolation from it. It would not be an exaggeration to say the entire episode led to a revolution in Israel in how people think about many of the issues connected with the Holocaust. After hearing survivors' evidence at the trial, such terms as "heroism" and "resistance" were understood in a much broader way than before, not only in regard to revelations of active physical bravery, but also in terms of spiritual-emotional courage (which had practical implications as well). Moreover, another result of the trial was that the survivors ceased to be an anonymous group within Israeli society and became flesh and blood human beings, with personal names and concrete life stories. This qualitative change led the Israelis to think more deeply about the Holocaust and its significance, which naturally became the subject of frequent and intensive public debate at that time. Among other results, many more people became aware of Yad Vashem's varied activities, in which high school students began to participate as part of their program of studies.

Holocaust, Heroism, and Rebirth as Elements in the Collective Memory

Another important and multifaceted change in the perception of the Holocaust in Israeli society began about five years later, in 1967, following the trauma of the Six Day War. For three tense weeks preceding the actual outbreak of the war, during which the Israeli army, including virtually all of its reserve units, was mobilized, feelings of great anguish and insecurity, along with associations related to the Holocaust, awakened within the Israeli public, including within its younger generation. Until that time the Holocaust was viewed as something that had happened "to them—there," that is, to the submissive ghetto Jews, and now they (the Israelis) suddenly found themselves faced with an ominous danger: that it might happen "to us—here." Following the victory and amidst the euphoria that followed it, these fears and thoughts swung about quickly and the pervasive feeling of impotence was replaced by an illusion of almost unlimited strength and power. It had taken only a few days for the eve-of-the-war dread to change into an exaggerated post-victory headiness.

In this way, after the Six Day War a combination of various aspects of the Holocaust, Zionist ideology, and Jewish history provided the justification for the "occupation"—or "liberation"—of the "territories" (the West Bank and the Gaza Strip) and of domination and rule over the Palestinians there, on the one hand and, on the other, a source of moral criticism of that very same rule, which the Israelis were "forced" to assume. There was at that time—and there still is—much political and moral controversy about this issue, and the repercussions and by-products of this situation are interpreted in different ways by various groups on the Israeli political spectrum.

* * *

The creation of the Holocaust memory doesn't lie in the hands of the country's leaders and legislators alone, nor is it the consequence of historical events and attitudes. Many different things influence this memory, some of them subconscious, and some of them based on research knowledge. As noted above, the academic research carried out in this field has an important role in constructing the nation's collective memory. Research of the Holocaust developed rapidly in Israel, especially after the 1967 war. Not only were faculties and research departments established in universities, but dissertations for master's degrees and doctorates were written on different aspects of Jewish life in Europe during the years of the Holocaust. The research carried out by Yad Vashem also expanded greatly during this period, and it was at this time that a committee of historians was designated whose responsibility was to instruct and guide the scientific research activity of the institution. Collections of primary source materials and periodicals dealing with Holocaust studies also began to appear at this time.

22   The Pain of Knowledge

This research activity affected not only the attitudes prevailing in the social and political reality of Israel, but also the character of the academic and intellectual discourse concerning the Holocaust and the degree of interest that it aroused. Since the early 1990s a large number of research papers have been written in Israel dealing with the creation of the memory of the Holocaust, some of which will be discussed below.

The book *The 1948 Generation: Myth, Profile and Memory*, by Emmanuel Sivan, deals mostly with the generation that grew up and fought during the era of the War of Independence and with the memory of those who fell in it.[3] (Among other topics, the author deals with the part played in the "1948 Generation" by Holocaust survivors, and with their proportion among the fallen.) The chapter entitled "Mourning, Bereavement and Memory" describes the forms of mourning and bereavement in Israeli society. These forms are expressed, according to Sivan, both in the creation of the memory of the Holocaust and in the memory of the Rebirth (i.e., Israel's wars, mainly the War of Independence), despite the difference in the character of these historical events. In discussing the Israeli historical memory, states Sivan, in general:

> [T]he way in which these events have become engraved in the collective Israeli memory is, of course, different from the objective historical reality, insofar as it can be known. In other words, the foundation myth of 1948 does not fit in with the facts—or at least with some of the main elements of these facts—regarding the characteristics of the 1948 Generation as they appear from the known or recorded facts, and certainly not from what is known about how that generation perceived itself.[4]

If this is true for the period of the War of Independence, which is a comparatively "easy" field for historical research, then it is true several times over for an occurrence as unprecedented, complicated, complex, and incomprehensible as the Holocaust.

Sivan's research is important insofar as the creation of collective memory is concerned not only in and of itself, but also because it compares this matter as it pertains to other difficult modern wars, particularly the First World War. In his opinion, many of the characteristics of this war bear strong similarities to those of the War of Independence. Sivan writes:

> The uniqueness of the War of Independence stands out most clearly in exactly the very same aspects in it and in its memory that are no different from the terrible

spilling of blood suffered by democratic societies compelled to fight in devastating wars in an era of mass mobilization. Even if each person is the only son of the Holy God, and even if the People of Israel is the Chosen People, still, all of those who stood and fought in the line of fire share many common attributes. Their uniqueness, if there is any uniqueness at all, is in the details—those of actual fact and those in the mind—which must be sought with the greatest possible fidelity. And it is these details that, in the words of the [French] poet Chateaubriand [1768-1848], constitute the soul of history; they are the nuances that express the uniqueness of the historical event, in the way that it occurred and in the way that it was experienced and stored in the memory.[5]

In this context we may say that the uniqueness of the Holocaust, too, will stand out even more clearly when various different aspects within it and within its memory are compared with those of other genocides in history.

And yet, as reflected in the research of this topic, the patterns of the memory of the Holocaust in Israel are exactly the reverse. An article by Yechiam Weitz, "Shaping the Memory of the Holocaust in Israeli Society in the 1950s,"[6] as its name indicates, deals with these patterns of memory in the years in which they were constructed, crystallized, and to a great extent institutionalized. Among the prominent forms of memory that Weitz specifies are the connecting links between Holocaust and Heroism and Holocaust and Rebirth, the strong emphasis placed on the national-Zionist lessons, and the desire to establish the State of Israel as the central, and perhaps the only, body responsible for preserving the memory of the Holocaust and for formulating its lessons. The main components of these forms of memory continue to serve as the central elements—and in many ways the dominant ones—of the forms of memory common today. This remains true despite the decades that have passed and the claims made in the last few years by different circles that they are too Zionist and overly tendentious.

It is also important to note that most of the discussions on this topic criticize the intended connection between the Holocaust and Heroism that is expressed, as seen above, in the Yad Vashem Law and by the "Martyrs' and Heroes' Remembrance Law" that established the status of Remembrance Day (Yad Vashem, it is important to reiterate, is defined as the "Martyrs' and Heroes' Remembrance Authority"). There can be no doubt but that the creators of memory in the young state, still struggling for its very existence, found it difficult to cope with the phenomenon of the Holocaust itself and endeavored to learn from it, and to elicit Zionist "lessons" in the Israeli context. Their purpose was clear: to foster the leitmotif of heroism. In Israel at that time the attitude towards the European Jews of the Holocaust period was characterized by expressions of criticism, antagonism, detachment, and disinterest, and sometimes even by alienation. The typical young Israeli often asked, openly or in some guise, and invariably with a great lack of empathy and understanding, "Why did the Jews go like sheep to the slaughter?" During those years the education system tried to give prominence to the many revelations of physical heroism among the Jews during the Holocaust, such as armed struggle, uprisings and partisan activity. In the decades that followed, the meaning of the concept of heroism was broadened, and the education system tried to find ways to elucidate revelations of resistance on the moral-spiritual level, such as the keeping of religious faith, fulfillment of the religious commandments despite conditions of terrible distress and need, the maintenance of human dignity, the sanctification of life, as well as the continued operation of institutions providing support and assistance. Although not always entailing physical struggle and resistance, these acts bore witness to the strength of the spirit and the bravery of the soul.

Weitz raises four questions that are linked to the deliberate formulation of the conscious memory of the Holocaust in Israel:

- What were the main ideological, national, and humanistic messages that were transmitted to the public during Israel's first decade?
- To what degree was the source of these messages founded in the 1930s and even the 1940s, the years during which European Jewry was persecuted and destroyed?
- Did all of the messages that were crystallized in the 1930s and 1940s find their expression in the collective memory of the 1950s?
- Why were some of the messages that crystallized in the earlier decades expressed in the 1950s as well, while others were hidden away ("selective seepage"), as it were, and lost?

The national-Zionist lesson of the Holocaust and the emphasis on the heroism of the fighters were the prominent elements in the formation of a perception of memory in the 1950s, according to Weitz. On the other hand, he claims, various other elements present in the Yishuv in the 1940s were banished from the collective memory, such as the fear of German conquest (which hovered ominously above the Yishuv in

Palestine, especially in 1942). Also banished was the ambivalent attitude that had developed in the country regarding Jewish resistance in Europe that, along with expressions of admiration, also aroused fear that it would result in the complete destruction of the remaining Zionist pioneering elements. Calling attention to certain acts on the one hand, while pushing aside or ignoring others completely on the other, was greatly influenced by "the desire to praise, extol, uplift, and glorify the Zionist and Eretz Israel ethos. Everything that conflicted with that goal or did not serve it was shunned as if it were anathema."[7]

The issue of the linkage between the Holocaust and heroism was also dealt with in an article by Muli Brug, "From the Top of Masada to the Heart of the Ghetto: Myth as History."[8] Brug discusses the central place of the accounts of the rebels on Masada and of the heroism of the fighters of the Warsaw Ghetto Revolt in Jewish historiography, and of the use made of both in forming the collective memory in the first years of Israel's statehood. He claims that the description of the brave stand of the fighters besieged on the top of Masada in the year 73 CE and the account of the struggle of the Warsaw ghetto fighters against the Nazis in the spring of 1943 were presented by the leaders of the Yishuv during the 1940s as symbols of a unique Jewish heroism. The agents of Zionist education enlisted these two episodes and presented them as historical parallels, viewing the revolt that broke out in the ghetto as a replication of the revolt that ended at Masada, and of its fighters as "brothers in arms." The centrality of the "sacrifice and heroism" motif in Zionism is what explains, according to Brug, the construction of these memory stories in such a way that, out of the vast mosaic of complex and horrendous events of the Holocaust certain elements and not others were emphasized. It is in this context that the heroes of the uprisings in the ghettos were sometimes presented—or in any case were perceived by many—as "Israelis" amongst the "Jews of the Exile" who yielded before their murderers and went, as it were, "like sheep to the slaughter." The construction of the narrative of the Jewish revolt in the Warsaw ghetto is, in Brug's view, a reflection of the decisive influence of Masada as the dominant myth of heroism the Yishuv prior to the establishment of Israel, and of the state during the first decades of its existence.

The connection between the heroism of the fighters on Masada and those in the ghettos is also discussed by Yael Zerubavel in her article

"The Death of Memory and the Memory of Death: Masada and the Holocaust as Historical Metaphors."[9] Zerubavel chooses to focus on the differences that occurred in Israeli society's perception of this connection as, in the course of time, the Masada myth gradually declined, or, at least, faded somewhat. She analyzes the place of the myths of Masada and the ghetto revolts as symbolic events serving as historical signposts that became part of the collective Israeli memory, and notes that this memory was constructed by a selective approach to the historical narrative. Zerubavel maintains that the collective memory of brave resistance that was established on the basis of these myths never became obsolete, regardless of the research and historical documentation that mitigated it. Zerubavel thus rebuts Pierre Nora's claim that history may push memory aside (see above, chapter 1) and attempts to prove that the memory itself may reduce history's scope of operation.

Contending with the Memory: Society and the Individual

The formative development of the Holocaust memory in the 1950s, as described in the articles discussed above, had significant and clearly Israeli-centered implications for the education system and for the way in which it attended to the commemoration and remembrance of the Holocaust, which at that time was not yet an officially studied subject. However, although changes in several of the components of the formation of the Holocaust memory undoubtedly did come about in the decades that followed, other elements remain unchanged and are firmly maintained more than fifty years after the establishment of the State of Israel.

The changes that have occurred in the attitudes of Israeli society toward the Holocaust in the last few years are the subject of an article by Daniel Gutwein, "The Privatization of the Holocaust: Politics, Memory and Historiography."[10] This article deals with the attitude of Israeli society towards the Holocaust and with the connection between the Holocaust and memory, historiography, and politics. In Gutwein's opinion, the construction of the collective memory of the Holocaust in Israel is a reflection of the ongoing processes that affect Israeli society and the parallel changes that occur in the Israeli collective identity. He claims, further, that three main periods can be identified in the process of the construction of this memory, in each of which one memory dominates and pushes competing memories to the sidelines:

- the period of fragmented memory;
- the period of nationalized memory;
- the period of privatized memory.

The period of fragmented memory begins with the shock of exposure to the atrocities of the Holocaust and the need to cope with its meaning; the period of nationalized memory begins with the Eichmann trial and its directions intensify following the Six Day War; the period of privatized memory begins in the 1980s and is part of Israeli society's confrontation with the political and moral dilemmas that arose following the Lebanon War and the first *intifada*. This period is characterized by an undermining of the feeling of personal security, a decline in social unity and a strengthening of the ethos of privatization, as well as general "post-Zionist" attitudes prevailing in both the Right and the Left.

Gutwein transfers the term "privatization" from the field of economics to that of politics and culture and uses the concept of "privatization of the Holocaust," but he also emphasizes the difference between his use of this term and that sometimes made of it in order to denote commercialization of the Holocaust memory. He relates to the post-Zionist approach to the Holocaust, which he analyzes and whose directions and goals he criticizes. The creation of different narratives about the Holocaust was accompanied by an increasingly strong division between disparate sectors and subgroups in the Israeli population, most markedly within ultra-orthodox Jewry and the Arab sector. In the ultra-orthodox society such particularistic narratives are created in many cases by casting the responsibility, and even the blame, for what happened in the Holocaust directly on Jews who assimilated and/or on the Zionists (the two sometimes being considered identical). In Arab society the narratives are created indirectly, for example by increasing the awareness of the *nakhbah* ("catastrophe," the Arab term for the events of 1948), sometimes by making extremely severe and sweeping accusations of what they claim was a genocide of Arabs that was carried out at that time in what became Israel. These trends have important ramifications for the identity of Israeli society, and they are likely to intensify in the coming decades. Because of this, it is of utmost importance to examine the Israeli education system and to ascertain whether or not it is aware of these processes, and how it contends with them.

A different focus on the question of the memory of the Holocaust is presented in the chapter entitled "Between Fear and Hope: An Ongoing Dialogue with the Holocaust," the epilogue of the book *Between Fear and Hope*, by Dan Bar-On.[11] The chapter presents the stories of the lives of five families of Holocaust survivors, each comprising three generations. Bar-On unveils the generation-to-generation transmission of the memories of the horrors in each of these families and combines them to form personal-familial paradigms through which he raises specific questions regarding the patterns of the Holocaust's memory in Israeli society and the continuing influence it has on the families themselves. In the first generation of these families Bar-On identifies a tension between two magnetic poles, one pulling, as it were, to look back at what happened in the past, "there," the other pulling to the reality of the present, "here." This tension between the two forces continues, of course, in different ways and to different extents in the second and third generations of the survivors' families. Another tension within these families, among both the survivors and their offspring, is that between the Holocaust as a directly endured, personal-familial experience, and as a national-historical event. Many of the survivors and their families find this national-historical appropriation of the Holocaust both difficult and problematic.

It is important to mention another book by Dan Bar-On, *Legacy of Silence: Encounters with Children of the Third Reich*, because of its unique perspective.[12] This book does not deal directly with the teaching of the Holocaust in Israel but with the "legacy" of the Holocaust in Germany. Its author relates to this issue from his vantage point as the son of a Jewish family that had fled Germany in 1933, in the early days of Nazi rule. Within the framework of his studies in social psychology, Bar-On returned to Germany fifty years after his family's flight in order to interview the now grown-up children of men and women who had filled various positions in the Nazi regime, including the S.S. These sons and daughters comprise a special group of people whose childhood and adolescence were invariably "protected"—screened by a veil of silence. The present reality, however, demanded, and continues to demand, that they contend not only with Germany's Nazi past, but also with that of their own parents. All of the differences notwithstanding, they, too, experienced the "silence" that was characteristic of Holocaust survivor-families in many countries (and apparently those in Israel as well), at least in the 1950s.

The main questions that occupy Bar-On in this book are: How do these individuals and their society contend with their private and their collective past? Is it indeed possible to repress or conceal, or to cover over or deny this past—painful and difficult as it may be—whether as victims, as murderers, or as bystanders? Is facing this past with honesty and integrity, including its "black pages," a necessary condition for the moral strengthening of future generations and for their ability to cope with so complex a reality?

It appears that there are, to this day, more questions than answers on this matter, and that that itself is perhaps one of the reasons for the gradual and slowly paced changes in how the collective memory of the Holocaust is formulated in Israeli society in general, and in its education system in particular. Small wonder, then, that in many of the books and articles that deal with this subject, the authors express reservations and criticism. It is in this context that the important question of the relationship between academic research of the Holocaust (history, historiography, and historiosophy) and the actual forming of the ways in which it is remembered arises again and again, and does so, among other reasons, according to what the establishment perceives as the needs of the state and its society.

Notes

1. Benedict Anderson, *Imagined Communities* (London and New York: Verso, 1983).
2. Ibid., pp. 205-206.
3. Emmanuel Sivan, *The 1948 Generation: Myth, Profile and Memory* (Tel Aviv: Ma'arakhot—Ministry of Defence, Israel) (Hebrew).
4. Ibid., p. 13.
5. Ibid., p. 14.
6. Yechiam Weitz, "Shaping the Memory of the Holocaust in Israeli Society of the 1950s," in Yisrael Gutman (ed.), *Major Changes in the Jewish People in the Wake of the Holocaust: Proceedings of the Ninth Yad Vashem International Historical Conference* (Jerusalem: Yad Vashem, 1996), pp. 497-518.
7. Ibid., p. 515.
8. Muli Brug, "From the Top of Masada to the Heart of the Ghetto," in David Ohana and Robert Wistreich (eds.), *Myth and Memory: The Evolution of the Israeli Consciousness* (Tel Aviv: Hakibbutz Hameuchad, 1996) (Hebrew).
9. Yael Zerubavel, "The Death of Memory and the Memory of Death: Masada and the Holocaust as Historical Metaphors," *Representations,* 45, Winter 1994, pp. 72-100.

10. Daniel Gutwein, "The Privatization of the Holocaust: Politics, Memory and Historiography," *Research Papers on the Period of the Holocaust*, 1998, pp. 7-52.
11. Dan Bar-On, "Fear and Hope: Three Generations of the Holocaust," in *Between Fear and Hope* (Cambridge, MA and London, England: Harvard University Press, 1995), p. 350.
12. Dan Bar-On, *Legacy of Silence: Encounters with Children of the Third Reich* (Cambridge, MA and London, England: Harvard University Press, 1989).

4

The Teaching of the Holocaust in Israel: Historical Processes

Textbooks reflect a society's prevailing attitudes and opinions. It is also possible to view them as agents that play an important role in the socio-cultural processes taking place in the schools, as do other factors that influence the society in general. The fierce polemic that has been going on in Israel since the early 1990s regarding the content of these books, especially in the field of Zionist-Jewish history, bears witness to the importance—perhaps exaggerated—of this matter in Israel.

Every education system is situated at the junction of past and future. Its main function is to prepare the current young generation for life in the future, and of ensuring the preservation of the society's past and present values. According to many traditional perceptions of education, the education system must equip its students not only with knowledge, but with affective experiences that foster social solidarity and identification with the cultural tradition of the society of which they are members.

In the first years of Israel's independent statehood, when the Zionist endeavor was still perceived as a revolution, the trend in the education system's role was to controvert the ideologies of the Exile and to nurture the paragon of "the new Jew." It was in this spirit that, both before the establishment of the state and in its first years, the education system in Israel encouraged the "sabra myth" and, along with it, a negation of the "Golah," the Exile, which often metamorphosed into a rejection of the "Jew of the Exile." The aspiration of the Zionist pioneers of the second and third waves of immigration (1904–1914, 1919–1923) was that their sabra children would be totally different from their own fathers, from whom they had sometimes parted under painful and agonizing circumstances. Since the Golah past was frequently perceived as a stain to be erased, the sabra son was frequently described as having arisen from nowhere: "Elik was born of the sea," wrote the Israeli author Moshe Shamir of his brother, who was killed in the War of Independence.[1]

This approach led to considerable conflict in Israeli society, arising mainly from the dissimilar convictions of secular Zionism, religious Zionism, and the non-Zionist, and even anti-Zionist, ultra-orthodox-religious streams. Given the complex state of affairs this created, the educational functionaries had to construct a curriculum that would deal with only certain selected events in the lives of the Jews in the Diaspora, and would cope with the tension between change and revolution on the one hand, and continuity on the other. It should be emphasized that, especially insofar as it touches on the teaching of the Holocaust, this would be the curriculum according to which Israeli youth would be educated, and that this young generation in fact felt that it was superior to the Jews of the Diaspora, from whose culture they were almost completely cut off.

Teaching about the Holocaust in Israel during Different Periods of Time

The researcher Dalia Ofer, in the chapter entitled "The World Reacts to the Holocaust: Israel," has suggested that the history of the teaching of the Holocaust in Israel be divided chronologically into two main periods, which she terms "The Zionist Period" and the "Humanistic Period."[2]

"The Zionist Period" (1948-1977)

It became clear in Israel, as early as the 1940s, that the young generation must be taught about various topics connected with the Holocaust and with its meaning. The country's leaders' and educators' main apprehension was that the memory of the Holocaust, and with it knowledge about the Jews of the Diaspora and their culture, would be lost—a phenomenon that could, in a way, fulfill Hitler's aim of "erasing" the Jews from the map of the world. Along with this, the matter of teaching this subject was accompanied by a persistent sense of discomfort that arose not only because the subject itself was beyond comprehension, either rationally or emotionally, but also due to the educators' fears about the severe emotional effects that exposure to the Holocaust might have on the young generation. In addition, as already noted many young Israelis had a preconceived negative image of Exilic Jews, which was supported by the literature taught in the schools. The modern Israeli literature tended to emphasize the poverty and humiliation that were the fate of East European Jewry and contained various different stereotypical descriptions of these Jews, some of which even had anti-Semitic overtones. Many young secular Israelis thus willingly cut themselves off from any identification with the chapter of the Exile in Jewish history.

At the beginning of the 1960s the subject of the Holocaust was included in two high school textbooks,[3] but an analysis of the chapters dealing with this subject in both of these books indicates that they were based on a strong and unequivocally ideological and emotional Zionist bias. In 1963 the Israeli Ministry of Education suggested the addition of "The Ghetto during the Holocaust" as an elective to the matriculation examinations. However, due to the paucity of study materials and of the teachers' knowledge in this subject, very few pupils registered for this course. Prior to the early 1970s, most of Israeli pupils' knowledge about the Holocaust was gleaned from ceremonial memorial ceremonies held within the educational framework, which until 1958 were not obligatory. Not only was there no systematic teaching of factual knowledge about the Holocaust, but what was transmitted was incomprehensible to the pupils and, in addition, almost completely isolated from any general historical framework. It was, moreover, meant to create an emotional reaction rather than an intellectual challenge. (The Holocaust was defined as a separate unit in the high school curriculum only in 1979, and the unit was added to the matriculation examination in 1981.)

The Eichmann trial took place in Jerusalem in 1961. One of the important goals of this trial was to bring the atrocities of the Holocaust, as well as its significance and lessons, to the attention of Israeli society, and to that of its young generation in particular. The trial did, indeed, prompt a profound change in the approach of young Israelis to this subject. They began to form a more positive approach to the Jews of the Diaspora and attempted to understand their desperate situation during the years of the Holocaust. Many of them felt, and even expressed, pride in the stand of the Jews during this period. Studies carried out among young people after the trial indicated that their readiness to learn about the Holocaust was even greater than what their teachers had estimated. (Also, and as expected, the secular pupils expressed a specific identification with the Jewish underground fighters, while the religious pupils expressed a specific identification with those who continued, even in those desperate days, to maintain the religious laws.) Despite this change in the approach of these young people to the subject, nothing was changed in the Ministry of Education's learning materials and programs, and the study of the Holocaust in Israeli schools remained very limited. Many teachers refrained from dealing with it because they were well aware that they lacked both the means and the basic knowledge needed to teach so sensitive a subject. The Ministry of Education, in cooperation with the Lohemei Haghettaot Museum (Ghetto Fighters Museum) did, however, initiate various teacher-training seminars, but these were few and far between, and far from satisfactory.

Thus, during the 1960s and until the end of the 1970s, no systematic program for the teaching of the Holocaust was developed by the Ministry of Education. A suggestion was made, however, that the subject be studied in the schools during several homeroom lessons in conjunction with the preparations for the ceremonies commemorating Holocaust Martyrs' and Heroes' Remembrance Day, and that it be considered one of the humanities subjects, which usually meant history and literature. Teachers received a very limited selection of learning materials, consisting of a small number of documents and parts of articles published by Yad Vashem, and were given the possibility of mounting exhibits connected with the day, comprised mainly of photographs and some documentary materials.

"The Humanistic Period" (1978 to the Present)

During these two and a half decades, the humanistic approach and values, as they pertain to the teaching of the Holocaust, were specifically emphasized. As a result of the activities of various different social and political factors after the Six Day War and the Yom Kippur War, the education system took greater interest in the teaching of this subject. In spite of the differences between them, these two wars awakened complex and deep questions, many of which also touched on the question of individual and collective identities within Israeli society, especially among the younger generation—subjects that seemed, until then, to be self-understood and simple but were revealed to be extremely complex. The two wars had awakened feelings of fear and anxiety and the comparisons made between them and, at times, with the Holocaust, by the media and politicians led historians and educators to realize how much the public lacked both knowledge and understanding of the Holocaust. Due to the fierce criticism leveled at the Ministry of Education, it could no longer ignore the question of Holocaust teaching in the schools and its responsibility to outline a learning program for the teaching of this subject. In 1979, as noted above, the Holocaust was finally defined as an independent unit of study in the high school curriculum and, in 1981, as part of the matriculation examination as well.

Dalia Ofer's division of trends in the teaching of the Holocaust, although logical and helpful in mapping the discussion of this subject chronologically, leaves room for doubt about the suitability of the definition of this latter period as "Humanistic." There is no doubt that processes leaning heavily towards humanistic values took place in Israeli society during these years, and that these processes also influenced the teaching of the Holocaust. However, the question of whether it is possible to determine that, as a rule, this was true for the field of education during the same period of time is less clear. The doubt regarding this is based on several facts:

- The Law for Compulsory Education, passed in 1953, which defined the educational goals of the State of Israel, was amended in 1980. The Knesset, the Israeli parliament, voted to add an amendment that established awareness of the memory of the Holocaust and of heroism as an educational goal. The purpose of this amendment was clear: to base, or to strengthen, the memory of the Holocaust and of heroism, and to do so particularly from a Jewish-Zionist perspective, as had been specified in the Yad Vashem Law in 1953. In practice, this amendment to the law established the basis for teaching about the Holocaust in all high schools in the country's education system, and was undoubtedly an important milestone in the process of expanding the teaching of this subject to the country's entire education system. (It is important to emphasize that this is the only "compulsory subject" that is anchored in law.) However, the fact that there was a decision to make the teaching of this subject compulsory—and above all from a Zionist-Jewish standpoint—rather than indicating a trend towards a humanistic and universal ethos,

testifies to exactly the opposite, that is, to a narrowing of its scope to a particularistic perspective.
- During this "humanistic period" the subject of the Holocaust was studied (until 1999) within the framework of "Jewish History," and thus separately from "World History." This alone narrows the "humanistic" approach.
- In visits of groups of youth to Poland, which began at the end of the 1980s, the emphasis has been on the Zionist perspective of the Holocaust (and remains so at the time of writing). Its Jewish perspective is emphasized less, and its universal one even less than that. In only a small number of the youth groups that travel to Poland do the group leaders deal, intentionally and in a significant way, with the connection between the Holocaust and humanistic or universal values.
- During this same "humanistic period" there were no changes in how the schools taught about instances of the genocide of other nations, and no real change in the Ministry of Education's directives regarding this subject (this will be discussed in greater detail in chapter 13). Although in April 2001, then Minister of Education Yossi Sarid announced that the subject of genocide would be studied in the education system, in reality nothing came of this.

Be that as it may, in the opinion of certain researchers the division into time periods is an important tool for analyzing the continually changing processes that affect the teaching of the Holocaust in Israel. Like Dalia Ofer, the researcher Ruth Firer, in her book *The Agents of the Lesson*, also discusses the teaching of this subject according to a chronological division, but proposes a third phase between the "Zionist" and "Humanistic" periods.[4] Firer calls the years 1961-1977, which encompass the Six Day War and the Yom Kippur War, the "Intermediate Period," and asserts that this period is characterized by the specific ramifications the wars have had on the teaching of the Holocaust. Firer also provides a comprehensive review of the changes made in school textbooks between 1948 and 1988. She follows the development of various aspects in the presentation of the Holocaust in readers for grade school and for Jewish history books prepared for junior and high schools. Along with this she examines how these specific aspects are treated in academic texts, especially those written for introductory courses required of university students undertaking a program in Holocaust studies.

Two articles, both by the researcher Nili Keren, are important to mention here: "Preserving Memory within Oblivion: The Struggle over Teaching the Holocaust in Israel,"[5] and "The Subject of the Holocaust in Israeli Society and in the Educational System in the Years 1948-1981,"[6] both of which deal with learning programs in this subject. These articles focus on the struggles to change the character and the content of Holocaust studies in Israel. Keren proposes a division into five periods for the teaching of the Holocaust.

1. From the establishment of Israel to the creation of Yad Vashem (1948–1953)
2. The period ending with the capture of Adolph Eichmann (1953-1960)
3. The period ending with the Six Day War (1961-1967)
4. The period ending with the Yom Kippur War (1967-1973)
5. The period ending with the ratification of the amendment to the "Compulsory Education Law" (1973-1981)

Within the framework of her analysis of the nature of the teaching of this subject in Israel, Keren asks a number of important questions:

- Should the education system be influenced by political and social processes in the country, or should it influence them?
- Is the political-public achievement expressed in the changes in the teaching of the Holocaust (the amendment of the Compulsory Education Law—making the teaching of the Holocaust compulsory) an educational achievement as well?
- Has the compulsory teaching about the Holocaust been followed by a greater awareness of its roots and the lessons that can be learned from it?
- Can the study of the period of the Holocaust contribute to the social, political, and moral character of Israeli society? And if so, how?

The penetrating conclusion that Keren presents is that insofar as the subject of the Holocaust was concerned, the education system had no influence on processes in Israeli society but, rather, the system was influenced by these processes. In her opinion the immediate and short-term needs of Israeli society took precedence over all other considerations. Keren quotes the words of the Israeli poet and Holocaust survivor Abba Kovner in a discussion about the teaching of the Holocaust in the Knesset's Education Committee:

> With all my heart I join those who warn against using the subject of the Holocaust as a spade to dig with, even if the digging is important, and even if at this moment the most important thing is to fortify the country and struggle with the problem of

emigration [from Israel]. If we use the Holocaust as a means, then the disillusionment when it fails to succeed will be terrible. The teaching of the Holocaust is a purposeful goal unto itself, but woe to this learning if it is done without soul-searching.[7]

The expansion of academic research of the Holocaust contributed to the creation of suitable learning materials and deepened the knowledge in this field. A new generation of teachers that could influence the introduction of changes in the teaching of the Holocaust arose in the 1970s and 1980s. Not only had these teachers been students and teachers in universities that carried out research on the subject, they themselves had been schoolchildren during the Eichmann trial, and then soldiers during the Six Day War and the Yom Kippur War. Together with historians and various educators they made known their pointed criticism of the way in which this the subject had been taught when they were pupils. An article entitled "Didactic Problems in the Teaching of the Holocaust," written by the historian and educator Haim Schatzker,[8] is known to have had an especially strong influence on the Ministry of Education and to have prodded it to reexamine its approach to the teaching of this subject.

At this same time, beginning in the early 1970s, a new general trend began to appear in the character of all of the curriculums in the schools: teachers were allowed to use their own judgment regarding the emphasis of certain elements in the content as long as this was done systematically. Three main approaches were prominent among this generation of teachers:

- The approach that underscored the need to strengthen the *Zionist identity* through the teaching of the Holocaust: This trend is recognizable in the textbooks written at the end of the 1970s and in use throughout the 1980s and even later. Their main message was that the Jews of Europe had been unable to read "the writing on the wall" because of their belief that Jews would share in the emancipation that was spreading throughout Europe. The Holocaust exploded these illusions, and *aliyah*, immigration to Israel, was a "lesson" to be learned from the Holocaust.
- The approach that underscored the educational trend towards *universal values*: The aim of those who supported this approach was that the pupils would focus on clarifying the meaning and the importance of their lives as humans, as Jews, and as Israelis through learning about the Holocaust. The study of this subject would provide for their intellectual needs as individuals seeking their identity and for their social needs as citizens of the country.

(This subject is dealt with in Arye Carmon's article "Teaching the Holocaust as a Means of Fostering Values."[9])
- The approach that underscored the aspect of *enriching general knowledge about the Holocaust:* This approach was the one most accepted by teachers and historians during the 1970s. In its supporters' opinion, pupils should be exposed to a great amount of information on the Holocaust, in the same way in which other topics are taught in history, rather than placing an emphasis on values and emotions. The purpose of teaching about this subject was therefore mainly a broadening of knowledge, and the way to achieve this was through systematic historical analyses of the main elements of this subject, and to do this in coordination with the reading of primary sources and broad comparative research studies. (In Israel during these years, Yisrael Gutman and Haim Schatzker's book *The Holocaust and its Meaning*, which exemplifies this approach, became the most widely used textbook on this subject.[10])

In any case, it appears that in Israel until the late 1990s, most of the textbooks dealing with the Holocaust gave varying degrees of prominence to its connection with Zionism. The books directed at younger children convey the Zionist lesson whose main precepts are "Remember" and "Do" (i.e., practical Zionist applications) while in those for adolescents the lessons of the Holocaust are based on an awareness and understanding of the significance of the Holocaust and are related to the existential and moral necessity for the existence of the State of Israel.

Nonetheless, towards the end of the 1990s significant changes began to appear in some of the textbooks used in both elementary schools and high schools. (Some of these books are discussed briefly in chapter 6, among them several that were published in the late 1990s or shortly thereafter.) In these more recent textbooks the approach that emphasizes the didactic importance of the acquisition of knowledge based on systematic historical analysis of the Holocaust has taken precedence over the ideological-emotional approach that characterized the textbooks in the past that, along with an ideological identification, were meant to awaken an emotional reaction in the pupils. The strongly Zionist emphases that were so prominent in the past, with their highly accessible ideological messages, have been modified. Most of the books now devote less attention to the Jewish connection to Holocaust than in the past and more to its general historical background, and thus attempt to provide explanations and insights for the Nazis' rise to power within the framework of world history.

Notes

1. Moshe Shamir, *With His Own Hands: Pirkei Elik* (Tel Aviv: Am Oved, 1951) (Hebrew).
2. Dalia Ofer, "The World Reacts to the Holocaust: Israel," in D. Wyman (ed.), *The World Reacts to the Holocaust* (Baltimore: Johns Hopkins University Press, 1996), pp. 836-923. (The discussion of the teaching of the Holocaust in Israel in this chapter is based to a large extent on Ofer's chronological division.)
3. Samuel Ettinger and Michael Ziv, *Chronicles* (Vol. 2/3) (Jerusalem, 1960) (Hebrew); Ephraim Shmueli, *A History of Our People* (Vol. 7) (Tel Aviv, 1961) (Hebrew).
4. Ruth Firer, *The Agents of the Lesson* (Tel Aviv: Hakibbutz Hameuchad, 1989) (Hebrew).
5. Nili Keren, "Preserving Memory within Oblivion: The Struggle over Teaching the Holocaust in Israel," *Zmanim*, Vol. 16, No. 64, Autumn 1998, (Hebrew) pp. 56-64.
6. Nili Keren, "The Subject of the Holocaust in Israeli Society and in the Education System in the Years 1948-1981," *Yalkut Moreshet: Holocaust Documentation and Research, 42*, December 1986 (Hebrew), pp. 193-202.
7. Keren, "Preserving Memory within Oblivion," p. 62.
8. Haim Schatzker, "Didactic Problems in the Teaching of the Holocaust," *Guidelines for Teachers of History*, 2, 1961 (Hebrew), pp. 11-15.
9. Arye Carmon, "Teaching the Holocaust as a Means of Fostering Values," *Curriculum Inquiry*, 9/3, 1979, pp. 209-228.
10. Yisrael Gutman and Haim Schatzker, *The Holocaust and its Meaning: A Teacher's Guide* (Jerusalem: Zalman Shazar Center, 1983) (Hebrew).

5

On Teaching the Holocaust: Didactic Aspects

Within the framework of the present book it is impossible to examine all of the didactic aspects of teaching about the Holocaust. We have chosen to deal here with those aspects that, in our opinion, are important for the success of such teaching—sometimes even decisively so—and comprise the "criteria of success" (which is a complex subject in its own right). Anyone engaged in the didactic aspects of teaching the Holocaust in Israel has discovered the great depth and breadth of the gaps between "theory" and "practice" in this field. Thus, for example, although historians and senior educators called for Jewish history to be taught within the framework of world history as long ago as the mid-1960s, this was begun in practice in the education system only at the end of the 1990s.

In any attempt to clarify the nature of the gaps between theory and practice, questions and answers suggesting the universalistic and particularistic perspectives of the subject inevitably arise. For example, is it possible to learn about the Holocaust and to truly comprehend it? This is a universal question with meaning and significance for all, and it is asked in Israel as well as in other places in the world. Both in Israel and elsewhere some of those attempting to answer this question "make do" with research and a search for the facts alone: There was a Holocaust, and it must be understood and taught, if only because it is part and parcel of historical reality. This is a universal answer to the universal question. The question of *why* the Holocaust should be taught, however, although also a universal one, evokes different answers in Israel and in the rest of the world. Some of these answers are also universal, and as such they are as valid for Israel as they are for the United States, France, Australia, and Germany, and so on. Others are particularistic, and evoke different specific answers in different countries. This topic will be dealt with in a later chapter that describes the teaching of the Holocaust in different places, other than Israel, throughout the world.

Teaching the Holocaust: Objectives

An answer to the important issue arising from the second question asked above—*why* the Holocaust should be taught—is dependent on the objectives of such teaching. Opinions about this, on both its universal and particularistic levels, vary considerably. As a rule the answers are divided into those seeking to emphasize the emotive aspect of the Holocaust memory and those emphasizing informative-learning goals and, hence, the importance of acquiring knowledge about it. This division is even more pronounced in Israel.

A more specific distinction between the different objectives is discussed by Haim Schatzker in his article "Didactic Problems in the Teaching of the Holocaust," (referred to in the preceding chapter).[1] Schatzker lists four different types of objectives:

- informative-learning;
- educational;
- societal;
- national-Jewish.

The first three may be defined as universal objectives; the last is clearly particularistic. There is, however, a particularistic dimension in each of the first three universal objectives as well, which constitutes an essential precondition for achieving them. During the first years of Israel's independence the teaching of the Holocaust's national-Jewish objective was undoubtedly the central one, with the informative-learning goal being added only somewhat later.

One of the functions of Yad Vashem is to provide the means for realizing all four of these purposes. This institution has, over the last few decades and especially during the 1990s, developed a broad range of educational activities that deal with the Holocaust. Among other projects, Yad Vashem established The International School Holocaust Studies, which is undoubtedly one of the most important such centers in the world. The activities of this school are guided by its educational program, which reflects the fact that Yad Vashem is the State of

Israel's national authority for remembrance of the Holocaust. The school's educational program is described as follows:

> The community in Israel and in the world sees Yad Vashem as the representative authority for memorializing the Holocaust, and its expectations derive from this perception. This status demands that The International School for Holocaust Studies represent the government of Israel in its educational activities. The school, whose perception is connected to a deep indebtedness to pluralism, sees this as an especially complex educational challenge. In dealing with the Holocaust there is an intrinsic value to both nationhood and pluralism that necessitates unceasing work to pave ways to deal with the Holocaust and the memory of the Holocaust as factors shared by the whole nation and, by extension, by all mankind. This is above and beyond any social, political, or religious view. Thus, any attempt, by any group, to appropriate the Holocaust and turn it into a tool for strengthening any ideology must be *deterred*.[2]

This statement goes on to affirm the uniqueness of the Holocaust, its influence on the forming of the Jewish identity, and its significance for the history of mankind:

> The Holocaust is a unique event in human history that has educational significance that must be learned and taught. The uniqueness of the Holocaust is in that it was an ideologically motivated attempt to murder all of the Jewish people and its culture. It was a sweeping operation, carefully planned, and was carried out with the cooperation of a bureaucratic administration, and with the use of modern up-to-date technology.
>
> We view the Holocaust as an important event in the formation of identity in Jewish society in general, and in that of the State of Israel in particular. The influence of the Holocaust is expressed in the national-collective dimension and sometimes in the personal-individual dimension. The process of the formation of Jewish identity draws from the world that preceded the Holocaust, among other things, and from the Holocaust itself, and seeks to confront the trauma of the Holocaust and the void that was created in its wake.
>
> The Holocaust carries significant weight in the history of mankind, and it presents, since its occurrence, questions of deep moral and ethical value for all of humankind.[3]

The main values of the educational approach of Yad Vashem's International School for Holocaust Studies, and those that guide its work and its activities include:

- A commitment to the continued existence of Jewry;
- Meticulous attention to historical accuracy;
- The inculcation of universal values;
- An emphasis on human dignity.

44 The Pain of Knowledge

A comparison between this educational program and those of similar institutions elsewhere in the world that deal with the teaching of the Holocaust is of considerable interest and will be discussed below (see chapter 12).

Against the prodigious public institution of Yad Vashem, the activity of one individual, Abba Kovner, stands out prominently. One of the leaders of the Jewish underground and of Jewish partisans, and one of the initiators and founders of the Diaspora Museum[4] in Israel in the 1970s, Kovner was also deeply engaged in many aspects of the teaching of the Holocaust, and of its inculcation and place in the long-range collective memory of the Jewish People. In an article entitled "From Generation to Generation" Kovner asserted that the educational imperative of those who survived the Holocaust is to "try to etch into the memories of future generations the difficult but genuine and true message of the present generation: that the life of the Jew who knew the Holocaust is a relentless tension between *blessed and damned*, between the sanctity of life and its cursedness."[5] Although Kovner does not deal with the didactic aspects of Holocaust teaching in this article in a direct way, his words carry the unequivocal implication that the realization that the Holocaust is not the obsession of its surviving remnants, and that its place is in the historical consciousness of every generation of Jews wherever they may be, is a necessity. Without this realization, Kovner believes, it is doubtful, if at all possible, to truly identify oneself with a living, positive, and creative Judaism.

Teaching the Subject of the Holocaust: Methodology

In the light of the objectives of Holocaust teaching described above, we shall briefly examine some of the different ways in which this can be done. The subject of the Holocaust is taught twice within the official history curriculums: first in junior high (middle) school (ages 13–14), and again in high school (ages 17–18). Although the official curriculum suggests allotting four to six lessons to this subject at the middle school level, it appears that most of the teachers actually devote considerably more time to it. At the high school level, as noted above, the Holocaust is a required subject, and is studied in depth in the course of thirty to forty lessons. All students are required to be tested in this subject, within the framework of the matriculation examination in history.

It is also worth noting that teachers in grade schools, and even in kindergartens, also teach this subject, although there is no Ministry of Education directive to do so. Pupils at all levels are exposed to the subject of the Holocaust on many different occasions within their school frameworks, and certainly more often than any other subject dealt with as part of their history studies.

An important article about this subject is "The Problems of Teaching the Holocaust Today," also by Haim Schatzker.[6] The author first discusses the objectives of Holocaust teaching in Israeli schools. He examines these from the earliest period in which there was didactic thinking in this field, which in his opinion began in the early 1960s, and then asks what constituted the underlying principles, the directions, and the objectives that guided the people who were working in this field. Schatzker also tries to identify the directions of change and innovation in the teaching of the Holocaust that, along with the changing reality of life in Israel, could have—and should have—been foreseen. He compares these with the changes that did come about in Holocaust teaching, and then points out various aspects that remain in need of change. On the basis of his research Schatzker recommends the following:

1. The teaching unit devoted to the Holocaust should begin with the background of the First World War, rather than with the aftermath of that war, as is usual; the unit should also deal with the part played in this war by various ethnic groups in Western Europe and the Balkans.
2. The Soviet Union and the fate of its Jews during the period of the Holocaust, a subject almost never treated in textbooks about the Holocaust, should be dealt with.
3. In deliberating on the reactions of the victims of the Holocaust under the conditions of terror thrust upon them, use should be made of texts on psychology, especially those relating to behavior under pressure.
4. European Jewry on the eve of and during the Holocaust is usually evaluated from the perspective of an "Israeli commando officer"—an insupportable and intolerable approach that should be completely uprooted.
5. Ways must be sought to incorporate the findings of recent research into existing learning programs and textbooks: "The incorporation of scientific approaches, the fruit of scientific research, can counterbalance recent simplistic, subjective, and ideological trends that seek a powerful and emotional lesson from the period of the Holocaust, which appear to be similar to the political, social, and economic threats facing Israel today."[7]

Another article that deals directly with the question of the objectives of Holocaust teaching and ways in which to achieve them is "Teaching the Holocaust as Education toward Values," by Arye Carmon,[8] who developed a learning program for this subject (discussed above, in chapter 4). Carmon specifies the educational approach that constitutes the basis of his program, according to which the Holocaust should be taught from the general perspective of "education toward values." In this article the author provides the details for how his program—which sets as its goal to foster certain, clearly defined values in adolescents—uses various different methods and content to serve this goal. Carmon's learning program is based on three underlying basic assumptions:

- It is imperative to cope with ambiguities.
- The degree of competence of adolescents to distinguish between different kinds of values and to contend with the process of adopting them must be taken into account.
- The relationship between value-oriented education and its subject matter must be considered.

In its optimal structure Carmon's learning program includes both the Jewish dimension of the Holocaust and its universal one, and consists of four parts:

- The socialization of the German adolescent in Nazi Germany;
- The conditioning of an S.S. man;
- Continuity and change in Jewish communities on the eve of the Holocaust;
- Moral dilemmas faced by Jews—as individuals and as groups—during the Holocaust.

Carmon's program constitutes an interesting and innovative attempt to deal with the Holocaust mainly from the perspective of education towards values. By its very nature this perspective is prone to tension between the "educational challenge" and the "learning challenge." It is of interest to note that in most countries other than Israel, the teaching of the Holocaust is more commonly found in the context of education towards values.

Evaluation of Programs for Teaching the Holocaust

It is well known that evaluating educational achievements is a multi-faceted and complex problem; evaluating programs for teaching the Holocaust is especially difficult, as well as sensitive, as it is dependent on a number of different subjective factors, among them the evaluator's viewpoint, the educational goals, the criteria used for the evaluation, and how these criteria are applied. While evaluation, examination, and self-criticism are extremely important elements—one may even say essential ones—in the successful result of every educational process, educational activities in general, and especially those related to Holocaust teaching in particular, are usually not equipped with the most suitable tools for accomplishing these objectives. Such evaluations also usually fail to yield the expected results, in addition to which they are not helpful in the continuing search for possible alternative programs.

Facing the Educational Aspects of Holocaust Studies

The article "Training Students for Teaching and for Dealing Educationally with the Subject of the Holocaust" presents research on and an evaluation of the subject of consciousness awareness of the Holocaust.[9] This was the subject of a three-day seminar carried out as part of teacher training in Bet Berl College; the seminar was held in the memorial and educational center located in Kibbutz Lohamei Hagetaot in the north of Israel. Since the year 1986 Bet Berl College, like other teacher-training colleges, has required most of its students to attend this concentrated seminar; study of the subject is a requirement for receiving a teaching certificate and, until the 1994–5 school year, was for all practical purposes the only compulsory course in the college. Bet Berl College drew conclusions from the results of this study that led to the development of a new program for training its students in coping with the educational aspects of the Holocaust. The new educational rationale adopted by the college in this field expresses a desire to deal with as broad a range of approaches to the "understanding of" the Holocaust as possible, while also realizing that "there will always be a gap between the desire to explain and the ability to fully comprehend what happened." The college's new program aims to present a model of involvement and educational responsibility that takes into consideration the full scope of approaches and dilemmas presented by this subject. The entire program is taught over three years, the seminar constituting only one of its components, and the active involvement of the college's teachers, pedagogical instructors, and students is expected. The students are required to prepare model learning programs for teaching about the Holocaust.

A study that evaluated a different program is described in an article by Sarah Guri-Rosenblit and Na'ama Tsabar Ben-Yehoshua.[10] The authors examined the effect of teaching the Holocaust through the "adopt a community" method on adolescents' knowledge about the Holocaust and on their attitudes towards it. The basis for developing this method was the assumption that pupils, at all grade levels, find it difficult to identify with the intangible concept of millions of victims in thousands of communities that were destroyed in the Holocaust. The "adopt a community" program suggests learning about the Holocaust through a more personal approach. In actuality, what is applied here is the principle of a "case study": in order to understand the broad range of events and about the lives of the Jews that preceded them, a class "adopts" one community and closely examines its history, life routine, organization, culture, and values, and its fate prior to and during the war. The program chosen for this research deals with the Jewish community of Vilna (Vilnius) and is geared to grades 8–9. According to the researchers' conclusions, in the experimental group that studied this program there was a significant change in the pupils' knowledge about the lives of Jewish communities in Eastern Europe during the period that preceded the Holocaust. In regard to the attitudes of these same pupils towards the past there was no significant change, no greater feeling of identification with the adopted community, nor any internalization of the need for learning about the Holocaust in general.

This is one example, of the few that exist, of an educational program for the study of the Holocaust that was accompanied by a study that examined the connection between the declared goals and the results that were achieved in the cognitive domain (knowledge) and in the affective domain (attitudes and identification).

In every educational situation there is a gap between "theory" and "practice" or, phrased differently, between the "vision" and the "deed." This gap is perhaps especially great in regard to the teaching of the Holocaust in Israel.

Despite the important place of the Holocaust in the Israeli education system, there is a dearth of in-depth research of the different kinds of educational activities in use in Holocaust studies, and of the teaching itself.

Both of these quandaries have yet to be addressed and have conclusions drawn.

Notes

1. Haim Schatzker, "Didactic Problems in the Teaching of the Holocaust," *Guidelines for Teachers of History, 2,* 1961 (Hebrew), pp. 11–15.
2. *Educational Program: The International School for Holocaust Studies* (Jerusalem: Yad Vashem, 1998) (Hebrew), p. 9.
3. Ibid., pp. 14–15.
4. The Diaspora Museum, an interactive educational institution located on the campus of Tel Aviv University, was created in the 1970s. Its main purpose is to enrich young people's knowledge of the history and cultural achievements of the Jewish people during almost 2500 years of life in the countries in which they were dispersed, and to strengthen relations between Israel and the present-day Diaspora.
5. Abba Kovner, "From Generation to Generation," *Yalkut Moreshet, 50,* April 1991 (Hebrew), pp. 13–16. (The emphasis is in the original.)
6. Haim Schatzker, "Problems in Contemporary Holocaust Teaching," in Rivka Feldhay and Immanuel Etkes (eds.), Education and History (Jerusalem: The Zalman Shazar Center for Jewish History, 1999) (Hebrew), pp. 447–455.
7. Ibid., p. 455.
8. Arye Carmon, "Teaching the Holocaust as a Means of Fostering Values," *Curriculum Inquiry*, 9/3, 1979, pp. 209–228; Arye Carmon, "Teaching the Holocaust as Education toward Values," in *Theory into Practice in Lesson Planning, 3,* 1980 (Hebrew), pp. 97–172.
9. Ofer Shiff, Yaakov Bar Zohar, Drora Kfir, and Tali Singer, "Training Students for Teaching and for Coping Educationally with the Subject of the Holocaust," *Dappim: Studies on the Holocaust Period, 23*, 1996, (Hebrew) pp. 7–26.
10. Sarah Guri-Rosenblit and Na'ama Tsabar Ben-Yehoshua, "An Evaluation of the Cognitive and Affective Changes about the Holocaust in Youth as a Result of Teaching the Holocaust through the Adopt-a-Community Method," *Theory and Practice in Planning Studies, 3,* 1980 (Hebrew), pp. 113–132.

6

Learning Programs in Israel

In this chapter we will briefly describe five of the many learning programs and textbooks for teaching the Holocaust that were developed in Israel during the 1980s and 1990s. These programs were not selected because they were "better," or "more correct" than others, or more prevalent, but because they exemplify the range of programs in use at the time of writing. Although the evaluation of these learning programs is in itself an important issue, it will not be dealt with here; the construction of a set of criteria for such evaluations may, however, evolve as a by-product of the present book.

Four of the five different programs described in this chapter deal with the Holocaust in a general, historical way; while the fifth does so through "the mirror" of literature. A few short sections or specific segments, such as "Educational Rationale," "Introduction," and "Teacher's Guide," are presented for elucidation. The fifth does so through "the mirror" of literature.

During the 1980s and 1990s one of the textbooks most highly recommended by the Ministry of Education for teaching the Holocaust, and the one most widely used, was *The Holocaust and its Significance: Teacher's Guide*, by Yisrael Gutman and Haim Schatzker.[1] In their discussion of the dilemmas that arise during the teaching of this subject, the authors present five main goals that teachers are advised to use as guidelines to help them in making didactic considerations and decisions[2]:

1. The pupils should acquire a basic body of information that comprises the historical event termed "Holocaust." Such a basis is necessary for making balanced judgments and evaluations, and for adopting an independent position. Only on the basis of such knowledge can we impart meaning to Holocaust Remembrance Day and its attendant memorial ceremonies, to literary

and other artistic expressions of the Holocaust, and to make it more meaningful than routine learning.

An additional aspect of the importance of this body of basic information lies in the constantly growing danger of the neo-Nazi literature that seeks to attenuate the magnitude of the Holocaust or to deny its very existence. Although even the most reliable information cannot have an effect on neo-Nazis themselves, factual knowledge is essential for those unable to refute such lies by virtue of their own experiences or memories.

2. The pupils should acquire an understanding and sensitivity to the structures and mechanisms that underlie the non-legitimate generalizations and stereotypical preconceptions in interpersonal relations that are liable to create the prejudices, fears, and hatred that can end in murder and holocaust.

It is the reflective awareness of these mechanisms that constitute the universal lesson of the Holocaust, a lesson significant to each and every human being and to every educational system whose orientation is drawn from the mistakes, the shortcomings, and the omissions of the past. The change in one's perception of the image of Man and of the nature of mankind is the universal lesson of the Holocaust, and the education of a person in accordance with this perception is the educational message of the Holocaust, while also aiming to prevent new holocausts.

3. The pupils must be able to discern the intrinsic links between the above structures and mechanisms and the totalitarian rule created in their light and that served to nourish them and to ensure their continued existence and development. They must be made aware of the danger of baseless and unproven myths, mass hysteria, and the cult of the personality. Above all, they must be aware of the danger of abandoning the imperative of personal morality and individual responsibility for one's actions, while creating a supra-personal morality of the state, the race, or anything similar, and which may be at variance from an individual's personal morality, thus releasing that individual from responsibility. An awareness of these dangers constitutes something of an education towards democracy and towards conscious and responsible civil behavior.

4. The pupils should be made aware of, and warned about, the danger of anti-Semitism in all of its forms, and able to correctly judge its place and importance in the Third Reich. The indiscriminate persecution and murder of Jews, without any distinctions or exceptions, were never marginal aspects of the Nazi ideology or of the Third Reich's policies. They were also neither a by-product of the conditions and circumstances created by the war, nor included in the category of class war, a policy towards minorities, war casualties, or any other inclusive term that attempts to avoid a confrontation with the core issues of the Holocaust.

The pupils must be made capable of distinguishing between different forms of anti-Semitic phenomena, as well as the roots and the significance of anti-

Semitism, and of perceiving that the murder of six million Jews was carried out not by an anonymous mechanism but by human beings—citizens, fathers, husbands, and sons; and that this was done with the agreement, through its silence or passive stand, of the entire world. Against this background the importance and the fundamental reasons for [Israel's] national existence become clear. The recognition of these issues and the lessons implicit in them are not specifically and solely Jewish goals but, rather, a mission and a goal in the broadest and most universal terms.

5. The pupils should become capable of comprehending the Holocaust from an historical standpoint, on the background of the immanent developments in the history of the Jewish people in recent times, and to include this perception in their analysis and evaluation of those ideological streams that sought the solution to the "Jewish question" in assimilation and integration amongst the nations.

The universalistic aspect of learning about the Holocaust, which is emphasized in sections 2 and 3 of the above guidelines, also characterizes the program prepared by Arye Carmon.[3] Carmon's program is unique in its attempt to develop a model for teaching the Holocaust from a more universalistic standpoint than that usually found in the Israeli education system, and in doing so without disregarding the particularistic aspects of the subject. The program's principles, problems, and practice are described in Carmon's "Teaching the Holocaust as a Means of Fostering Values" which, with certain called-for modifications, was also studied in the United States and in Germany. Its universalistic goal is clear from the presentation of the principal aim that underlies the program: "The major objective of the universal dimension is to heighten the student's awareness of the critical function of individual responsibility in a democratic society." The content of "Teaching the Holocaust as a Means of Fostering Values" is based on multifaceted data in four main sections:

> In its optimal format, the program has two dimensions: the universal and the Jewish. As such it is meant principally for a Jewish student body, but the program has also been fashioned in a shorter form for non-Jewish students [in the upper grades in secondary schools] in democratic societies. . . . The universal format includes four sections:
>
> Section I. The socialization of a Germans adolescent in Nazi Germany
> Section II. The Socialization of the Secret Service Man
> Section III. Moral Dilemmas of Jewish Individuals and Groups during the Holocaust
> Section IV: The Meaning of Life in the Post-Holocaust Era

Section I. Socialization of the Germans during the Third Reich. This section deals with:
(a) *significant elements in the socialization of a German adolescent in the 1930s*, the historical factors that led to the development of an irrational entity, and the adolescent's immediate home, school, and extra-curricular environment. The human tendency to stereotype is discussed . . . ; (b) features of *socialization and the personality* in the formation of political and moral identity are clarified theoretically; (c) *life within an antirational entity*, including propaganda and distinctions between individual moral dilemmas within the antirational entity; (d) the avoidance of individual responsibility, including discussion of tendencies of the individual to obey authority vs. the necessity for individual responsibility.

Section II. Socialization of the Secret Service man during the Third Reich, including:
(a) *social conditions of the Secret Service man*; indoctrination, social conditioning; the norms and techniques that foster behavior and moral judgments are discussed and compared; (b) stages in the implementation of the destruction machinery: clarification of elements of the "Final Solution," *Einsatzgruppe*, death camps, etc.

Section III. Response of Jewish individuals and groups in "nonlife" situations created during the Holocaust, including moral dilemmas relating to the "Jewish councils," active resistance, and passive resistance.

Section IV. The meaning of life in the post-Holocaust era; aims at summarizing the entire program on the basis of various accounts pertaining to moral, humanistic, and theological issues.

The objectives the program wishes to develop in the student as a prerequisite to realizing broader aims are based on the following:

A. Knowledge and comprehension
   1. Knowledge of the basic facts
   2. Fostering the ability to conceptualize (in the fields of history and the social sciences)
   3. Fostering the ability to reach valid generalizations on the basis of substantive data
   4. Initiating the use of research skills—locating and collecting relevant information
B. Fostering of critical thinking
   1. Identification of central issues and underlying assumptions
   2. Evaluation of evidence and of classified documents and drawing warranted conclusions
   3. Ability to formulate and analyze reasonable hypotheses as well as to evaluate their validity
C. Developing an awareness of the potential dangers inherent in the human tendency to stereotype

D. Fostering of autonomous attitudes
   1. Development of a rational approach to human behavior, as far as possible, based on an understanding of the structure of human behavior and its direct and indirect causes
   2. Development of tolerance towards the behavior of others, based on empathy and ethical norms
   3. Development of the assumption of individual responsibility for deeds of social significance

A prerequisite essential to the achievement of these objectives, and thus an objective in itself, is to free students from their preconceived judgments and preconceived images insofar as they are the result of external, emotional, and uncritical pressures.[4]

At the end of the 1990s a "new wave" of textbooks for learning about the Holocaust appeared, among them *Shoah: A Journey to Memory* by Nili Keren,[5] and *Shoah and Memory* by Yisrael Gutman,[6] the latter a textbook for the upper high school grades and one of a three-part series of textbooks dealing with the world and the Jews in recent generations. (Note that the words "Shoah" and "memory" both appear in the titles of these two books.)

In her Introduction, Keren presents her book in the following way:

The book before you discusses in detail three main groups of people: the perpetrators, the victims, and the bystanders. The main protagonists of the story of the Holocaust are, of course, its victims. The vast majority of these victims left behind the story of a life cut short, small bits of memory, or sometimes only a name. Those who survived to see the day of their liberation had experienced years of terror during which they tried, day-by-day and hour-by-hour, to preserve their human dignity in the face of an absence of humanity that surrounded them on all sides. After their liberation they had to cope for many years with the scars that remained on their bodies and on their souls.[7]

While Gutman, in his Introduction, writes as follows:

Shoah and Memory presents comprehensive information about the Holocaust and its ramifications. It examines the period of the Holocaust from two main perspectives: as a part as the totality of events of world history and of Jewish history, and as an attempt to derive from this period of terror meanings that will contribute to the crystallization of our present-day self-awareness as Jews and as human beings. . . .

Shoah and Memory is meant to provide a teaching-didactic dimension to the Holocaust and to its ramifications—a subject that is considered beyond human comprehension. During the last few years interest in the Holocaust as an event indicating

56   **The Pain of Knowledge**

a turning point in the history of the Jewish people has grown, and its impact continues to grow with time, both in Israel and in the world. In addition, new sources have also been uncovered that reveal much information concerning the Holocaust.

In *Shoah and Memory* an attempt has been made to deal with these developments. The book presents a broad historical context for an examination of the events of the period that is based on a broad range of historical, artistic, literary, and philosophical sources. The book attempts to contend with the questions of how such an event was possible in the twentieth century, and why the helpless and powerless Jews were turned into the enemies and the victims in the confrontation between the great powers. The book also focuses on additional issues, such as the Holocaust and the establishment of the State of Israel, the rehabilitation of the survivors, and the memory of the Holocaust and its place in the Jewish consciousness today.[8]

Regarding both of these books we chose to examine the similarities and the differences between how they portrayed the question of how the world's response to the Holocaust was represented and which rescue attempts of the different countries were described.

A fifth textbook, *Testimony and Identity 1938–1946: The Holocaust as Reflected in Literature,* by Mikhal Popowsky, is an example of the possibility of dealing with the subject of the Holocaust from a perspective other than an historical one.[9] In this textbook, which is actually an anthology, poems and explanations of them are presented in chronological order and serve as the background for a short description of the events that occurred during that given period of time.

The poem below, selected from the reader for the seventh grade (and included in the new curriculum for literature in the middle schools), is a representative example of the contents of this book. The author, Iakovos Kambanelis, a non-Jewish Greek writer who fought against the Nazis, was arrested and incarcerated in Mauthausen for two and a half years.[10] His poem "Song of Songs," which is one of the six-part "Ballad to Mauthausen," touches on certain aspects of the attitude of the world to the victims of the Holocaust in a unique way:[11]

"Song of Songs"

How lovely is my love
in her everyday dress
with a little comb in her hair.
No one knew how lovely she was.

Girls of Auschwitz.
    girls of Dachau
    have you seen the one I love?

We saw her on the long journey.
She wasn't wearing her everyday dress
    or the little comb in her hair.

How lovely is my love,
Caressed by her mother,
    kissed by her brother.
No one knew how lovely she was.
Girls of Belsen
    girls of Mauthausen
    have you seen the one I love?

We saw her in the frozen square
    with a number on her white arm
    and a yellow star over her heart.

How lovely is my love
    in her everyday dress
    with a little comb in her hair.
No one knew how lovely she was.

Through its delicate poetical phrasing and its allusions to the biblical Song of Songs (Song of Solomon), the reader's attention is drawn to seemingly trivial details rather than to abstract generalizations. In this way, the poem evokes a personal identification with a specific figure (a young Jewish girl in this case). These special qualities are likely to create a greater willingness on the part of the pupil to devote more attention not only to the poem itself but also to the historical details, or to a "dry," historical analysis of the period of the Holocaust.

Notes

1. Yisrael Gutman and Haim Schatzker, *The Holocaust and its Significance: Teacher's Guide* (Jerusalem: Zalman Shazar Center, 1983) (Hebrew).
2. Ibid., pp. 4–5.
3. Arye Carmon, "Teaching the Holocaust as a Means of Fostering Values," *Curriculum Inquiry*, 9, 3, 1979, pp. 209–228. A parallel article appeared in Hebrew as *The Holocaust: A Subject for the Upper Levels of the General School* (*Teacher's Guide*) (Jerusalem: Ministry of Education and Culture, 1981).

58   The Pain of Knowledge

4. Ibid., pp. 217–219.
5. Nili Keren, *Shoah—A Journey to Memory* (Tel Aviv: Sifrei Tel Aviv, 1999) (Hebrew).
6. Yisrael Gutman, *Shoah and Memory*, in the series "The World and the Jews in Recent Generations" (Jerusalem: The Zalman Shazar Center for Jewish History, 1999) (Hebrew).
7. Keren, *Shoah—A Journey to Memory*, p. 3.
8. Gutman, *Shoah and Memory*, p. 5.
9. Mikhal Popowski, *Testimony and Identity 1938-1946: The Holocaust as Reflected in Literature* (Tel Aviv: The Center for Educational Technology, 1994) (Hebrew).
10. Ibid., p. 52.
11. Iakovos Kambanelis's poem, set to music by Mikis Theodorakis and sung movingly by, among others, Maria Farantouri, won broad attention throughout the world. The version presented here was translated from the Greek by Gail Holst Warhaft.

7

Holocaust Martyrs' and Heroes' Remembrance Day

In Yehuda Amichai's poem "And Who Will Remember the Rememberers?" quoted in the epigraph, he asks:[1]

> What is the correct way to stand at a memorial assembly?
> Erect or stooped, pulled taut as a tent or in the slumped posture
>   of mourning, head bowed like the guilty or held high
>   in a collective protest against death,
>   eyes gaping frozen like the eyes of the dead
>   or shut tight, to see the stars inside?
> And what is the best time for remembering? At noon
>   when shadows are hidden beneath our feet, or at twilight
>   when shadows lengthen like longings
>   that have no beginning, no end, like God?

In this chapter we ask how "we stand at the memorial assembly" by examining the commemoration of Martyrs' and Heroes' Remembrance Day in Israel's education system. The ceremonies held in Israeli schools on this day play a central role in the schools' calendar and in the pupils' emotional experiences. Bestowing an official, solemn status on such commemorations for educational purposes is a well-known and familiar phenomenon throughout history, and especially in the history of religions and nations. As in the ancient empires, modern national states have also established and exploited the use of ceremonies as a vehicle for celebrating their victories; they have turned such ceremonies into educational tools for instilling in the masses the fundamental principles of the dominant national doctrine.

In their article "Ceremonies, Education and History: Holocaust Remembrance Day and Memorial Day [for the Fallen in Israel's Wars] in Israeli Schools" the authors, Avner Ben-Amos and Ilana Bet-El, claim that both religious and national state establishments were, in most cases, meticulous in making a clear differentiation between their ritual ceremonies and those marked in official educational institutions.[2] In the case of Israel, according to these researchers, the education system, which the Jewish Yishuv in Palestine established and the state continued to develop after its founding, is unique in that it weaves such ceremonies into the framework of the official education programs, with the aim of increasing its educational efficiency.

The assemblies commemorating Martyrs' and Heroes' Remembrance Day and Memorial Day have been the most central of all ceremonies observed in Israeli schools since the establishment of the state.[3] Although the central importance of these ceremonies has been retained during all of these years, their character and their form and content have undergone changes and modifications, and it appears that the uniformity that characterized them in the past has, to a certain degree, weakened in the course of time. According to the authors the ceremonies for Martyrs' and Heroes' Remembrance Day should be examined within the sequential framework of the national holidays that begin with Passover (in late March or early April) and end with Jerusalem Day (around mid-May):

> This continuity has great emotional power and binds together the fate of the Jewish People throughout its generations with that of the Jewish People living "in Zion" [i.e., in its own land] within a broad historical framework characterized by a recurring cycle of loss and redemption. This cyclic theme begins with Passover, which in its modern nationalist embodiment has been turned into "The Festival of Freedom." The narrative of the Exodus from Egypt provides a deep historical anchor for the Jewish People, simultaneously creating its basic character as a people in an ongoing struggle against distress, striving for freedom and a return to the Land of Israel. Holocaust Memorial Day, which falls a few days after the end of Passover, marks the modern attempt to destroy the [Jewish] People, and the revolt in the ghettoes is the spark of heroism that will again appear in the Land of Israel; Memorial Day marks the memory of the sacrifice that must be made in order to attain the yearned for freedom, which is celebrated on Independence. A few weeks later, the next stage in the realization of freedom is marked by Jerusalem Day, the anniversary of the capture of the Old City of Jerusalem, as a national-Jewish event, and one that also wavers between the poles of loss and redemption. The sequence of these holidays thus marks the threat of loss, surmounting the loss, and rebirth—in ancient times with the help of God, and finally, in the modern era, by the strength of the People itself. In the ceremonies of both of these memorial days there are recognizable military and religious influences that make their educational dimension even more complex.[4]

Although certain structural changes in the school assemblies marking Holocaust Memorial Day were added to the ceremonies as early as the 1960s, most of them after the Eichmann trial, according to the authors, the ceremonies still preserved their traditional content and the distinction between the praiseworthy ghetto fighters and partisans and the passive victims of the Nazis. The changes in the attitude towards the Holocaust that came about in the aftermath of the Six Day War (in 1967), and deepened following the Yom Kippur War (1973), led in the course of time to a new phenomenon, one that also affected the form—but not the content—of the Holocaust Remembrance Day ceremonies: the educational tours of high school pupils to Poland (which are discussed in chapter 8). After their return from Poland these pupils undertake the role of "emissaries" of the Holocaust victims, thus creating a new tradition in the ceremonies based largely on their own experiences, and through them of the Holocaust survivors' experiences. (Usually a survivor, a "living witness" of the Holocaust, participates in each such visit to Poland, and the pupils thus become "witnesses of the witnesses," as it were.)

In Ben-Amos and Bet-El's opinion, despite the great similarity between the memorial ceremony for those who fell in Israel's wars and that for Holocaust Remembrance Day, the very fact that a new tradition developed is itself evidence of a basic difference between them: Memorial Day for the Fallen, which deals with the ongoing reality of a violent struggle between the State of Israel and the Arabs, has an established, stable format; Memorial Day for the Holocaust, which relates to a one-time event of the past, is influenced by the changes in Israeli society's collective memory, and its ceremonial format is therefore more flexible.

An example of an unusual attempt to introduce a dramatic change in the character of Holocaust Remembrance Day is a ceremony carried out in 1995 in the Kedma School, whose student population was largely of Mizrahi descent (Jews from Arab-speaking countries), and is located in the disadvantaged Hatikva neighborhood in Tel Aviv. That year the school decided to change the traditional ceremony by adding to it an emphasis on the issue of racism and human suffering as a universal problem. To do this a seventh ceremonial torch was added to the six that symbolize the six million Jews murdered in the Holocaust, and was dedicated to the murder of other groups and peoples. (It is worth noting, in this context, that in discussions preparatory to the opening of the

U.S. Holocaust Museum in Washington, D.C. regarding the shaping of the memory of the Holocaust in the United States, Rabbi Yitzchak Greenberg, later the museum council's director, raised the idea of kindling a seventh candle on Holocaust Remembrance Day in memory of the non-Jewish victims of the Holocaust.) The Kedma School's ceremony elicited strong reactions in different circles of the Israeli public that claimed that Holocaust Remembrance Day must emphasize the uniqueness of the Jewish Holocaust, and that the lighting of the seventh torch detracts from this uniqueness. In the heat of the controversy questions arose regarding the complex relations between the Mizrahi and the Ashkenazi Jews in the country—both within and beyond the context of the Holocaust—because the Kedma School unquestionably also tried to raise the issue of the ethnic-class gap within Israeli society. This subject was dealt with in an article, "Holocaust Remembrance Day in Progressive Eyes: Ethnicity, Class and Education in Israel," by Tamar Barkay and Gai Levy (and see below, chapter 9).[5] In connection with this ceremony in the Kedma School the authors maintained that:

> The ceremony in the Kedma School diverged from the customary format only in the lighting of a seventh torch in memory of the victims of racism and the persecution of peoples throughout history, but this was a virtual battle-cry not only regarding the memory of the Holocaust but also because of its significance for the national memory as a whole, and thus for the very essence of the Israeli identity.[6]

A dedication for the seventh torch was written by the school's principal, Sammy Shalom Chetrit, and declaimed, along with the lighting of the seventh torch, by a Holocaust survivor:

> We, Jews of the third generation since the nation's liberation and independence, with great reverence, wish to draw from the fire of the torches in memory of the six million Jews, victims of the Nazi Holocaust, a seventh torch, to be displayed for the entire world to see.
>
> We have the tragic privilege of standing here to remember and to forewarn: no nation, no culture and no group of people is immune to hatred, racism, persecution or extermination.
>
> Xenophobia, persecution and annihilation of the other is a social phenomenon, which could infect any society, at any time.
>
> We do not intend, God forbid, to mitigate the pain of the memory of our people, nor do we wish to compare one Holocaust to another.

Our only wish is to remind all human beings that persecution and extermination of the "other" are man-made monsters, created by the hands and minds of human beings, as other nations, races and members of different religions and ethnic groups have learned throughout the history of mankind. We must remember that only Man can overcome these terrible monsters. We, the offspring of the survivors of the most terrible catastrophe of all, today standing here with heads held on high, pray for peace and fraternity between nations, religions, races and cultures.[7]

The authors of the article relate to various different reactions to this ceremony:

The reactions that followed a news item about the unique format of the Holocaust Remembrance Day ceremony in the Kedma School several days prior to the event itself [and after it as well] veered between complete opposition to ardent support. Those negating it reacted, sometimes even with rage, either against the requisition, as it were, of this day from the collective Jewish memory, or to the suggested prominence of the difference between the historical experiences of Ashkenazi and Mizrahi Jews. The supporters, too, expressed recognition of the importance of Holocaust Remembrance Day for its national Israeli-Zionist content, but also of the fact that this recognition is anchored in the less ethnocentric perception of national identity.[8]

It appears in any case that despite the changes that have occurred in the course of time in their character, and notwithstanding the fact that the uniformity that characterized them in the past has somewhat lessened, the ceremonies marking Martyrs' and Heroes' Remembrance Day still constitute a significant factor in drawing the Zionist-Jewish lesson of the Holocaust (as demonstrated by the stormy controversy surrounding the Kedma School affair). And yet, it appears that in spite of the fact that the importance of these ceremonies in constructing the memory of the Holocaust (as opposed to the teaching of the subject) remains firm, its influence as an affective emotional factor has diminished to some degree. This is perhaps a result of the transfer of the focus of the "Holocaust experience" to the visits of Israeli high school pupils to the extermination camps in Poland, as we shall see in the next chapter.

Notes

1. Yehuda Amichai, in *Open Closed Open* (translated from the Hebrew by Chana Bloch and Chana Kronfeld) (New York, San Diego and London: Harcourt, 2000), stanza 3, pp. 169–170.

64   The Pain of Knowledge

2. Avner Ben-Amos and Ilana Bet-El, "Ceremonies, Education and History: Holocaust Day and Remembrance Day in Israeli Schools," in Rivka Feldhay and Immanuel Etkes (eds.), *Education and History: Cultural and Political Links* (Jerusalem: The Zalman Shazar Center for Jewish History, 1999) (Hebrew), pp. 457–479.
3. On this see: Don Handelman, "State Ceremonies of Israel: Remembrance Day and Independence Day," in *Models and Mirrors: Towards an Anthropology of Public Events* (Cambridge: Cambridge University Press, 1990), pp. 191–223.
4. Ben-Amos and Bet-El, "Ceremonies, Education and History," pp. 473–474, 477 (without the footnotes).
5. Tamar Barkay and Gal Levy, "Holocaust Remembrance Day in Progressive Eyes: Ethnicity, Class and Education in Israel," *Politika*, 1, 1999, pp. 27–46 (Hebrew). An English version of this article appeared as "The Kedma School: An Alternative to the Ashkenazi, Classist and Ethnocentric State School System," in *News from Within*, vol. XV, no. 6, June 1999, pp. 26–32.
6. Barkay and Levy, "Holocaust Remembrance Day in Progressive Eyes," pp. 36–37.
7. Barkay and Levy, "The Kedma School," pp. 26–32.
8. Barkay and Levy, "Holocaust Remembrance Day in Progressive Eyes," pp. 36–37.

8

Journeys of Youth to Poland

Towards the end of the 1980s several high schools began, at their own initiative, to conduct visits of pupils to Poland, and in 1989 Israel's Ministry of Education also began to initiate similar trips. Almost from the very beginning these visits generated public debate about their character and purpose, their content, and how they were carried out. In the last few years the visits of these groups have nonetheless taken a central place in the teaching of the Holocaust and in the formation of its memory. It is estimated that during the first few years of these visits a total of about 10,000 eleventh- and twelfth-year pupils took part in them, mostly to Poland but some to Czechoslovakia and Hungary. According to Ministry of Education data, the number increased in the last few years of the twentieth century, to 18,000 and even 20,000 pupils each year, and in 2005 to about 28,000, which is about one-fifth of the pupils in the relevant grades. About one-third of the pupils participated in the visits within the framework of the Ministry of Education's programs, the remainder through school-organized delegations. In addition, a procession of delegations from both Israel and the Diaspora, the "March of the Living," is held in Poland every two years. The "March of the Living" is officially recognized by Israel. Since 2001 delegations totaling more than 1000 Israeli soldiers and officers have also begun to visit the extermination camps every year.

The journeys to Poland arouse strong emotional reactions in the Israeli teenagers who participate in them. The preparations, the visit itself, and the pupils' "working through" of their impressions after their return to Israel constitute a unique educational-learning framework based on an emotional-affective experience. Nonetheless, several questions must be addressed: Can—and should—such visits become one of the pivotal educational and formative factors in the lives of the Israeli youngsters who participate in them? Are these visits the answer to the education system's difficulties in transmitting Zionist values? Or do they in fact stifle serious engagement with the problems of Zionist-Jewish education because they merely give the impression that they provide the answers to these issues?

Questions of a different kind surround the issue of youth delegations that visit Germany, which are funded at least in part by German organizations and institutions. The young Israelis on these trips visit local sites connected with the Holocaust and also meet with their German peers, which some people disapprove of in principle. The fact that German organizations are involved with these trips, they contend, has an influence on the entire venture and is therefore liable to present certain difficulties with young people who are sincerely trying to clarify and to understand various complicated and abstruse issues, with all of the emotional problems they entail.

In her article "The Journey to Poland as the High Point of an Educational Process," Tova Tzur presents the positions taken by the Ministry of Education on this matter.[1] In her opinion these visits have great educational import. The most important proof of their relevance for teachers, pupils, and parents, she claims, is the increasing number of schools that send delegations of their pupils to Poland, although participation is entirely voluntary, and despite the fact that organizing them is difficult and complicated both financially and socially.

As noted earlier, there are also those who, because of the unavoidable "tourist" component of the visit in Poland, but also for other reasons, have reservations about them. For example, Jackie Feldman, who claims in his article "At the Death Pits and under the Israeli Flag Flying Above: Israeli Youth Delegations to Poland in the Footsteps of the Holocaust and their Meaning" that these trips add a new and tendentious ritualistic structure in time and space to the existing ones that have long since been dictated by Holocaust Remembrance Day,[2] and to a lesser degree by Yad Vashem, as described in previous chapters:

> The visit presents Poland as a Jewish cemetery. The concentrated exposure of the pupils to a world of death, Poland of the Holocaust, strengthens the place of Israel as the center of the world of life. The Holocaust survivors who accompany the journey as "living witnesses," the teachers, and the guides (most of whom are children of survivors) represent two biological generations in the transmission of the tradition. The pupils acquire an identity as third-generation children of the Holo-

caust, not through their genealogical origins but as the young members of the Jewish collective living in Zion. The inter-generation composition of the delegation, the narrative of the "living witnesses," and the prominent display of the national [Israeli] symbols during the visit, together serve to signify to the pupils that the genealogical connection is less binding than the connection of each Jew to his country.

Feldman notes three important components of the visits to Poland characteristic of this new pattern:

- The preparatory program;
- The structure of the visit and the selection of sites to visit;
- The ceremonies prepared by the pupils during their visit in Poland.

He finds elements of pilgrimage in these visits, and concludes that they form part of the phenomena meant to bestow legitimacy of national goals through ritual:

> Through their ritualistic activities the pupils declare themselves to be proud survivors. In doing this they internalize the memory of the Holocaust. Their personal experience at the remains of Auschwitz and their return to Israel is melded into the experience of the death camp survivors and their immigration to Israel. In this way they internalize the Holocaust as the State of Israel's foundation myth. . . .
>
> In terms of the duration of the Poland visits and the intensity of the emotional reactions they incur, there is no known parallel in any other known civil memorial ceremonies. Both the ceremonies and the journey itself are rituals in space and in time. The participants do not view themselves as tourists: they are pilgrims to the sites of the destruction of their people, pilgrims in search of their identity. In contrast to the usual pilgrimage to the *axis mundi*, around which the world turns, this is a descent to the *anus mundi*, the lowest depths—the black holes of the death camps, centers of the World of Death and the antithesis of all sacred values. It is this descent to the lowest depths that sanctifies the place of Israel as the antithesis to Auschwitz, as the center of the World of Life.
>
> The procession through "the Valley of Death" causes a change in status that is, in general, characteristic of pilgrimages as rites of passage. Their personal identification . . . with the State [of Israel] and with its self-perception allows them to turn from passive receptors of the experience into its active reporters, into adults with the moral responsibility of transmitting the testimony of those who have died and that of the aging "living witnesses." Upon their return to Israel they themselves become "witnesses." Through the telling of their experiences in Poland to others, through their vitality as young Israelis, and through their future service to the country, the participants embody the Jewish People that survived the Holocaust and was reborn in a strong and independent State of Israel. . . .
>
> As in other religious pilgrimages, the powers that be—in this case the education system—try to channel the visit's charismatic power by briefing the pupils, equip-

ping them with suitable symbols, setting a timetable and establishing the limits and the rules of behavior at the pilgrimage sites. Flourishing the symbols brought from Israel (flags, memorial candles and blue-and-white jackets) and conducting rituals (most of which are prepared in Israel before the trip) are the state's tools for channeling the flood of experiences, which can overwhelm the pupils. At the high point of the visit, at the crematoria of Birkenau, the delegation holds a ceremony, "At the Death Pits and Under the Israeli Flag Flying Above." The pupils constitute the connecting link between the death pits and the flag of Israel, between the past and the future. At the Warsaw ghetto memorial they raise their flags and victoriously sing the national anthem, *Hatikva* ["The Hope"], immediately before boarding buses for their return flight to Israel.

However, in all of these there is no unified ideology that can dictate how diversified groups of sixteen-year-olds should react or what to do about their experiences following their return to Israel. Some of them search for experiences that will change their lives. They want to see and to experience what cannot be experienced a second time. Some of them even confuse the [death] camp of the past with its remains at present, and they say that they saw and experienced Auschwitz. The trip as a whole places the return to Israel as the highest goal and sanctifies living in Israel here and now. At the end of the trip, at home with their families, the participants feel spiritually uplifted; but they are also troubled. They tell about their experiences, their fears and their good fortune. But above and beyond their strengthened feeling of belonging to their country and their greater awareness of the validity of the existence of a Jewish state, questions arise that they have not previously thought about—questions about their grandparents, about God, about Man's nature, and about themselves.[3]

Feldman maintains that in its comprehensive reach and in the speed with which it developed, this new ritual pattern has no parallel with those of any other "civil religion" in the world. (The term "civil religion," which will be referred to again below, has been accepted since the 1970s by sociologists, historians and political scientists, although there is no general agreement about its exact definition. It is possible to understand it as a system of beliefs and practices to provide a stamp of approval on the social order, to unite the population around a shared value system, and to enlist the utmost strength of all of the group's members in order to carry out social objectives or tasks.)

Although Feldman notes certain problems regarding these visits, he also sees their important effects when they succeed in making an emotional and intellectual impact on the youngsters. Adi Ophir, however, in an article entitled "On Feelings that Cannot be Expressed in Words and on Lessons that Cannot be Questioned," puts the emphasis on their negative side.[4] Like Feldman, he too views these trips as pilgrimages having a religious or quasi-religious purpose, but he emphasizes their economic-profit aspects (e.g., the interests of travel agencies) and their decidedly political overtones. In his opinion, the "priestly establishment" of this new religion is trying to crystallize three main articles of faith amongst the young generation:

- A belief in the uniqueness of the Holocaust as a singular and incomparable genocide;
- A belief in the uniqueness of the Jews as sacrificial victims;
- A belief that the Holocaust proves the justification of Zionism.

In Ophir's opinion the visits to Poland are not intrinsically a religious phenomenon, and certainly not a "civil religion," which by definition belongs within the environment of a civil society, but a "state religion"— in other words a "religion" fashioned or brought into being not by the country's citizens but by its institutions.

Be that as it may, and despite not a few reservations about the youth visits to Poland, the number of participants has increased rather than diminished over the years. And yet, to the best of our knowledge, there has not, to date, been a scientific evaluation of their educational value (other than a few academic studies for master's or doctoral degrees that dealt with this subject). In other words, the "results" of these trips have not been investigated, and certainly not by the responsible bodies.

The fact that so significant a government authorized educational activity has not been investigated in-depth, despite the sometimes sharp criticism directed at it, is in itself surprising. Another cause for concern is that in many cases the "journey" to "death" may not only be the "high point of the educational process" but its last one as well, unless it is followed by an educational activity whose purpose is to prompt the pupils who participated in the tour to work through the meaningful experience they have had, to evaluate it, and to examine its bearing on their Jewish and their Israeli identities. This is rarely done, and it may even be claimed that, paradoxically, the visit to Poland makes it easier for the youngsters to *not* contend with the arduous problems of their identity as Jews and as Israelis.

In the spiritual and emotional wasteland, and the quest for the matriculation certificate, that usually characterize the high school years, the journey to Poland can become a question-raising experience filled with great significance as well as one that awakens a sweeping and disturbing storm of emotions. It can therefore be an overpowering formative event in the lives of Israeli youth—which is something that, in our opinion, should not happen: the Holocaust and Israel's wars should not be, as they are at present, the dominant elements in the Jewish identity of many young Israelis.

Again, we still do not know what effect the trip to Poland has on the Israeli-Jewish identity of the youngsters who take part in it, neither immediately nor in the long run. But it is possible to claim that through these voyages the ideological content of Zionism, which had been severed from Judaism, has returned, via the crematoria, to its origins in Europe. The Israeli youngster's attitude to the Jewish People is mediated by the Holocaust: the connection is therefore with a Jewish People that has died, and not with the vital, living Jewish People. The visits do not connect the young participants with the intellectual richness of the now-lost vibrant past and its flourishing culture, but with a past of helpless victimhood and misery, destruction and death. In Auschwitz they do not see how people lived; they see how they were destroyed. But: Who were these murdered people? How did they live? What were their lives like? What was their world like? What were their religious beliefs? What were their cultural and intellectual values? About these things the voyage to Poland offers very little enlightenment.

It appears that one cannot seek—nor it is possible to find—one's national identity in ashes or amongst crematoria. A situation in which death camps become the main realms in which the young Israeli encounters the Jewish people of the Diaspora, even if the intention of these encounters is to glorify the idea of the Jewish revival, should not be allowed to occur. By allowing such encounters, Israel increasingly becomes a nation united "by virtue of" a shared tragedy; a people that is, actually, a function of a chain of disasters. In this way the Holocaust, like the expulsion of the Jews from Spain in 1492, for example, becomes but another in the long series of catastrophes that have befallen the Jewish People, calamities that began in the distant past and have continued to the present.

Notes

1. Tova Tzur, "The Trip to Poland as the High Point of an Educational Process," *Beshvil Hazikaron* [In Memory's Path], 7, 1995, pp. 5–7 (Hebrew).

2. Jackie Feldman, "Delegations of Israeli Youth to Poland in the Wake of the Holocaust and their Object," *Yalkut Moreshet*, 66, 1998, p. 86 (Hebrew). And see also: Jackie Feldman, "Defining the Israeli Collective through the Poland 'Experience'," *Israel Studies*, vol. 7, No. 2, Summer 2002.
3. Feldman, "Delegations of Israeli Youth," pp. 96–101, passim.
4. Adi Ophir, "On Feelings that Cannot be Expressed in Words and on Lessons that Cannot be Questioned," *Beshvil Hazikaron* [In Memory's Path], 7, 1995, pp. 11–15 (Hebrew).

9

About the Attitudes of Israeli Adolescents towards the Holocaust

Most of the research dealing with the attitudes of young Israelis towards the Holocaust has been carried out from the perspective of their Jewish or Jewish-Israeli identity. Although most of the studies on which the discussion below is based do not focus on the influence of the education system on these attitudes, they do reveal meaningful information about this influence and illustrate, among other things, the need for more comprehensive research of this aspect both of their attitudes towards the Holocaust and of the impact of the teaching of the Holocaust.

The results of the studies carried out to date indicate that during the 1980s and 1990s there was a gradual but continuous weakening among young Israelis of their feeling of "Israeliness" and a strengthening of that of their "Jewishness," along with the significant changes in their attitude towards the Holocaust. The Holocaust became a central factor, and sometimes *the* central factor in the formation of the Jewish identity of these young Jewish Israelis. (A parallel phenomenon has also been noted in some sectors of the Jews in the Diaspora.) This has had an unquestionably strong influence on the crystallization of the individual Jewish-Israeli identity of these youngsters as well as on their collective identity, in terms of both their subjective self-image and their attitude towards the non-Jewish world.

The pronounced upward trend of the salience of the Holocaust in the historical consciousness of the Israeli-Jewish youngster, which was noted in all of the studies, was undoubtedly influenced by the increased efforts of both the formal and the informal education systems, in school learning programs and in extra-curricular activities such as visits to museums and centers for learning about the Holocaust (e.g., Yad Vashem, Ghetto Fighters House, and others) and, since the late-1980s, visits to Poland, as described above (chapter 8). This upward trend is indicated by the number of participants in short, one-day to three-week seminars and courses held in the framework of Yad Vashem's International School for Holocaust for Holocaust Studies: 110,000 elementary and high school pupils in 1999 and 50,000 young Israeli soldiers and officers participate in these courses each year.

A study conducted among students of education or in teacher training examined which history subjects were the ones most taught in high schools and in various post-high school frameworks, such as teachers' seminaries and colleges. These courses included: history of the Jews in the nineteenth and twentieth centuries; the Holocaust; Zionism; the Arab-Israeli conflict; Israeli society; and Diaspora Jewry. It was shown that the two most-studied subjects are the Holocaust and Zionism; much less studied were courses connected with the Arab-Israeli conflict; the least studied were courses about the life of the Jews in the Diaspora and the history of the Jews in the nineteenth century.[1]

While these studies did not compare the level of *learning* with the students' level of *knowledge* of these topics, the respondents themselves (i.e., future teachers) estimated, in self-assessment questions, that they had far greater knowledge about the Holocaust than about any of the other subjects, including Zionism. This was true for all three of the Jewish educational sectors in Israel—state, state-religious, and independent ultra-orthodox religious.

In another study of a similar sample population, the subjects (also students at colleges for education) attested to the fact that they themselves had almost never studied anything, either in high school or in the college, about Christianity, Islam, racism, or fascism. Regarding the Holocaust, on the other hand, they had learned "a great deal" or "a considerable amount" during organized visits to museums, from Holocaust Martyrs' and Heroes' Remembrance Day assemblies, at study days, from individual lectures devoted to this subject, and the like.[2]

The results of these two studies raise many additional questions. For example: What is the significance of the fact that the Holocaust is studied more in Israel—apparently very much more—than any other subject in the field of modern Jewish history? What place do Holocaust studies have within the framework of general Jewish history studies and within the education system's framework in general? What is the significance of the fact that a topic such as "Racism," as an independent subject, is not taught practically at all in Israel's education system?

Although there is still sufficient latitude for further and deeper research of Israeli youngsters' attitudes about the Holocaust, there are, nonetheless, an immense number of articles about the place of the Holocaust in Israel society and in the formation of the Israeli identity. And yet, there is one very specific issue about which there is not so much as one academic discussion: the effect of inter-ethnic relations on attitudes towards the Holocaust. It is interesting that the vast research literature on relations between Ashkenazi and Mizrahi Jews in Israel[3] has also paid no attention at all to this issue, and the question of the attitudes of Israelis of Sephardic descent is almost never even mentioned. We therefore do not know if and how the ethnic origins of youngsters in these sectors of the population affect their attitudes towards the Holocaust, nor what educational implications may be inferred from this. It seems that this subject, so deserving of attention and research, is still avoided, possibly because, despite its relevance for the education system in Israel, it raises too many apprehensions.

Nonetheless, it is important to note that although the variable of ethnic origin was not examined either specifically or in-depth in various studies of the attitudes towards the Holocaust of teenagers and young adults studying in various different school frameworks, there were no findings indicating that ethnicity was a significant factor in the subjects' attitudes.[4]

In studies of high school students in Israel, too, no significant differences were found for the variable of ethnic origin on the question of identification with victims of the Holocaust. Researcher Uri Farago claims that this is because of an attitude towards the Holocaust that has become the accepted norm in Israel (at least at the outward level), apparently due to the influence of the education system.[5] In his opinion, the education system has succeeded, intentionally, in creating a norm of identification with victims of the Holocaust, and that this is one of the reasons for the great similarity in the respondents' answers, despite their different ethnic backgrounds. Although there are no research findings for it, some observers claim that the lower the socio-economic and educational status of the subjects (e.g., pupils in some of the trade schools), the lower the level of identification with this norm.

While Farago views such an increasingly well-formed attitude among the young generation as a "norm," Charles Leibman defines it as a "myth."[6] He claims that the Holocaust is the central myth of Israel's "civil religion," but emphasizes that a myth is not something untrue or non-historical but is, rather, a-historical: it relates to real events that occurred at a given time and in a certain place, and that can in theory be proved to have occurred. In either case, however, myths not only arouse strong emotions and impart social values; they add additional strength and authority to both.

The attitudes to the Holocaust of young Israelis was examined from a different angle in an article by Dan Bar-On and Oron Selah, which compared the attitudes of Israeli youngsters to their immediate surrounding reality (in terms of their attitude to Arabs, national identity, and democratic thinking and political tendency) and their attitudes to the Holocaust, and found a reciprocal connection—a "vicious circle"—between the two.[7] In the authors' opinion the Holocaust is often "recruited" by circles of both the Israeli Right and Left to present their political views, especially in regard to national affinity, but also in regard to the Arabs and to democratic thinking. What happened in the Holocaust is viewed by the Right as proof that Israel must be strong, because the dependence on others has been shown to be of no avail, while the Left claims that Israel must be mindful of not doing to other minorities what was done to the Jews. This, they claim, has created a "vicious circle" of attitudes towards the Arabs: affinity to national issues and democratic thinking on the one hand, and of political conclusions and "behavior" in regard to the Holocaust on the other. Such circular thinking precludes a deeper processing of these elements, one that can lead to a more complex worldview of the events of the past and of the present, one in which both the Right and the Left avoid the use of shallow slogans.[8]

* * *

The issues raised in the articles surveyed above oblige us, as Israelis, to ask ourselves if our society, including its political and education systems, has not willfully turned the Holocaust into an instrument in the service of national purposes. More concretely: Will the process of the strengthening and intensification of the division between sectors that has characterized Israeli society in recent decades, and the even more recent "privatization of the memory of the Holocaust" (discussed in chapter 3), which has been occurring in the last few years, affect Israeli society's attitudes to the Holocaust, and that of its education system within it? And if so, in what way or ways? A warning about this can be discerned in the sharp statements on matters touching on the Holocaust voiced by various members of the ultra-orthodox, largely Mizrahi political party, Shas, and by some of the rabbis associated with it, among them a renewed attack on the positions and activities of the Zionists during the period of the Holocaust—pronouncements that led to fierce public controversy and criticism.

The question also arises of whether the processes of polarization between the different sectors of Israeli society, and within its education system as well, have not created, de facto, different programs for teaching the Holocaust and for forming its memory. Programs such as these are liable to further exacerbate the tension that already exists between these sectors.

Notes

1. Yair Auron, *Israeli-Jewish Identity* (Tel Aviv: Sifriat Poalim, 1993) (Hebrew), pp. 89–128.
2. Yair Auron, Gila Zalikovitz, and Nili Keren, *Attitudes of Trainee Teachers to Anti-Semitism and Racism* (Tel Aviv: Seminar Hakibbutzim, 1996) (Hebrew).
3. Mizrahi Jews are descendents of those who originally came from Arabic-speaking countries of the Middle East; Sephardic Jews, of those from Mediterranean countries; and Ashkenazi Jews, from North European countries.
4. Yair Auron, *Israeli-Jewish Identity*, p. 112.
5. Uri Farago, "Attitudes toward the Holocaust among Israeli Students—1983," *Studies on the Holocaust Period*, Vol. III (Tel Aviv: Hakibbutz Hameuchad, 1984) (Hebrew), pp. 159–178.
6. Charles Leibman, "Myth, Tradition and Values in Israeli Society [The Holocaust Myth]," *Midstream*, 24:1 January 1980, pp. 44–53. See also: Charles Leibman and Eliezer Don-Yehiya, *Civil Religion in Israel* (Berkeley: University of California Press, 1983).
7. Dan Bar-On and Oron Selah, "The Vicious Circle of Israeli Youngsters' Attitudes towards their Actuality and towards the Holocaust," *Psychologia—Israeli Journal of Psychology*, Vol. 2, No. 1, September 1991 (Hebrew), pp. 126–138.
8. Ibid., p. 136.

10

About the Attitudes of Israeli Arabs towards the Holocaust

An article written by Saalam Gubran, an Israeli Arab active in various frameworks attempting to develop methods for teaching the subject of the Holocaust conjointly to Jews and Arabs, appeared in the monthly journal, *Beshvil Hazikaron* (In Memory's Path), published by Yad Vashem's Education Department. In it Gubran wrote:[1]

> The historical process of establishing an Israeli-Palestinian and an Israeli-Arab peace obligates the shedding of historical stereotypes and distortions. This necessitates recognizing one's counterpart and of understanding the aspirations of the human being on the other side. Within this framework there is also the need for a new approach, by both the Arabs and the Jews, to the subject of the Holocaust.

The main question that we have to ask ourselves insofar as the Arabs of Israel are concerned is, is it important for young Arabs who grow up and receive their educations in Israel to learn about the Holocaust? And if so, why? And how? While the Holocaust is actually taught in Arab schools in Israel, it is presented through a Zionist-Jewish perspective, and there are, to date, no studies that can help us to evaluate the effects of this approach on the youngsters in the Arab sector and on their attitudes to the Jews.

As discussed in the preceding chapter, we do not even know exactly how the teaching of the Holocaust in the Israeli education system affects the attitude of Jewish society itself. We also lack research evidence on the question of how the Holocaust affects relations between the two societies—Arab and Jewish—in Israel. We also do not know the Holocaust's effects on each side's perception of the Arab-Jewish conflict, or the effect of the fact that the Palestinians, both within Israel and outside of it, use terms similar or identical to those used for the Jewish Holocaust for their own tragedy: They usually use the term *naqba*, which means "tragedy" or "catastrophe," for what happened to them in or as a result of the War of Independence in 1948. (The Jewish Holocaust is called *al-karissa*, meaning disaster.) Many Palestinians inveigh against the fact that the subject of the naqba is not studied in Israeli schools at all. Along with an emphasis on the qualitative differences between the Holocaust and the *naqba*, it is important to keep in mind that in the Israeli-Arab society, as in the Israeli-Jewish society, the sense of being victims and victimization are important components of the group's self-identity.

The issue of mutual recognition of the national memory of "the other" by each of these two groups is discussed in an article entitled "The Palestinian Control over the Memories of the Holocaust and the Naqba," by Ilan Gur-Ze'ev and Ilan Pappe.[2] The authors claim that the central streams of Zionism have consistently denied the *naqba*, and have systematically disputed any role of the Israelis in the Palestinians' suffering. They consider this one of the things that, among others, influenced Palestinian perceptions of both the Holocaust and the *naqba*. Different and even conflicting positions to this can be found in Palestinian reactions: from complete negation of the Holocaust through indifference, to recognition of its occurrence while minimizing its scale and moral implications, and to full recognition of the event and its moral and universal significance as a unique stage in the history of human evil. The authors of this article express their hope that Palestinians and Israelis will be able to hold a critical dialogue free of ethnocentrism that will enable them to confront both the unique memory of each of the two groups as well as the unique memory of "the other."

For many years both Jews and Arabs have brought the subject of the Holocaust into the on-going dispute around the question of the Palestinian-Israeli conflict, with each of the sides usually distorting the historical facts. This combination of highly sensitive national issues is a dangerous mixture, and one that provides convincing proof of the need for a serious, in-depth study of this matter, perhaps mainly in regard to the aspects that are connected with teaching the Holocaust.

As noted above, the feeling of victimhood constitutes an important component in how the Palestinians identify themselves—both those who are citizens of Israel and those living elsewhere—in the same way as it does for Jews living in and outside Israel. It is therefore necessary for all those contending with the question of the attitude of Arabs to the Holocaust, and desiring to promote the development of a new approach to this issue, to recognize the pervasiveness of this feeling.

At the time of writing, pupils in the upper grades of Arab high schools in Israel are required to take a half-unit course (approximately forty-five classroom hours) in the history of the Jewish People in modern times, about half of which deals with the Holocaust. (It is important to note that these pupils are also exposed to the subject of the Holocaust within the framework of their studies of European history of the twentieth century in high school.) Those who are interested in pursuing broader studies in history can choose the Holocaust as one of their electives (which only very few do, possibly due to the lack of suitable textbooks in Arabic on this subject or because of their distance from it). We thus do not know whether the teaching of the Holocaust in Arab schools, as carried out today, brings the Arab pupil closer to the subject, and to the Jewish citizens of the country, or, perhaps, does just the opposite and intensifies the tension and distance between them.

A dismal picture of the situation at present arises from the pages of the chapter "The Arabs and the Holocaust" in David Grossman's *Present Absentees*.[3] Grossman, a prestigious Israeli writer, asked Arab pupils if they feel that the Israeli Jews treat them like the Germans treated the Jews:[4]

> These youngsters did not hesitate. From every side calls of agreement were heard. When I noted that Israel is not trying to annihilate the Palestinian people, neither from racial nor any other motives, a boy named Na'im called out to me: "It's exactly the same thing there and here! The same thing-the State of Israel wants to get rid of the Arabs, wants to annihilate us!"
>
> "To destroy?"
>
> He thought for a moment: "Okay, if not bodily, then spiritually! Okay, if not our bodies, then our spirits! Prevents us from studying our national poets! Destroys us in terms of our values!"
>
> As he spoke he became more and more belligerent. "They want us to assimilate in the society, to become Israelis . . . that we cut ourselves away from the other Arab peoples . . . that we forget what the Palestinians are! That isn't destruction in your eyes?"

It is important that if, in the future, a new learning program for Arab pupils in Israel is prepared, it deal seriously with such claims as these, and that it be written in a way suitable to the needs of the Arab population of the country. Since Grossman wrote these things in 1992, however, the Ministry of Education has taken no steps to change the face of the existing situation.

The same heading, "The Arabs and the Holocaust," as that used by Grossman for the above-quoted chapter is used by many writers dealing with this topic, and is the focal point of an article by Azmi Bishara about the connection between the Arabs and the Holocaust, which appeared in *Zmanim*, a prestigious Israeli historical quarterly:[5]

> "The Arabs and the Holocaust" is not only a very mysterious topic . . . it is also provocative and suspicious. What is the meaning of the heading "The Arabs and the Holocaust"? It is perhaps first worth clarifying the fact that this heading and the combination "The Jews and the Holocaust" are not close in meaning. Nor can it be compared with a title such as "The French and the Holocaust" or "The Germans and the Holocaust." It is more like "The Indians and the Holocaust"—meaningless! The question that this title elicits is not a relevant one, and it is thus possible to discuss it only scholastically. The conjunction "and" here has the status of jack-of-all-trades. It can connect anything with anything, the trouble being that this is so only in a heading, only in language, and not in the reality. But in a certain way, titles, expressions, and myths themselves constitute reality.
>
> The Arabs have become bound in a roundabout way to the history of the Holocaust—although perhaps it would be better to say to the history of the post-Holocaust period. The Palestinians are the indirect victims whose homeland was taken from them by the direct victims. All attempts to make any connection between them and the Holocaust are suspect. Words can have magical power, and only words can bestow legitimacy on such a connection.

Bishara's article elicited a sharp critical response by the Holocaust historian Dan Michman, who claimed that Bishara wanted to strip the Jewish dimension from the Holocaust. He also rejected Bishara's axiomatic dictum that the Palestinians were the ones who paid the price of the Holocaust. As for the title, Michman considered the title "The Arabs and the Holocaust" the most neutral wording imaginable.[6]

In responding to Michman's claims Bishara accused him of distortion, of taking things out of context, and even of "deliberately turning upside-down what I claimed in the article."[7] He added that, "it is difficult to not perceive the paternalistic, arrogant tone that found its way into this response, which I am not convinced belongs in an academic journal."[8] Bishara essentially rejects Michman's claim in the matter of stripping the Jewish dimension from the Holocaust, and explains that this claim is based on the premise that the universal meaning of the Holocaust negates its unique significance for the Jews.

This polemic exemplifies, among other things, how problematic and complex the sought after dialogue between the two peoples will be, especially regarding the Holocaust and the *naqba*. It is also an indication of how difficult it sometimes is to separate academic research and debate from political and ideological claims and discourse.

An examination of the situation at present reveals a dismal fact: the State of Israel invests great efforts to bring the horror of the Holocaust to the attention of diverse populations in the world (every official visitor to Israel visits Yad Vashem), but for various reasons—which undoubtedly should be clarified—has till now refrained from doing so, at least in a suitable manner, before the Arabs of Israel living in their midst. An unusual and notable exception is the recently published *Outlining the Holocaust for Arabic Speaking Students*, which appeared in both Hebrew and Arabic.[9]

With the recent emergence of a few unique programs, however, there are hopeful signs that this situation can be changed. These programs are carried out under the aegis of various educational programs oriented to the Arab sector, and sometimes in joint Arab-Israeli non-governmental learning frameworks such as the Ghetto Fighters' House, the Moreshet Center in Givat Haviva, the David Yellin College in Jerusalem and, in cooperation with the national memorial institute Yad Vshem. The scope of these innovative programs is unfortunately very limited at the time of writing. In 2003, a very significant initiative of Israeli Arabs was realized when, in order to arrive at a better understanding of the Jews and identification with their suffering, a group of 200 Israeli Arabs and Jews visited concentration camps in Poland. The changes in the perceptions and attitudes of both sides, to which these and similar activities will hopefully lead, will undoubtedly be gradual and slow.

Notes

1. Saalam Gubran, "The Arabs and the Holocaust: A Historical and Realistic Perspective," *Beshvil Hazikaron* [In Memory's Path], 17, 1996 (Hebrew), pp. 15–18.
2. Ilan Gur-Ze'ev and Ilan Pappe, "The Palestinian Control over the Memories of the Holocaust and the Naqba," in Ilan Gur-Ze'ev, *Philosophy, Politics and Education in Israel* (Haifa and Tel Aviv: Haifa University and Zmora Beitan, 2000) (Hebrew), pp. 99–123. See also: Ilan Gur-Ze'ev, "Holocaust/Naqba as an Israeli-Palestinian

Homeland," in *Destroying the Other's Collective Memory* (New York: Peter Long, 2003), pp. 25–50.
3. David Grossman, *Present Absentees* (Tel Aviv: Hakibbutz Hameuchad, 1992) (Hebrew).
4. Ibid., pp. 131-132.
5. Azmi Bishara, "The Arabs and the Holocaust: Analyzing the Problems of a Preposition [sic—Conjunction]," *Zmanim*, Vol. 13, No. 53, Summer 1995 (Hebrew), pp. 54–72.
6. Dan Michman, "Arabs, Zionists, Bishara and the Holocaust: A Political Campaign or an Academic Study?" *Zmanim*, Vol. 13 (Responses Section), Autumn 1995 (Hebrew), pp. 117–119. Azmi Bishara is an Israeli-Arab scholar who became a leader of an Israeli-Arab political party and, at this writing, is a member of the Knesset.
7. Azmi Bishara, "On Nationalism and on Universalism," *Zmanim*, Vol. 13, No. 55 (Responses Section), Winter 1995–1996 (Hebrew), pp. 102–105.
8. Ibid.
9. Irit Abramski (ed.), *Outlining the Holocaust for Arabic Speaking Students* (Jerusalem: Yad Vashem and Ghetto Fighters' House, 2000) (Hebrew and Arabic).

11

To Remember or to Forget?

Who will I remember, the living? the dead? Who will I forget? the dead? the living? What else is there for me to do but to remember and to forget, to live and die, to fear and hope?

These are the words of a woman interviewed by Dan Bar-On and quoted in his book *Fear and Hope: Three Generations of the Holocaust*.[1] There can hardly be a better way of expressing the difficulty, individual and collective, surrounding the question of remembering and forgetting about the Holocaust. During the first decades after the Holocaust there was concern over the possibility that the memory of the Holocaust might be lost forever. Today, some people are worried about it being remembered "too much," and there are also, as discussed above, some who claim that it is being used, and even exploited, for purposes completely unrelated to the Holocaust itself.

A critical approach to the question of the place of the memory of the Holocaust, mainly within American Jewry but also, to some degree, in Israeli Jewry as well, was brought to light in the book *Holocaust in American Life* by Peter Novick, a professor of history at the University of Chicago.[2] In his opinion, the needs of American Jewry and of the United States as a great power during the late 1940s and the 1950s determined to a large degree the place of the Holocaust in American memory. He asserts that during those years it was both discomfiting and unacceptable in American public life to talk about the Holocaust. This was not, as some others have claimed, due to feelings of shame or guilt that awakened among the Americans because of their failure to do anything about the Holocaust while it was being carried out but, rather, due to the significant changes that were taking place at that time in the world order as a result of momentous ideological shifts. By this Novick means, of course, the Cold War between the West and the East that was then at its height: the Soviet Union and its satellites, who together with the United States had fought as an allied force against Nazi Germany, was now the enemy, and the German enemy was now an ally. Since any discussion of the Holocaust would not only be inefficacious but even detrimental at this time, Novick considers this the explanation for the muting of the of the Holocaust's memory during those years. It appears that the needs of the hour did, indeed, push the claim of the recent past to the sidelines.[3]

A different critical approach is that of Norman Finkelstein, in *The Holocaust Industry: Reflections on the Exploitation of Jewish Suffering*."[4] The reactions to this book, which is undoubtedly both unbalanced and tendentious, were extreme. Finkelstein asserts that since the Six Day War in 1967, American Jewry has been utilizing the Holocaust in order to defend the interests of Israel. He claims that this protective position of American Jews first appeared when Israel had already won a decisive victory and was no longer in need of such defense. Thus, in his view, the subject of the Holocaust was raised and continues to be used only to thwart public condemnation of Israel's rule over the Palestinians and the occupied territories.

In Israel in the mid-1990s the debate on the place of the Holocaust in the national memory was connected with various aspects of the polemic between "Zionists" and "post-Zionists." While the subjects of these debates do not exactly overlap, the arguments themselves, on both sides, have intensified because of them. Many articles on this subject have appeared in newspapers and periodicals in the last few years, and a considerable number of academic papers dealing with them have also been written. Some of the debate revolved around topics directly connected with the period of the Holocaust, such as the extent of the rescue efforts made by the Zionist movement, the attitude of the Yishuv to the survivors of the Holocaust, and other hard questions.

Another much-debated subject is connected to a greater extent with the present: the use and the "exploitation" of the memory of the Holocaust by Zionism and by Israel. The "post-Zionists"—whose positions are stated mostly by academics—contend, among other things, that the state is to a great extent interested in this subject in order to strengthen its claim that only Zionism is the solution for anti-Semitism. They also assert that the Holocaust is used in Israel for fostering the Zionist-Jewish identity, as well as for furthering other national interests that have to do with the Arab-Jewish struggle. Much, as indicated, has been written about this subject. For example, there is a 600-page anthology, *Post-Zionism and the Holocaust*, containing hundreds of articles, mostly from newspapers, written between the years 1993–1996. But even this vast collection could not include all the articles on these subjects that were published during this short period of time.[5]

Three particular newspaper articles that appeared in 1988 are of special interest in relation to our subject of the memory of the Holocaust. The first one, entitled "On the Right to Forget," was written by Yehuda Elkana, a professor of philosophy, who had lived through the Holocaust as a child:

> I have recently become more and more convinced that it is not personal frustration, as a socio-political factor, that drives Israeli society's attitude to the Palestinians but, rather, a deep existential fear that is nourished by a certain interpretation of the lessons of the Holocaust, and from a readiness to believe that the whole world is against us and that we are the eternal victim. I view this ancient article of faith, shared by so many today, as Hitler's tragic and paradoxical victory. Two peoples came out of Auschwitz: a minority that asserted that "this will never happen again," and a frightened and fearful majority that asserted that "this will never happen *to us* again."
>
> If these were the only two possible lessons, I would obviously have believed in the first one for my entire life and would have seen the second one as a disaster. All that I say here is not in support of one or the other of these perceptions, but in support of the normative claim that any lesson of life or any perception of life based on the Holocaust is a disaster. Without disregarding the known historical importance of the collective memory, an atmosphere in which an entire people determines its attitude to the present and plans its future by relating mainly to the lessons of the past is disastrous for the future of a society that desires to live in relative peace and relative security in the same way as do all the nations.
>
> History and collective memory constitute an inseparable part of a people's culture, but allowing the past to be the controlling factor in determining the future of a society and the fate of a people should not, and must not, be allowed to happen. The very existence of democracy is in danger when the memory of victims of the past is an active factor in the democratic process. All of the ideologists of fascist rules understood this very well. It is not by chance that most of the research on Nazi Germany deals with the political myths of the Third Reich. Dependence on the lessons of the past in order to build the future and use of the suffering of the past as a political claim are like having the dead participate in the democratic process of the those still living. . . .
>
> I see no greater danger for the future of the State of Israel than that the Holocaust has been systematically and intensively instilled in the consciousness of the Israeli public, including that very large part of it that did not experience the Holocaust and, also, the generation of sons and daughters that were born and grew up here. For the

first time I see the full weight of what we did when during tens of years we sent each and every child in Israel to visit Yad Vashem, again and again. What did we want these young children to do with this experience? Without explaining, we mindlessly and even heartlessly declaimed "Remember!" For what? What is the child supposed to do with these memories? For many hundreds of them the photographs of the horror may be understood to be a call for hatred. "Remember" may be understood to be a call for endless and blind hatred.

It may be important that the world at large remember. Even of that I am not sure, but it is not our concern in any case. Each and every people, including the Germans, will determine its own way and according to its own considerations if it wants to remember. We, on the other hand, must forget. I do not see at the present time a more important political and educational role for the leaders of this nation than to take a stand on the side of life and to dedicate themselves to building our future, and not to occupy themselves, day in and day out, with the symbols, the texts, and the lessons of the Holocaust. It is their duty to uproot the historic "Remember" from our lives.

What I have written is unsparing, and unlike my usual writing it is couched in black-and-white terms. This is neither by chance nor because of a passing mood. I found no better way of calling attention to the seriousness of the situation. In reality, I know very well that a nation does not, and should not, completely forget all of the chapters of its past. And there are, of course, other myths that are vitally necessary for the construction of our future, such as the myth of [Jewish] excellence or that of [Jewish] creativity, and it is certainly not my intention that they stop teaching the history of our people. I have tried to fight against the continuation of setting the Holocaust as the central hinge of our national existence.[6]

Many articles were written in response to this one by Elkana. Two of them, the first by Boaz Evron and the other by Yisrael Eldad, both intellectuals, express antithetical stands. Evron agrees with Elkana's position and continues in the same vein and in a similarly sharp way and, for similar reasons, goes on to attack the youth visits to Poland. Evron claims that these journeys—which he labels "education towards fascism and escape"—were conjured up as a "device" to forestall young people's leaving the country:

Behind the "device" there is no intention to teach the real history of this period (which is complex and more lacking in "lessons" than anything the inventors of the "device" can imagine), or to honor the memory of the victims. For those, they would not have allocated such generous sums of money.

The objective is different: it is "to frighten" the [Israeli] youngsters, to instill in their minds the idea that "the whole world is anti-Semitic" and that all of the Jews, sooner or later, face the danger of a Holocaust, and that there is no escape from their gathering together in fear, in Israel, and to station themselves, weapons in hand, against the hostile world. This is the true purpose of what in Israel is called "teaching the lessons of the Holocaust."

Needless to say, this is the complete opposite of the original goal of Zionism (and even more so to that of the *kibbutz* movement):[7] to live in the Land as a free and normal people among other free peoples, with respect and mutual understanding, open to them and contributing to them, and not as a frightened community of refugees shutting itself away from the whole world.

Not only is this not the remedy for the illnesses of Israeli society, but:

[W]ithin a few years the inventors of this "device" will discover that the groups that they sent to Poland will generate on the one hand fascists of the worst kind (for "we are allowed" to carry out any atrocity, because "everyone wants to see us destroyed"), and on the other, a mass flight to other countries. And there will also be some in whom there will be a combination of these extremes.[8]

A completely different opinion, as can be expected, was expressed by Yisrael Eldad in an article in the same newspaper, "The So-called Forgetting of the Holocaust," in which he sharply attacks Elkana's views:

In my comments on the Holocaust of Forgetting I do not mean, of course, that moral, educational, psychological atrocity that has now fallen upon us by the "command" ordered by Professor Yehuda Elkana to forget the Holocaust. And if not for the position this man fills as director of the Van Leer Institute,[9] which is so closely connected with the Ministry of Education, with various intellectual projects and with publishers, it would not of course even have been worthy of being mentioned in any sane and serious newspaper. It may be that this man, who is himself a "Holocaust survivor," has psychological reasons for forgetting, and is of course entitled to do that, if he is able to, but is to demand such a thing from the Jewish People and from Israel desirable?[10]

Eldad goes on to criticize not only the intellectual-political objectives and proposals that Elkana represents, but also the groups and circles that foster what he calls "the Holocaust of forgetting the Holocaust." In Eldad's opinion this approach is encouraged by the religious and orthodox streams of Jewry that ignore the meaning of the Holocaust and do not contend with it, accepting it as ordained by God. He claims that even Zionism is guilty of the fact that there isn't greater awareness of the fundamental thesis according to which "the Exile itself, in all its forms, is a disease, a disaster, a pathology—that is the Holocaust."

The on-going controversy about the place of the Holocaust in historical memory in Israel and about how to articulate it have, and will continue to have, long-ranging ramifications on the political and ideological standpoints of Israel's citizens, especially of the younger ones.

Insofar as education about the Holocaust in general is concerned it has great importance because it constitutes the basis of the teaching of this subject in the future.

Notes

1. Dan Bar-On, *Fear and Hope: Three Generations of the Holocaust* (Cambridge, MA and London, England: Harvard University Press, 1995), p. 350.
2. Peter Novick, *The Holocaust in American Life* (Boston: Houghton Mifflin, 1999).
3. Novick, "That is Past, and We Must Deal with the Facts Today," in *The Holocaust in American Life*, pp. 85–102.
4. Norman Finkelstein, *The Holocaust Industry: Reflections on the Exploitation of Jewish Suffering* (London: Veriso, 2000).
5. Dan Michman (ed.), *Post-Zionism and the Holocaust: The Role of the Holocaust in the Public Debate on Post-Zionism in Israel (1993–1996): A Collection of Clippings*, Research Aids, Series No. 8 (Ramat-Gan, Israel: Bar-Ilan University, 1997) (Hebrew).
6. Yehuda Elkana, "On the Right to Forget," *Haaretz*, March 2, 1988.
7. Evron is referring here to the fact that the first visits of youth to Poland were carried out by high schools of the kibbutz movement.
8. Boaz Evron, "Education towards Fascism and Escape," *Yedioth Ahronoth*, March 4, 1988.
9. An esteemed independent academic institution in Jerusalem.
10. Yisrael Eldad, "The So-called Forgetting of the Holocaust," *Haaretz*, April 14, 1988.

12

On the Teaching of the Holocaust Around the World

Throughout the world the teaching of the Holocaust, in both elementary and high school frameworks and in universities, is intended and constructed for students, few of whom are Jewish. In view of this, there are a number of questions, all having varied but important implications, which can and should be asked.

For example, it is important that we examine whether a young African American living in a poor and crowded Washington D.C. slum should learn about the Holocaust—and if so, why? And, along with this, whether he should learn about his ancestors' fate (which some will claim was their "genocide" or "holocaust")—and if so, why? And, also, why was no attention given to this latter subject until the past few decades, much in the way that the Holocaust was pushed aside? Moreover, is there any connection between these two subjects—and if so, what is it? And, finally, if these subjects are studied—what content, and how much time, should be devoted to each of them?

The answers to questions such as these are neither unequivocal nor of a kind, but they all have some degree of universal relevance. In other words, insofar as the subject of this book—the Holocaust as a genocide of the Jewish people—is concerned, and beyond its specifically Jewish orientation, they touch upon problems that concern all human beings, wherever they may be. Those teaching the subject of the Holocaust must therefore seek and understand its universal lessons, whose main points are connected with the war against fascism, racism, and oppression, and with the struggle for democratic society and against injustice anywhere. In this matter it is important to reiterate that in Israel the Holocaust is learned mostly in a particularistic national-Jewish or Zionist-Israeli-Jewish context, as described in detail in the preceding chapters.

As noted in the introduction of this book, we have chosen to focus mainly on the teaching of the Holocaust in the United States and Germany, as this provides a comprehensive dimension and comparative perspective that can, in our opinion, contribute to a deeper understanding of the broad range of topics with which we deal. We will begin our descriptions, however, with a brief discussion of how the teaching of the Holocaust is dealt with in France and Great Britain, two countries in which interesting and significant changes have been initiated over the course of time.

On the Teaching of the Holocaust in France and in Great Britain

France

The last few years have witnessed an ongoing public controversy in France in regard to the memory of the Holocaust, how this memory can or should be transmitted to future generations, and the ways in which the subject of the Holocaust is taught. The very existence of such a controversy is an indication of the difficulties caused by the connection, whether direct or oblique, between the memory of the Holocaust and its actual history, a problem found to be even more complex when considered in terms of its educational aspects. The reverberations of this controversy in France are also indications of, among other things, the connection between the national memory of the Holocaust in France—with all of the specific questions encased in this memory—and the question of how it is to be taught.

One of the reasons that it is only in the last few years that the teaching of the Holocaust was initiated in France is linked to the country's long and slow process of freeing itself from memories of the "Black Years," the Vichy period (1940–1944). These years were deeply etched in the collective memory of the French people as a particularly difficult time. Haunted by the memory of the Nazi occupation and collaboration with it, about which an unceasing stream of questions, furor, guilt feelings, and fierce polemic continues to flow, France has lived since then with what is known as the "Vichy syndrome." Many French people would be happy to erase those four years from the history of their nation.

Since its liberation in 1945 French society has seen the development of two myths—one Gaullist and the other communist. These two myths dominated the national discourse for many years, reaching a peak between the end of the Algerian war in 1962 and the students' revolt in 1968. Both the Gaullist myth and the communist one, by nurturing the heroic dimension of the French Resistance answered the psychological and political needs of French society in its attempts to minimize the extent of French collaboration with the Germans and the significance of the Vichy period in general. Both ignored, among other things, the uniqueness of the reaction of the French Jews to the occupation and the extent of their participation in the struggle against the German occupiers during this period. It is important to keep in mind that the suffering of the Jews of France, like that of Jews in other countries, was due to their being Jewish, and not because they were French, and that this was also the main, although not the only, reason for their voluntary enlistment in the struggle against the conquerors. Some of the underground Jewish fighters themselves testified to the fact that as Jews they had no alternative but to take up arms and fight against the Germans.

The French historian Henry Rousso has suggested four stages in the development of France's collective memory of the period of the German conquest and occupation, based on Freud's definition of the mourning process:[1]

1. Unfinished mourning (1944–1954)
2. Repressions (1954–1971)
3. The "Broken Mirror," through which only parts of the past are seen (1971–1974)
4. The return from the Repressions (after 1974)

In the French education system, it is possible to identify a period of denial, which lasted from 1954–1960, followed by a "period of banalization" in the teaching of the Holocaust, which lasted until 1980. While teaching of the Holocaust was begun during these two decades, many of the complex and disturbing questions that begged for answers were avoided, especially those about France's responsibility for the fate of its Jews and those about French collaboration with the Nazis. Only in the 1980s did signs appear of real attempts to cope with these issues in the teaching of the Holocaust.

Nonetheless, as we shall discuss below, in France both awareness of and knowledge about the Holocaust are much greater than in many other countries, and certainly in comparison to results found in surveys conducted in the United States. Moreover, it appears that in France, the problems encountered in dealing with the traumatic events of the past, which were neither dealt with nor internalized earlier, return and erupt in various kinds of stormy affairs—especially those connected with collaboration with the Germans and with their policy of destruction—and in debates about historical revisionism and denial of the Holocaust. These affairs did, however, contribute, in their own way, to the public's increased awareness of the subject.[2]

The articles discussed below appeared in the prestigious French periodical *Débat*, an intellectual, non-Jewish publication that devoted considerable space to the question of the memory and the teaching of the Holocaust, as did other French periodicals and the media, all of which have dealt with this subject in the last few years. The debate between the writers was focused around the question of whether the Holocaust should be taught in French high schools within the framework of compulsory subjects, or as an elective course. This led to questions about the subject's content and goals, as well as about the specific influence of the ramifications of the Holocaust on the worldviews of French youngsters today.

An article that appeared in this issue of *Débat*, entitled "Pédagogiser la Shoa?" ("Should the Holocaust be Taught?"), written by Emma Shnur, an educator and the daughter of Holocaust survivors, stirred up public controversy.[3] In this article Shnur argues that in spite of its problematic nature this subject should be taught in France within the high school framework, but as an elective course. She goes on to explain that the present state of the education system in France does not allow for it to deal with the complex and difficult implications that inevitably arise when dealing with the Holocaust in a manner suitable for all of its pupils:

> We shall return to the middle of the century and to its shameful secret: the concentration and extermination camps. We considered ourselves cultivated people, masters of ourselves and of our futures: we do not stop to ask ourselves questions about the most disturbing enigma of all, and the one that opens our eyes to an amazing possibility about ourselves—the possibility of a derangement that is not bestial but, as befits a modern era, industrialized, rational, based on efficient productivity methods, and camouflaged as a well-organized morality.
> On the fiftieth anniversary of the Warsaw Ghetto Uprising and the fiftieth anniversary of the discovery of the camps—the term "liberation of the camps" is intentionally not used here—the belated trials of aged defendants finally brought to

justice for their collusion in the organization of the deportations [of Jews to the camps], and all of the memorial ceremonies inanely forced upon us by the round number of years—all of these force us to return, at least partially, to the past, long guarded as a secret. In this process one prominent and repetitive motif stands out, and never fails to surprise me: the oft-repeated declaration about the obligation to remember and to impart the memory of the Holocaust to future generations. How can it be that no one is seized by doubts, or frightened by such a great responsibility, and with a clear conscience? And when there is a discussion, it revolves only about the desired form—novels? television? learning in schools?—of bequeathing this memory. Is it not conceivable that someone will bring claims for the right to forget . . . and is it possible?

I am neither for nor against. But I am troubled by this internal conviction, which does not distinguish anything problematical. I suspect that the convinced are unaware of the ramifications of transmitting this memory. The educators' good intentions are liable to be discovered as no more than the quickest way to relieve a guilty conscience. Before placing an unbearable burden on the shoulders of the young, it is our duty to face one challenge—to understand what happened. This is not easy; and whosoever takes this challenge upon himself should think twice before so easily declaring "ce devoir de transmission" ["this necessity to transmit"].

Shnur raises arguments similar to those of Yehuda Elkana, and goes on to explain that the much repeated slogan of "To remember so that such a genocide 'shall never happen again'" is not only a sign of overly optimistic views, but proof that what happened has not been fully comprehended. She maintains, on the basis of her own experience, that transmitting such knowledge to young people is either impossible or unsuitable, and may have a negative impact on their perception of human nature.

Shnur tries to distinguish between intuitive feelings and logical explanations in order to discuss moral standpoints, "but not in the light of an existing morality, or one that has already been translated into universal terms." She seeks, rather, attitudes that have to be patched together from principles, conditions, experiences, and emotions, using whatever meager means are available.

Under the heading "to teach or to drive to despair" Shnur concludes her contentions:

To expose, detail-by-detail, the process of destruction and the camps' organization of killing, to delve into the macabre ceremonials in which the so-called "scientific" medical experiments were carried out, to take this voyage into the obscure secrets of systematic dehumanization—do we really have the right to impose such a thing within the framework of compulsory school lessons? I firmly maintain "no."

At the age of seventeen or eighteen, she asserts, the high school student is too overwhelmed by his own self-awakening and by the demands and concerns of his last year or two of studies, and what awaits him after them, to be able to devote the necessary thought to the deeds of Doctor Mengele and his like, and to the reasons underlying them. While the subject of the Holocaust should be offered as an elective course, as a compulsory subject it might lead, according to Shnur, to traumas that the teacher can neither foresee nor recognize, and that he or she cannot deal with.

> The students must, of course, learn exactly what occurred under the Nazi regime and during the Second World War—through history textbooks, literature, films.... To teach them about the many faces of totalitarianism as it appears in the horrifying character of Nazism in its day-to-day deeds is a difficult task: the "mercy killings" of the mentally ill, the development of sport in the youth movements, the hunting down of homosexuals, and the ecological protection of nature.... The students must of course learn about the existence of the camps and about various aspects of the destruction. But they must not be compelled to confront the experience of the concentration camp in the classroom....
>
> In order to return to being human we have to forget. Not that I am advocating oblivion here. But it is necessary to create a situation in which we will have to look deep within ourselves only after we have established several elementary beliefs.

Shnur asserts that the real thing that has to be considered is the thinking that we of the present generation must do. We have to reconsider the tradition, examine the history, return and examine the new humanism again; such work has been done in the last half century and is still far from finished.... The question is not whether Auschwitz should be brought into the curriculum, but what constitutes the culture that will provide a suitable answer to the challenges of our era and that has to be transmitted to the public. The culture that is suitable to the challenges of our era will assimilate what Auschwitz forces us to know, but only after a period of mourning and melancholy. It will allow us take heed of its implications, but without continuing to harp on the death camps. "For everything there is a season, and a time for every matter under heaven . . . a time to mourn" and a time to complete the mourning—a time to forget.

> Adorno maintained that after Auschwitz art is not possible; and the poet Joseph Brodsky answered, "Of course. But not only art; neither is breakfast." This interchange is the perfect expression for what I am making such a great effort to say.

> Let us abandon the fantasies of redemption that we nurtured through the teaching of the Holocaust. There are people who will want to know, and they must be given the possibility of knowing. Others will prefer not to know too much, and that is their right. There will be a memory, or other memories that are more or less the same; there will be history; and there will be works of art that will express what history cannot transmit. And there will be unavoidable and perhaps felicitous forgetting.

Other discussants in this debate took issue with Shnur's opinion, and suggested ways of teaching the subject—despite the difficulties it entails—to all high school pupils in France, that is, as a compulsory subject. Jean-François Forges disagrees with Shnur about memory as a matter of choice, as well as about the study of this topic only to those who really want to learn about it:

> Where have we ever heard that children, and especially children, will choose bitter facts, that are considered necessary, rather than stories with happy endings? Children do not comprehend that history has depth. They do not yet know what we owe to the suffering, to the happiness, and to the creativity of those who came before us. Many children, like most adults, deny society's responsibility for the past. Education is meant to arouse awareness in our belief in the ancient idea of the paternity of all human beings. To bestow this feeling of solidarity on children—that is the basic thing we are responsible for, and even, should we so desire, to present them with a pretentious, but necessary, utopia, on which all educational efforts are dependent. If we believe that the school years are not the right time for transmitting the memory, if we fully accept "unavoidable and perhaps felicitous oblivion," we lose the one and only tiny chance of preventing a return of barbarity. We will forget everything; there will be only the personal and secret memory of each victim and his or her family, as they seclude themselves in their pain. And then the way is open for another round.[4]

Forges concludes that schools or school curriculums that do not allow or fail to transmit the memory of the crimes—of which Auschwitz is the most extreme expression—are defective and do not fulfill their civil task: rather than blaming the school system, official curriculums have to be created that include reading Primo Levi and watching Claude Lanzmann's *Shoah*, not only so that certain pupils succeed in their final examinations, but so that they succeed to progress somewhat in knowledge, moral values, and culture, especially through the mediums of literature of the camps and the Holocaust:

> Refusing to discuss Auschwitz in the schools will result in transferring the responsibility for transmission of the memory to the media. The schools surely have deficiencies, and there are teachers who are Holocaust-deniers or

irresponsible. However, most teachers work quietly and with no undue commotion to transmit the memory of the Holocaust, faithful to the demands of truth and humaneness. . . .

Educating against Auschwitz . . . presents the demand for an attitude of respect for one's fellow man in the daily lives of both children and adults, and first of all in the school itself. If this is based on Levi and Lanzmann, such education is an invitation to struggle. If we do not talk about Auschwitz, in the most despairing possible way, we will lose the possibility of going through the process of mourning without forgetting Auschwitz, which will surely repeat itself one day in the history of mankind; and we will also forget the absolute necessity of assailing Auschwitz in the various different forms, small and large, in which it still exists today and will continue to exist tomorrow. If the teachers do not lead in this struggle, in this education, then who will?

Another participant in this same debate, Philippe Joutard, is also in favor of teaching the Holocaust as a required subject. In his view it is not only "a mission possible" ("Une tache possible," which is also the name of his article), but an imperative:[5] He claims that the Second World War cannot be studied, as it is in the eleventh and twelfth grades, without a focus on Nazism and, thus, on the Final Solution, and on how the horror of these were gradually revealed with the discovery of the death camps. To ignore these, he continues, would not only be a severe distortion of the "historical truth," but a moral sin. Joutard agrees with Emma Shnur's evaluation of the problematic nature of teaching the facts of the Holocaust: these facts cannot be presented in the same way as the facts of other types of knowledge because the perverse cruelty and perversion that they portray is not bestial but moral. But, Joutard explains:

> We have no choice also because of what is happening all around us: aggressive, uncompromising Holocaust-deniers are courting our pupils and, even more than them, public opinion. One or two events shock the school system every year. Since pupils are Internet-literate and use it easily, they are exposed to Holocaust-denial propaganda, a danger that should not be underrated. And I doubt the effectiveness of the supervisory and oversight mechanisms.

In a different article in the same periodical, Shnur responds to the other discussants' comments and summarizes her claims. She asserts that it is very difficult, indeed practically impossible, to provide "a real Holocaust education," with its weighty moral aspects and the values that are part of it, to all students in high schools:

> There is no point in thinking that education against Auschwitz can be accomplished through emotion, compassion, and dogmatic affirmations; after

Auschwitz—and because of Auschwitz—it is necessary to educate for independent judgment and egalitarian dialogue with even greater resolve and firmness. We have no choice; any other possibility is neither desirable nor acceptable.[6]

The importance of this debate cannot be exaggerated. On the premise that there is a desire to intensify the teaching of the Holocaust, not only in France but elsewhere as well, the question is how to do so while preserving an appropriate didactic level and without banalizing its content. Considering all of the sensitive and complex issues it entails, how are the teachers, those of today and those of the future, to be prepared for teaching this subject? How are they to be taught to cope with questions of immediate relevance in a present-day reality in which, as before, xenophobia and the exclusion of sub-groups and "others" continue to exist and thrive? These and similar questions exemplify why the teaching of the Holocaust cannot be left in the hands of any one particular bureaucratic group, and they indicate how much thorough research, deep thought, and teaching experience is required.

Great Britain

Significant reactions to the Holocaust began to be heard in Great Britain, as noted earlier, in the 1990s. The British government announced its intention to designate an official memorial day for the Holocaust and for victims of genocide throughout the world only in October 1999. Tony Blair, prime minister at that time, declared that Great Britain did not intend to forget—nor could it forget—the millions of Jewish and other victims murdered by the Nazis and their collaborators. The British Ministry of Interior called upon the broad public to respond to this announcement and to suggest a suitable date before the law was placed before the Parliament. The Ministry also asked the public for suggestions and recommendations for appropriate ways of marking this day. (The very fact that the government called for the active participation of the public in these questions is in itself notable.) The date chosen was January 27—the anniversary of the liberation of Auschwitz-Birkenau. (Among the other proposals were June 12, Anna Frank's birthday, and 27 Nissan, the Hebrew date of Holocaust Memorial Day in Israel.) It is important to repeat that this day was to be dedicated to the memories of all victims of the Nazi rule and to the memories of all victims of genocide throughout the world.

Holocaust Memorial Day in Great Britain was marked for the first time on January 27, 2001. (It was marked for the first time in Italy on the same day.) A dispute arose, however, around the events that were planned to mark the day, among other reasons because the government broadened its framework in such a way that in addition to its commemoration of the Holocaust, which was cast as the center of the events, the tragedies that befell other groups or peoples were also commemorated. Thus, the ceremonies also observed the murder of the Roma (Gypsies), the mentally handicapped, and homosexuals, all of whom Hitler considered as undeserving of the right to live, as well as events of genocide in Cambodia, Rwanda, and the former Yugoslavia. A particularly stormy controversy arose over the question of whether to mark the genocide of the Armenians during the First World War, and only after vociferous arguments over the course of two months, and just two days before the designated day, was an invitation extended to an Armenian delegation, which included two survivors, to participate in the official, central memorial ceremony. According to the original plan, the Armenians were not to have participated in the ceremony at all, the ostensible reason being that this memorial day was intended only for events that occurred during and after the Second World War. The decision to invite the Armenians came about only after Armenians and others in the British public accused the government of surrendering to pressures exercised by Turkey, which refuses to recognize that an Armenian genocide occurred, and makes every effort to assure that no other country does so.

In Great Britain, as in France, researchers and educators are engaged in related issues that arise when teaching the Holocaust. Among others, their deliberations deal with such questions as whether, and how, the Holocaust and other genocidal events should be linked, and how and to what extent their universal ramifications should be emphasized.

An article by Bruce Carrington and Geoffrey Short, "Holocaust Education, Anti-racism and Citizenship," examines the potential in the teaching of the Holocaust for fostering concepts of good citizenship.[7] Special attention is given to the Holocaust as a subject that can contribute to education against the phenomenon of racism in general. This article, based on an empirical study carried out in general and Catholic parochial schools in southeastern Great Britain, probes the pupils' understanding of the phenomenon of racism, and especially their ability to identify and to deconstruct racial stereotypes. The study also attempted to examine the pupils' evaluation of the possible contribution that learning about the Holocaust can make in preparing young people for active citizenship in a pluralistic democracy. While the researchers are cautious about reaching sweeping conclusions from their small sample, they believe that the teaching of the Holocaust can be an important factor in the teaching of subjects connected with human rights and racism in general as long as care is taken to avoid equating various different manifestations of racism with the specific phenomenon of the Holocaust.

There is no doubt that the Holocaust can be a pivotal factor in how various education systems deal with the phenomenon of racism. However, there is also no doubt that this subject must be dealt with through a clarification of the unique elements of the racial theories of the Nazis.

Reactions to the Holocaust in the United States

The Jews in the United States Prior to the Holocaust

Jewish immigration to the United States occurred mainly in three waves. The first wave, in 1654, consisted of a very small and short-lived group of Jews who worked for the Dutch West India Company. This was followed by a limited but continuous flow of Jewish immigrants, largely of Spanish-Portuguese origin, who at first integrated into various branches of trade and merchandising, and then gradually entered the free professions.

The "second migration" occurred between the years 1820 and 1880, and consisted of European Jews, most of whom were from areas in or influenced by Germany, from which they fled because of political instability and repression, and the economic deterioration that began in 1848 and continued for the next decade. The latter stage of this wave included growing numbers of Jews from Eastern Europe. Most of these immigrants integrated into the budding American economy as skilled craftsmen or in some form of petty commerce, roles they had filled in their countries of origin. At the end of this wave of immigration, and prior to the main influx of immigrants that was yet to follow, the Jews of the United States constituted one of the largest Jewish communities in the world.

The "third migration," which consisted almost entirely of Jews from Eastern Europe, began in 1880 and peaked during the first decades of the twentieth century, following the Kishinev pogrom (1903) and the Russian revolution of 1905. After a hiatus caused by the First World War, it continued with intensified force until it was severely restricted by a new law. The Jews of this wave lived in considerable poverty, barely subsisting from work in needlecrafts and light industry or as peddlers. The National Origins Immigration Act, enacted in 1924, drastically reduced the possible number of newcomers.

Despite comprising only 10 percent of the total influx of immigrants arriving in the United States between 1830 and 1930, this Jewish community became the largest in the world. By 1826, Jews in America had already acquired full civil rights in all but three of the states existing at that time, and they encountered very little anti-Semitism, at least until the second decade of the twentieth century. Beginning in the 1920s and 1930s, and due to a general fomenting of racist ideas in the country at that time, as well as the economic policies initiated by the United States to discourage immigration, anti-Semitism began to develop and grow. The massive numbers of Jews that had arrived during or just before these years from Eastern Europe were the targets of contumely and scorn, especially by Protestant Christians, who opposed the United States policy of large-scale immigration. This anti-Semitic approach was expressed in various ways, among them by limiting the number of Jewish students admitted to the more prestigious universities, exclusion from certain residential areas or from becoming members of certain clubs or societies, and impeding their advancement in, or even preventing their entrance into, the business world.

The United States during the Holocaust Era

The reaction of the United States to the Holocaust fell far short of fulfilling the humanistic and democratic values that were the professed ethical pillars of the American people. During the years that preceded the actual annihilation of Jews (1933 to 1941), when the United States (and many other countries) could have opened its gates to them, it failed to do so. Three main reasons can be cited for this:

- The Great Depression of the 1930s;
- Nativism and isolationism (xenophobia);
- Anti-Semitism.

The great economic depression of the 1930s led to an atmosphere of anxiety and insecurity. When unemployment reached 25 percent many Americans feared that immigrants would take their jobs, and even during the war, when the United States needed as many working hands as possible, the pervasive fear that jobs would be scarce after it was over persisted.

The trends towards nativism and isolationism that prevailed in the United States during the 1920s intensified during the thirties under the slogan "America for the Americans." These trends were connected, in part, to apprehensions regarding the negative cultural influences that immigrants might have on American society, a fear held by many, and by the perceived need to uphold various myths held by the native-born Americans.

The anti-Semitic trends that had developed gradually in the United States during the 1920s continued, and even intensified, towards the end of the thirties and in the early forties. Anti-Semitic publications (such as *Protocols of the Elders of Zion*, fabricated documents first published in Tsarist Russia, that accused the Jews of a conspiracy to rule the world) proliferated and were spread throughout the country, thus strengthening the anti-Semitic trends and contributing to the closure of the United States to Jewish refugees. Even after Kristallnacht in 1938, when it became painfully clear that the Jews of Germany had to leave the country, and when world leaders, led by President Roosevelt, condemned the situation, the quota policy of the United States was not changed. (The United States began to take significant steps to rescue the European Jews only in August 1942.)

In the autumn of 1942, when there was incontrovertible knowledge of the systematic murder of Jews throughout German-occupied Europe, and after heavy pressure was exerted on the government—not only by Jewish organizations but by some Christian leaders as well—the American government began to act, hesitantly, to rescue Jews. In January 1944, under the pressure of various quarters, Roosevelt established a government agency, called the War Refugee Board, which tried to help those who had survived the Nazi destruction. This agency received little support from Roosevelt's government and was connected, for all practical purposes, to the Treasury Department, which received most of the monies that flowed to it from Jewish organizations and not from the government. It was in any case too little and too late.

The United States after the Holocaust

The Second World War ended in Europe in May 1945. The victorious Allies immediately had to deal with many problems, among them the immensely chaotic one of eight million "displaced persons" (DPs) living in the areas now under the control of the Western allies. In an extraordinary extensive operation they succeeded in returning seven million to their homes, but one million others remained homeless, among them between 50,000 and 100,000 Jews who had survived the camps and the ghettos, a number that doubled to 200,000 within the year. Since the British refused to allow 100,000 Jews living in DP camps throughout Europe to enter Palestine, over which they still held the Mandate, the United States government was compelled to seek other solutions. Only in 1948, under pressure from both Jewish and non-Jewish organizations, and after a difficult and exhausting process, was a law passed that increased the immigration quota, but this quota would include all refugees displaced by the war, not only Holocaust survivors.

The Holocaust also influenced U.S. policy vis-à-vis the government's attitude to the question of the establishment of a Jewish state in Palestine. At the beginning of the 1940s the activities of pro-Zionist groups heightened and were supported by various non-Jewish elements. In the autumn of 1944 about two-thirds of the members of both houses of Congress were in favor of such a Jewish state, but the government was more hesitant and, apparently, conditioned its support on a Zionist agreement to a partition of Palestine. When it finally came, U.S. support for the establishment of the State of Israel, and concern with its continued existence and the sustainment of a special relationship between the United States and Israel were all determined to a great extent by the Holocaust, and by the need to ensure that such an atrocity would never happen again.

The United States was involved in matters touching on the Holocaust in the period following World War II when Nazi war criminals were brought to trial. Of more than 5,000 German war criminals that the countries of the West found guilty, 1,814 were convicted by U.S. tribunals established for this purpose (of the 462 death sentences imposed, 283 were carried out).

Until 1952, therefore, the United States was engaged in dealing with three important matters linked to the Holocaust: the DPs, the establishment of the State of Israel, and the prosecution of Nazi war criminals. Notwithstanding these acute issues, the Holocaust itself received little attention during the postwar years and the two decades that followed. Even within the Jewish leadership in the United States there was a tendency during these years to keep the profile of the Jewish question very low, especially since after 1944 there was a significant decline of anti-Semitism in the country.

Most Americans thus took no notice of the Holocaust during the 1950s, and of those who did, most were affected by *The Diary of Anne Frank*, which was published in the United States in 1952. The great success of this book was followed by a stage version in 1955 and a Hollywood film in 1959. This well-known book depicts the inner life of the young Anna Frank and the events of the Holocaust serve only as the background of the personal story. In the stage play, and even more so in the film, the Jewish aspects of the story were obscured, apparently in order to endow them a stronger universal appeal. Two other books that dealt with the Holocaust appeared in the 1950s and were widely read at that time: *The Wall*, by John Hersey and *Exodus*, by Leon Uris. The first dealt with the revolt in the Warsaw ghetto, the second with clandestine ("illegal") immigration of Holocaust survivors to Palestine, and both stressed the heroic aspects of these events. Despite the considerable public interest they aroused, these popular novels engaged the subject of the Holocaust melodramatically, and only superficially.

A real and perceptive interest in the Holocaust and the fate of the Jews began in the United States only in the 1960s, following the trial of Adolph Eichmann in Jerusalem. The trial was broadly reported in all the media and captured widespread attention. For a full year it was headlined in American newspapers, and thousands of articles were written about it. Before the trial began, and during its first stages, the American media focused on various legal aspects of the case, such as the infringement of Argentina's sovereignty by the Israeli kidnapping and spiriting of Eichmann out of the country, and the jurisdictional right of an Israeli court to prosecute a crime committed outside of its domain and even prior to its existence. At first, public opinion tended to oppose Israel's action, but as the trial progressed this gradually changed. Most of the American newspapers presented Eichmann as a symbol and a warning about the dangers of racial hatred and of dictatorial rule, and asserted that the Holocaust must be documented for the public, among other reasons, as an educational tool. And yet, in spite of the trial's high media profile and the public's great awareness of it, according to different surveys most Americans failed to internalize its deep moral significance. In actuality, its messages did not reach an appreciable part of the American public.

By sheer coincidence, and perhaps somewhat symbolically, the Eichmann verdict was announced on the same day that the first screening of the Hollywood film *Judgment at Nuremberg* took place. In this film, directed by Stanley Kramer, the universal message of the Holocaust stands out prominently: the film presents the Jews as but one of many victims of the Nazis. Other Hollywood films produced between 1962 and 1979 similarly deal obliquely with the events of the Holocaust. For example, in the 1976 film *Voyage of the Damned*, directed by Stuart Rosenberg, the Holocaust is dealt with as a Jewish event, but its main protagonist is the German captain of the St. Louis, a steamship carrying Jewish refugees fleeing Germany. It is noteworthy that many books dealing with the Holocaust from a Jewish standpoint were published in the sixties, among them the novels written by Elie Wiesel.

An artistic work that commanded great attention during this period was a drama written by the German playwright Rolf Hochhuth in which he severely criticized Pope Pius XII for not condemning the murder of the Jews by the Nazis. His play *The Deputy*, first staged in 1963, put the tangled issue of Christian-Jewish relations on the agenda, especially the role played by anti-Semitism in Christian theological doctrine. The Christian-Jewish dialogue that developed after the Holocaust led to a gradual cessation of anti-Semitic preaching as part and parcel of Christian dogma and, along with it, to a still partial recognition of the wrongs inflicted upon the Jews due to the silence of the Christian establishment as a whole during the Holocaust. (An historically significant step in this direction was made by Pope John Paul II on the occasion of his visit to Yad Vashem in the year 2000.)

In 1961 the first comprehensive academic study on the subject of the Holocaust, *The Destruction of the European Jews*, by Raul Hilberg, was published. It was revised and republished in 1985, and is still considered one of the most important works on the Holocaust. However, not only did it receive little press coverage at the time; questions were even raised as to the necessity of books on this subject at all. It is interesting that despite its undeniable importance, and the fact that repeated editions have been published in several languages, this valuable study has yet to be translated into Hebrew (probably also because of the writer's positions regarding the Jewish reactions during the Holocaust, and regardless of its unquestionable research value).[8]

Along with the changes in American public opinion about the Holocaust brought about by the books, films, and stage plays, and due to the shift that was then beginning to be felt in Jewish-Christian relations, there were also changes in the attitudes of various different strata of American society to the Jews. The decline in anti-Semitism that had begun at the end of the Second World War continued and accelerated in the ensuing decades, and for all practical purposes any obvious form of anti-Semitism, such as limiting the percentage of Jewish students admitted to certain universities, disappeared almost completely by the sixties.

Notwithstanding the decline in anti-Semitism, during the two postwar decades the Holocaust received relatively little attention, as discussed above. This changed significantly during the 1970s, one of the main factors being a large number of activities held in memory of events of the Holocaust, or connected to them in some way, a slightly belated reaction to the Eichmann trial. During the trial itself, many of the things revealed in it were still too fresh and painful, even to the American Jews; many of them had lost relatives in the Holocaust and had to come to terms with the questions of their own response and that of their country's government to what had happened in Europe during that era, as well as with their attitudes to the survivors who had arrived in the United States after the war. By the 1970s all were better able to view the Holocaust from a more objective perspective, especially since the Jews of the United States were now living in a more secure and free society, almost free of anti-Semitism. American Jews could now openly relate to Jewish matters, including the unique character of the Holocaust as a tragedy of the Jewish People. The Holocaust survivors living in the United States and still alive in the 1970s strengthened this consciousness: after arriving physically and emotionally shattered, most of them had rehabilitated their lives, raising new families and establishing themselves economically. During their first years most of them tended to refrain from talking about the past, among other reasons because the long-established American Jews discouraged it—a phenomenon that occurred, it should be noted, in both Israel and in Europe at that time.

It appears that this silence was due to a combination of various emotional and psychological factors that made it difficult for the survivors to speak about their experiences, along with social pressures connected to the unwillingness of those around them to hear about them. Cracks in this wall of silence began to appear during the Eichmann trial in the early 1960s, but only in the 1970s did they break open and the survivors begin to speak publicly about themselves and what they had experienced, thus becoming an important factor in developing an awareness of the Holocaust. In the United States during these years, other events, mainly the Six Day War in 1967 and the Yom Kippur War in 1973, strengthened the unique Jewish identity of American Jews, and with it a desire to also strengthen the memory of the Holocaust, not only amongst themselves, but also within the general American public.

Along with these changes in the 1970s, synagogues and churches in the United States began to hold ceremonies or services to mark a day of remembrance for the Jewish victims murdered in the Holocaust. The date chosen for this was April 19 (the day in 1943 on which the Warsaw Ghetto Uprising broke out), the day on which even before the end of the Second World War several Jewish groups in the United States had already begun to mark as a memorial day. In 1946 the Board of Orthodox Rabbis had already called for a day of remembrance, but their suggestion was not accepted at that time. Only thirteen years later, in 1959, was the anniversary of the day on which the Warsaw Ghetto Uprising broke out established as the remembrance day for all Jewish victims of the Holocaust. This was changed in 1961, when it was decided that Memorial Day for the Warsaw Ghetto Uprising and for the Jewish Victims of the Holocaust would be marked in the United States on the same day that it is marked in Israel, that is, on 27 Nissan in the Jewish calendar, which due to a different system than that of the Gregorian calendar, falls on a different date from year to year.

Also during these same years several high schools and universities began to offer courses in the Holocaust, a number of memorial sites were established, conferences and conventions were held about it, and a few educational centers devoted to the subject were opened. Films and prose and poetical compositions about the Holocaust, as well as scholarly research studies, began to appear and were more and more accepted by the broad public, and as this acceptance grew, it contributed to the motivation of additional writers and researchers to engage in the subject.

By 1978 the subject had become sufficiently interesting for the production of a four-part television series, entitled *Holocaust*, which was broadcast coast-to-coast at primetime. One hundred and twenty million people—that is, approximately one-half of the entire American public—saw at least one of the episodes. The series chronicled the destruction of European Jewry by the Nazis through the (fictional) story of the life a Jewish family, and although it was denigrated for portraying the Holocaust melodramatically and overly "sanitized," it succeeded in impressing the immensity of the atrocity on the consciousness of broad sectors of the American public, an awareness that led to an ongoing interest in the subject that continued for several years. Since then a large number of cinematic and television films have been screened in the United States, including, in 1993, *Schindler's List*, directed by Steven Spielberg, which had an especially strong impact. It drew the interest of both the general public and the critics, making a particularly powerful impression on younger people, most of whom had not seen *Holocaust* and who now had acquired at least a general understanding of the Nazi genocide of the Jewish people. The overall positive reactions to *Schindler's List* were not affected by many commentators' faultfinding, which criticized the film for being inaccurate historically, for its stereotypical representations of Jews, and because its protagonist was a Nazi, as well as for various other defects.

Memorial Activities

In the same year in which *Holocaust* was broadcast, 1978, and at the initiative of the American president, Jimmy Carter, the President's Commission on the Holocaust was formed and charged with making recommendations for the appropriate measures for memorializing the Holocaust and its victims. The commission, headed at first by Elie Wiesel, proposed the establishment of a museum and the continued observance of a remembrance day on the same day as it was marked in Israel. The museum, eventually built in Washington, D.C., was to be educational in character, and President Carter was insistent that it commemorate all victims of the Nazi regime, and not only the Jewish ones, a directive that led to much trenchant and impassioned discussion. Built in the center of Washington and opened in 1993, the museum includes large exhibition halls and educational and research centers.

The exhibits document the atrocities and murder of other groups committed by the Nazis, such as the Roma, Poles, Russian war prisoners, and homosexuals, but the museum's emphasis is undeniably on the Jewish Holocaust, the *Shoah*. The museum is open 364 days a year, including national and religious holidays (it is closed only on Yom Kippur, the Jewish Day of Atonement), and is operated and funded by the U.S. Department of the Interior. Its fifty-five-member U.S. Holocaust Memorial Council is appointed by the president of the United States. By the beginning of the year 2004 twenty million people—adults and children—eighty percent of whom were not Jewish, had visited it and participated in its educational activities, and many different schools, organizations, and institutions, as well as individuals, have used its documentary and research facilities.

Even before the construction of the Holocaust Museum in Washington was begun similar museums were being planned all over the United States. In addition to their memorial elements, most of them offer library and research facilities, as well as educational programs for schools and community institutions. One particularly interesting museum is Beit Hashoah—Museum of Tolerance, erected by the Simon Wiesenthal Center in Los Angeles in 1993. Among its other exhibits, the museum has a multimedia presentation that is mainly about the Holocaust but also elucidates the consequences of intolerance in general, in the past and in the present.

In addition to museums, from the late 1970s on memorial monuments and educational centers, mainly associated with universities and colleges, have been established throughout the United States. These centers provide library facilities that include learning aids such as films, videocassettes, and slides, and assist schools in the preparation of curricula and study materials on the Holocaust. They also offer teacher training courses, fund adult education, and hold lectures and various other activities connected with commemorating the memories of the victims of the Holocaust. Many of them also organize conferences and seminars, and publish bulletins, research papers, and bibliographies that include survivors' testimonies. Repositories of these recorded testimonies contribute greatly to perpetuating the memory of the Holocaust because such personal accounts transmit not only factual information, but something of the survivors' emotional anguish as well. In a project set up by Steven Spielberg to document the victims of the Holocaust, almost one hundred thousand testimonies have already been videotaped. It is important to mention again that Holocaust survivors are the source of much of the initiative for these projects, as well as for the actual activities associated with them. Despite the pain, they have shared their personal experiences of the Holocaust with the public at memorial assemblies, in radio and television programs, and by speaking to classes in various schools throughout the country.

Enormous efforts have likewise been devoted to the writing of memoirs, of prose and poetry, of stage plays about the Jewish Holocaust and, needless to say, of academic research. The outpouring of written materials on this subject apparently reached a peak at the end of the 1980s, but has continued to flow unceasingly since then. There are but few events in the history of mankind that have generated so great a corpus of creative endeavor, both artistic and academic, in so short a period of time as has the Holocaust. Interest in the subject intensified after the Nobel Prize for Peace was conferred on Elie Wiesel in 1986 in recognition of his life work in perpetuating the memory of the Holocaust.

Educational Activities

As public awareness increased, and undoubtedly also due to it, interest in the pedagogical and academic aspects of the Holocaust also increased. In the field of formal education it had been included in the curriculum of only a very small number of schools and colleges prior to 1970, but this began to change at that time. In most academic frameworks it was included in the lessons on Jewish history or the history of the Second World War, but in the 1980s many academic institutions began to offer full six-month or one-year courses in the subject. These courses, usually given as one of the electives for a B.A. degree in history or theology, drew thousands of students, who thus gained a thorough overview of the Holocaust. More detailed and serious courses towards master's and doctoral degrees were also opened, and these focused on literary, sociological, psychological, philosophical or historical aspects of the subject.

In spite of the interest described above, and although much progress has been made, the Holocaust has not become a standard subject in American high schools. As of 2004 at least twenty of the fifty states have passed legislation regarding the teaching of the Holocaust, and in twenty-six states there are Holocaust academic standards. However, in many hundreds of schools throughout the United States it is taught as a non-required part of the lessons on American or general history, or within special lessons on Nazism and the Second World War. These lessons usually have two goals: to impart basic information about the Holocaust, and to instill such basic humanitarian values as democracy, tolerance, acceptance of the "other," and the importance of personal responsibility and the struggle against religious or racial prejudice. In the teaching of these lessons the teachers use audio-visual learning aids, literature, films, lectures and discussions, workshops and role-playing, and so on. A vast amount of material is available in the form of literature, computer programs, fictional and documentary films, posters, and videocassettes. In addition, various Jewish organizations, among them associations of Jewish Holocaust survivors, provide summer programs for pupils, some of which take place in America, others in Poland or Israel. The Holocaust is dealt with in considerable depth in these programs, among other subjects.

The Holocaust in textbooks. The interest in the subject of the Holocaust and efforts to introduce it in school curricula have been far greater than the place it was given in textbooks and the way in which it was presented during those years. A study carried out in 1970 examined and compared twenty textbooks on American, European, and world history written for high schools and colleges. The results of this study showed that in most of them the Holocaust was mentioned only briefly and superficially, or not at all. Only one of them provided accurate and detailed information on the subject, two others included short but important chapters, and a fourth textbook was found to be full of errors. No significant improvement was found in another survey, from the end of the 1970s: almost half of the textbooks examined contained only one paragraph about the Holocaust, most of the rest had only one sentence; moreover, most of them contained inaccuracies. Several surveys indicated that the situation in regard to textbooks for college students was even worse.[9]

A certain improvement began to appear in the 1980s, and seems to have continued and even intensified in the 1990s. Nevertheless, researcher Glenn Pate concluded that the treatment of the subject of the Holocaust in American textbooks is far from satisfactory: they lack sufficient data, fail to deal with the important lessons that are called "in order to safeguard our future," and they rarely provide examples that may be used as important tools for enhancing the teaching of the subject within the framework of other disciplines.[10]

The textbooks available during those years do not reflect the fact that the American public was increasingly interested in Jewish subjects in general, and in the Holocaust in particular. During that same period of time there was a parallel increase in Holocaust denial, including the claim that the Jews had "invented" it in order to besmirch the good name of the Germans, to receive monetary restitution, and to win world support for the establishment of the State of Israel. This claim, heard previously in Europe, was based on the "premise" that the evidence—including eyewitness reports and documentary films—was likewise entirely fabricated. This notion won the support of various extremist groups, and in the 1970s those who held such views attempted to give them an academic basis through such books as *The Six Million Swindle*, by Austin J. App, published in 1973, and *The Hoax of the Twentieth Century*, by Arthur Butz, which appeared in 1976. Both of these writers asserted that the Jews of Europe were not annihilated, that the evidence was faked, and that it was all actually concocted in the fertile minds of the Jews to serve their own goals: the establishment of a Jewish state. All of these claims were wrapped in "scientific" dress, including the publication of an historical periodical. This trend received particularly widespread attention in the early 1990s when the "Holocaust-deniers" placed paid-for announcements in the newspapers of several universities. Despite such efforts, it remains clear that the American public tends, by and large, to disagree with such "claims" and gives full credence to the Holocaust having happened. (In Great Britain and in France these majorities are comparatively greater.) It has been shown clearly that in general the American public also supports education in the subject of the Holocaust, despite the fact that most of these Americans themselves have only limited knowledge about it.

Claims have been made that since the 1980s American interest in the Holocaust has become more restrained, and perhaps has also declined. And while books, films, courses, monuments, and other works of art continue to appear, the rate at which they do has decreased. Be that as it may, it is clear that the national and universal importance of this subject has become rooted in the American public's consciousness. As we have tried to show here, although necessarily in brief, the Holocaust has left its mark on education, literature, filmmaking, and academia, and on American society and its culture in general. American public opinion has reached a consensus about the need for commemorating it, and there is agreement, at least at the declarative level—and largely due to the influence of the Holocaust—that the state must be actively involved in preventing any recurrence of any genocide, in any place. In practice, however, the state's activities do not fulfill the spirit of this consensus.

In *Holocaust in American Life*, mentioned above, author Peter Novick attempts to investigate how, and especially why, the status of the Holocaust in the United States underwent so thorough a metamorphosis, in both the Jewish awareness and that of the public at large, from a subject rejected and ignored to one whose importance is now unequivocal. How, then, did the Holocaust become a dominant component of the American Jewish identity and of Jewish communal life? And how did it capture a place for itself in all the corners of the country's educational system and in its public discourse? In explaining American society's complete disregard and even rejection of the Holocaust survivors in the past (characteristic mainly of the 1950s), Novick asserts that the source of this was not guilt feelings for America's not having done whatever possible while it was being carried out, as many claim, but rather the political needs of the postwar years: to contend with the Cold War and the threat of totalitarianism, i.e., Stalinism, which had come to take the place of the Nazi menace.[11]

How to teach the Holocaust. Two important texts, the first of which appeared in 1982 and the second in 1994, represent two educational approaches that have strongly influenced the teaching of the Holocaust in the United States in recent years: *Facing History and Ourselves*,[12] devised by a group of teachers in 1976, and *Guidelines for Teaching about the Holocaust*,[13] published by the United States Holocaust Memorial Museum in Washington, D.C.

Facing History and Ourselves is an international nonprofit organization of educators and professionals (both Jewish and non-Jewish alike) whose mission is to engage students of diverse backgrounds, studying in middle schools and high schools and in teachers colleges, in an examination of racism, prejudice, and anti-Semitism in order to promote the development of a more humane and informed citizenry. By studying the historical development that led to the Holocaust, and its lessons, as well as other forms of collective violence, students make the essential connection between history and the moral choices they confront in their own lives.

Facing History and Ourselves provides Facing History teachers with staff development in the form of workshops, institutes, and seminars. Facing History teachers also have access to an assortment of books, periodicals, speakers, and videotapes for classroom use, mainly about the Holocaust but about other cases of genocide as well. The program originally included a comprehensive chapter on the Armenian genocide, but this section was reduced greatly in the 1994 revision of the program. In 2004, however, Facing History published a new resource book, *Crimes Against Humanity and Civilization: The Genocide of the Armenians*. This book focuses on the history of the Armenian genocide and examines how that history has informed the growing international human rights movement. The stories of Armenians, although particularistic, raise universal questions for everyone.

Over the past two decades, 11,000 teachers have participated in Facing History workshops and institutes, and the program reaches approximately 1,000,000 students annually. It is used in public schools, in independent and parochial middle schools and high schools, in colleges and universities, technical and vocational schools, adult education programs in the United States and Canada and, more recently, South Africa, France, England, Ireland, Germany, the Czech Republic, and former Soviet countries.

Through the teaching of the Holocaust, the program presents the pupils with questions about the role and the responsibility of the individual in society, and encourages them to deal critically with the complex issues of human and social relations and to beware of being satisfied with facile or simplistic answers to any of these complex problems. The project's point of departure is that learning about the past should generate critical thinking about the present and the future. Questions of a personal nature are also raised, such as, "What would I do in such a situation?" Despite general agreement about the importance of this project, there is some criticism of its educational approach, its goals, and its one-sidedness.

In the preface and the introduction to the 1994 revised edition of Facing History's resource book, the executive director of the project,

Margot Stern Strom, asserts that in their everyday life all Americans are recipients, in both small and large ways, of the consequences of life in a racially and ethnically diverse nation. Because the struggle for change is also a struggle for the nation's "conscience and future," it should be dealt with in its children's education. The children in American schools, she continues, have managed to assimilate a store of racial and religious stereotypes. Although we teach our children that "sticks and stones may break my bones but words can never hurt me," they know a different reality: "They are well aware that words of hate degrade, dehumanize, and eventually destroy. Indeed, much of the violence that threatens our society has its roots in bigotry and hate." Strom believes that hate and bigotry are at the root of the greater part of the acts of violence we are witness to in today's society. How, then, she asks, do children, sometimes at a very young age, acquire the language of hatred? She asserts that they are educated to it, that many of them internalize not only the language of hatred, but also its message.

In order to win the struggle for the future, the nation's children must receive an education that will prod them to think and to care about the fate of others. Young people have to be helped not only to ask themselves the questions that highlight possible situations in which they are liable to react with indifference to the suffering of "the other," but also what they can do actively to prevent them; they have to be taught the value of their right as citizens, and trained to be able to accept personal responsibility for their acts and deeds. Above all, they must be taught the brutal and tragic chapters in the history of mankind, and not only those that glorify success. Young people, says Strom, have to confront past injustices, so that they will understand the value of freedom, appreciate the differences between people, and will seek and work towards justice in their own time and in the future. She quotes Hannah Arendt's argument "that we can put past evils into the service of a future good only by squarely facing reality." Strom also quotes the Nobel prize-winning Russian-Jewish poet Joseph Brodsky who claimed that evil is not an aberrant or uncommon disorder outside of human existence but "a reflection of ourselves: of human negative potential"—that cannot be assailed unless it is understood. Moreover, Strom continues, learning history is the pupils' key to their ability to analyze events of the past critically, to examine them in the perspective of time, and to understand the implications of moral decisions. In this way each pupil becomes cognizant of the fact that the world in which he lives is the result of the decisions made by individuals and groups, and that every decision, even the smallest, may lead to a decisive effect—for good or for bad.

Thus, in Facing History the pupils learn to recognize that hundreds of decisions, small and large, right and wrong, have driven history, and in this way they internalize the fact that the courses history takes are not unavoidable. They learn that the answers to complex questions about racism, anti-Semitism, hatred, and violence are not simple, and that the solution to social injustice and moral iniquity is neither easy nor swift. What the project mainly seeks to teach, Strom explains, is what their teachers did not succeed in teaching her and her generation: that since history is largely the result of human decisions, there are things that can and must be prevented from happening. In order to ensure that these teaching goals are achieved, education must have a moral dimension. The Facing History project is based on educational principles and on the premise that there is a connection between freedom and education towards moral values; it is anchored in the precept that only a people that values its own freedom will raise its voice against injustices elsewhere.

Under their teachers' guidance the pupils learn to examine the roots of racial, religious and ethnic hatred, and the results of such hatred. Gradually they begin to understand that the gazes of the people that look back at them from the blood-filled mirror of history are no different from their own. This gradual discovery is made in several ways, and, since each chapter of history has both particularistic and universal significance, through a critical engagement with the history of the Holocaust as well. Thus, the events that led to the Holocaust are not to be perceived as "their history," but as "our history"—for it is a history that touches all of us. It is possible to find in various events that preceded the Holocaust similarities to many others: slavery in the United States, the annihilation of the Native American nations of both South and North America during colonization, the genocide of the Armenians, mass murders committed by the Japanese in China in the late 1930s and during the Second World War (the "rape of Nanking" is one of these), those committed in the U.S.S.R. under Stalin and, more recently, mass murders in Cambodia, Laos, Tibet, and Rwanda.

Despite these possible examples, the initiators of the project chose, for several reasons, to focus on the Holocaust. First of all, learning about the Jewish Holocaust is the most efficient way to induce deep thinking about the issues connected with genocide in the twentieth century. Secondly, there is an abundance of documentation—not only testimonies and memoirs provided by those that lived through it, but also records and photographs left by the perpetrators and bystanders—all of which demonstrate the destructive consequences of prejudices, fear, and lies. The documentation also vividly illustrates the danger hidden in charismatic leaders who take control over the masses in various manipulative ways, by appealing to people's fears and anxieties, and by exploiting the ignorance of young people. Finally, it is important to focus on the Holocaust, because it completely demolished the axiomatic premise that scientific and technological progress is always for the benefit of humanity, and the assumption that the driving force that raises our sensitivity to others and our desire to understand them is embedded within the liberal western culture.

The Holocaust forces us to face deep and perturbing moral questions, and their implications for our faith, our deeds, and our ability to distinguish between good and evil. It constrains us to contend with the question of the fate of those banished from the "universe of obligation," as were the Jews, the Gypsies, and other groups. When learning about the Holocaust the pupils can fully grasp the fact that human rights are neither self-evident nor automatically conferred on each and every human being, but are dependent on a society that bestows them and on its ability—and its readiness—to defend them. Facing History is thus first and foremost a project that facilitates the in-depth teaching of universal themes—themes that are connected with the history of the events that led to the Holocaust, which Strom unyieldingly maintains is a unique occurrence, unparalleled by and incomparable with any other mass murder.

Despite the importance and success of this project, it has not a few critics. Two of the most important of them are the historian Deborah Lipstadt (who became well-known internationally at the end of the 1990s due to a libel case brought against her by the English Holocaust-denier David Irving) and the Holocaust historian Lucy Dawidowicz. Lipstadt, noting that the Facing History and Ourselves project is the most influential model for teaching the Holocaust in the United States, criticizes it less for the way the Holocaust is approached and more with the context into which it is placed, which is, in her opinion, overly universal.[14] She asserts that this approach, which addresses a broad array of various other heinous injustices, including the Armenian genocide and violent manifestations of racism in American society, "elides the differences between the Holocaust and all manner of inhumanities and injustices." Lipstadt claims that "[w]hile positing the Holocaust as unique, *Facing History* presents the mass murders in Cambodia, Laos, Tibet and Rwanda as examples of the same phenomenon"—and thus comparable to the atrocity of the Holocaust. She agrees that while each of these was a horrific tragedy, all are different from the Holocaust, and that the Holocaust cannot be relativized since it is not a matter of comparative pain, but what was at the root of the genocidal efforts. "At times," Lipstadt asserts, "instead of making historiography relevant, *Facing History* distorts it."

Lipstadt exemplifies her claims by quoting from the 1982 edition of the project. In it, she claims, "a historically fallacious" parallel is drawn between the Holocaust and the atomic bombings of Hiroshima and Nagasaki by claiming that they share certain "basic principles." Then, after the project planners themselves advise against making too close a connection between these two terrible events, they provide six pages of suggested readings and activities on the topic, including some about the dangers of nuclear war. Although this emphasis on nuclear war was moderated in the revised 1994 edition, and the Holocaust is presented there as a unique event, the mass murders in Cambodia, Laos, Tibet, and Rwanda are given as examples of the same phenomenon.

Lipstadt maintains that to say that the Holocaust is not the same as other more local and less bureaucratized and single-minded examples of mass killing is not to rule out all points of comparison. Ultimately, the only way we learn is through comparison. But the Holocaust remains unique for two primary reasons. It was the only time in recorded history that a state tried to destroy an entire people, regardless of an individual's age, sex, location, profession, or belief. And it is the only instance in which the perpetrators conducted this genocide for no ostensible material, territorial, or political gain.

In its chapter on American racism, Lipstadt continues, the project's approach borders on the ridiculous: To exemplify how the African Americans reacted to generations of racial discrimination, its writers bring Louis Farrakhan. However, they fail to mention—other than one brief note that parts of his message "stereotype and demean other groups"—his use of traditional anti-Semitic slurs to deliver his message of African American pain, nor do they note that he spoke of Hitler as a "great man."

Lipstadt's criticism notwithstanding, she views as commendable the project's overall goal—to bring students to examine their own lives. In her opinion, however, only the facts themselves should be taught, and the students allowed to make their own comparisons. Mainly, care must be taken to avoid sending such misleading messages, for instance, that the Holocaust is just one in a long chain of inhumanities, or that every case of ethnic defamation bears the seeds of a holocaust. As an example of teaching the Holocaust that is "relevant but without relativizing," Lipstadt cites the U.S. Holocaust Museum in Washington, D.C., which will be discussed below.

Lucy S. Dawidowicz, also an historian of the Holocaust, addresses—and fiercely criticizes—another aspect of Facing History: the connections it makes between the Holocaust and present-day realities. She inveighs against the project's attempt to encourage the pupils to come to conclusions about the present on the basis of the reality of a past so unique as to be virtually incomprehensible.[15] The controversy that arose over the Facing History and Ourselves project spurred her to write a fairly long-ranging article evaluating the teaching of the Holocaust in secondary schools in tens of districts and states all over the United States. Since education in the United States is not centralized, it is difficult, according to Dawidowicz, to determine what is taught in different states, and how. However, it is clear, according to a 1988 survey, that it does not receive the attention it merits, if only because history in general, as a discipline, is not given the attention it merits. As background, she notes that at least half of the pupils in primary and secondary schools learn no world history or western civilization at all, and that lessons termed "global studies" or "world civilizations" have replaced them, in what she calls an "omnium gatherum of pop anthropology, sociology, geography, history and art appreciation," and that history studies have been pushed aside in favor of the special interests of various oppressed groups such as blacks, Hispanics, women, and Native Americans ("irreverently labeled 'oppression studies'"). As for Holocaust studies, in some schools opposition arose on such bases as that "it creates a bad atmosphere toward German-Americans in this country," or that apart from the Jews it is irrelevant to various other groups.

Despite these claims, the murder of European Jewry is now gradually being given a greater place in American education than in the past, but, according to Dawidowicz, not within the framework of history per se, but as part of the aforementioned "global studies" and "world civilizations." In schools in New York State study of the Holocaust is mandatory, and many local school boards or departments of education develop their own curricula (usually with the help of various different textbooks that sometimes bring incoherent or even erroneous information).

Dawidowicz examined twenty-five curricula, all of which endeavor to provide two things: basic information, and appropriate moral education. She found that they are better at the first than at the second: they describe *what* happened better than they explain *why* it happened. In any case, in most of the textbooks "the English language is mutilated ... with errors grammatical as well as typological, misspellings of names, wrong titles, sloppy mistakes—which reflect prevailing educational standards," and, moreover, factual errors are not uncommon.

In addition to lectures and discussions, films, and the written materials, most of the curricula use simulation and/or role-playing games in which the pupils act out the roles of perpetrators, victims, and judges. Such activities can become particularly problematic emotionally when, for example, pupils over-identify with their role as victims or as perpetrators or even release sadomasochistic urges. The curricula usually have serious shortcomings in their content: they tend to begin with a description of Hitler's Nazi regime with no information about the Weimar Republic that preceded it, or to deal with Nazi anti-Semitism under generalized headings such as "prejudices" or "racism," "scapegoating" or "bigotry" rather than the specific "anti-Semitism," and more then ten of them do not even mention the fact that anti-Semitism existed long before the Nazi regime. Only a few curricula contain information about Jewish history in Europe prior to the rise of the Nazis, a view that could put a more "human face" on these Jews, as against that of the Nazi propaganda.

As far as moral lessons are concerned, all of the curricula come, more or less, to the same conclusion, with variations only in how they get to it. Many quote (often incorrectly) George Santayana's well-known "[t]hose who cannot remember the past are condemned to repeat it," or say as much in a different way. Most of the teaching declares that its goal is "to teach students the inevitable consequences of hatred, prejudice, bigotry, and scapegoating," to try to educate towards tolerance and respect for religious, ethnic, and cultural differences, and the vast majority focus on "individual responsibility" rather than "obedience to authority" as the key to moral behavior.

Dawidowicz claims that while it is very difficult to determine the effectiveness of any of these curricula, they all have certain common shortcomings that are plainly discernible. Most of them present the facts, as we have already noted, but—

> Though most recite the facts, they do not stress the centrality of premeditated mass murder as an instrument of policy. But the more serious failure, to which I have already alluded, is the omission of the history of anti-Semitism—and especially its roots in Christian doctrine—as necessary background to the murder of the European Jews. To be sure, Christianity cannot be held responsible for Hitler, but the Nazis would not have succeeded in disseminating their brand of racist ant-Semitism had they not been confident of the pervasiveness, firmness, and durability of Christian hatred of Jews.

Because this is undoubtedly a very sensitive subject, and in order to avoid offending the largely Christian student population of the United States, most of the curriculums completely omit it. The strategy used to get around this topic is circumvention: non-specific terms such as "scapegoat" and "prejudice" are used instead of the problematic "anti-Semitism"; the term "scapegoat" is not difficult to explain or for pupils to understand: every child knows how easy it is to blame an innocent and helpless kid for any problem that arises.

Problems of this kind also arise, according to Dawidowicz, in Facing History, whose guidelines explain that "hatred of Jews invariably reflects larger crises in society which directly affect the lives of all." But the significant question is: Why are the Jews chosen again and again throughout history to be the scapegoats?—and this question, she repeats, is neither asked at all, nor, of course, answered. The concept of "prejudice," too, is mentioned in its universal context, but not specifically in regard to anti-Semitism. When they try to explain the general terms, most of the learning materials focus on individual attitudes, beliefs, and opinions—an approach that "conceives of prejudice as a psychological or mental-health problem"—and fail to point out that moral attitudes, beliefs, and opinions have become part of public policy and law.

Dawidowicz also takes exception to the broad use made in the project, and in many other curriculums, of the definition of the murder of

European Jewry as one of many genocides, such as the murder of Native Americans or of the Armenian people or, indeed, any other group. In the same way, she objects to the murder of homosexuals or Jehovah's Witnesses being used for comparison, as there is no historical evidence that the Nazis ever planned to exterminate either of these as a group.

In regard to the moral lessons that the Facing History project does transmit, some are inappropriate to the subject being studied, for example, the parallel drawn between the Holocaust and "a potential nuclear holocaust." The most frequently taught lesson, in an indirect way, is political. It is usually presented in unequivocal and simplistic terms regarding moral choice: "conforming" (which is immoral) is compared with "resisting" (which is moral); and "following the dictates of one's conscience" (good) is juxtaposed with "obeying authority" (bad). To illustrate the dangers of these, some of the curricula bring the well-worn example of Adolph Eichmann, thus creating considerable confusion between obeying authority as a personal trait and doing so because of ideological convictions. (Some learning programs bring as an example the case of Lt. William L. Calley who, in 1968, killed unarmed Vietnamese citizens in the village of May Lai, and was tried for doing so.)

In general, Dawidowicz finds that what the Facing History project tries most to impart is the moral lesson that obedience and conformity are "not morally admirable qualities," and that they are critical components of totalitarian societies. The author disagrees with this inference and argues that the study of totalitarian societies has shown that the "critical ingredient . . . that elicits obedience under duress, even to unjust laws" is terror. Moreover, she asks herself whether American children, who live in a completely liberal country, need at all to learn the virtues of disobedience. Insofar as conscience is concerned, she asserts that we cannot rely upon conscience when facing unfamiliar and complex moral questions. For this, Dawidowicz sums up that we must rely on a higher order of morality, "the fundamental moral code of our civilization and of the three great religions," and the commandment "Thou shalt not murder"—which she considers the primary lesson of the Holocaust.

It is, of course, possible to reject certain components of the Facing History project and to disagree with some of its premises, but it clearly offers a meaningful way of teaching the history of the Holocaust not only as one of many past events that already belong to history, or as a topic with relevance not only to Jews as Jews, but for its pertinence for our present reality as members of humanity anywhere in the world.

In Israel, too, where the Holocaust is a mandatory subject in schools, and for which abundant learning materials are available, much can be learned from both the achievements of the Facing History project and the critics' views of it, and from the assessments reported by its teachers and educators. It would be advantageous to consider incorporating certain elements relevant to Israel's specific situation, and to determine whether the project's rationale can be used as the framework for developing a curriculum for teaching the Holocaust to Arab-Israeli pupils.

United States Historical Memorial Museum (USHMM): Guidelines for Teaching about the Holocaust. A second important project, mentioned above, is the Guidelines for Teaching about the Holocaust developed by the United States Historical Memorial Museum in Washington, D.C. The primary aim of this project, which has proved to be highly successful, is to "promote education about the history of the Holocaust and its implication for our lives today." The guidelines are directed mainly at educators, and as such provide a list of the methodological guidelines to be considered when teaching this subject:[16]

1. DEFINE WHAT YOU MEAN BY "HOLOCAUST."

   The Holocaust refers to a specific event in 20th century history: The systematic, bureaucratic annihilation of six million Jews and their collaborators as a central act of state during World War II. . . . Although Jews were the primary victims, up to one half million Gypsies and at least 250,000 mentally or physically disabled persons were also victims of Nazi genocide. As Nazi tyranny spread across Europe from 1933 to 1945, millions of other innocent people were persecuted and murdered. More than three million Soviet prisoners of war were killed because of their nationality. Poles, as well as other Slavs, were targeted for slave labor, and as a result tens of thousands perished. Homosexuals and others deemed "anti-social" were also persecuted and often murdered. In addition, thousands of political and religious dissidents such as communists, socialists, trade unionists, and Jehovah's Witnesses were persecuted for their beliefs and behavior and many of these individuals died as a result of maltreatment.

2. AVOID COMPARISONS OF PAIN.

   . . . Avoid generalizations which suggest exclusivity, such as "the victims of the Holocaust suffered the most cruelty ever faced by a people in the history of humanity." One cannot presume that the horror of an individual, family or community destroyed by the Nazis was any greater than that experienced by victims of other genocides.

3. AVOID SIMPLE ANSWERS TO COMPLEX HISTORY.

   A study of the Holocaust raises difficult questions about human behavior, and it often involves complicated answers as to why events occurred. Be wary of oversimplifications. . . .

4. JUST BECAUSE IT HAPPENED, DOESN'T MEAN IT WAS INEVITABLE.

   Too often, students have the simplistic impression that the Holocaust was inevitable. Just because an historical event took place, and it was documented in textbooks and on film, does not mean that it had to happen. This seemingly obvious concept is often overlooked by students and teachers alike. The Holocaust took place because individuals, groups, and nations made decisions to act or not to act. By focusing on those decisions, we gain insight into history and human nature, and we can better help our students to become critical thinkers.

5. STRIVE FOR PRECISION OF LANGUAGE.

   [. . . Try to] help the students distinguish between categories of behavior and relevant historical references, to clarify the differences between prejudice and discrimination, collaborators and bystanders, armed and spiritual resistance, direct orders and assumed orders, concentration camps and killing centers, and guilt and responsibility. . . .

6. MAKE CAREFUL DISTINCTIONS ABOUT SOURCES OF INFORMATION.

   Students need practice in distinguishing between fact, opinion and fiction; between primary and secondary sources, and between types of evidence such as court testimonies, oral histories, and other written documents. . . .

7. TRY TO AVOID STEREOTYPICAL DESCRIPTIONS.

   . . . How ethnic groups or social clusters are labeled and portrayed in school curricula has a direct impact on how students perceive groups in their daily lives. . . .

8. DO NOT ROMANTICIZE HISTORY TO ENGAGE STUDENTS' INTEREST.

   . . . Accuracy of fact must be a priority. For example, people who risked their lives to rescue victims of Nazi oppression provide useful and important role models, yet an overemphasis on heroic tales in a unit on the Holocaust results in an inaccurate and unbalanced account of the history. It is important to bear in mind that probably less than one-half of one percent of the total non-Jewish population under Nazi occupation helped to rescue Jews.

9. CONTEXTUALIZE THE HISTORY YOU ARE TEACHING.

   Events of the Holocaust, and particularly how individuals behaved at that time, must be place in an historical context so that students can begin to comprehend the circumstances that encouraged or discourages these acts.... Encourage your students not to categorize groups of people only on the basis of their experiences during the Holocaust: contextualization is critical so that victims are not perceived only as victims. Although Jews were the central victims of the Nazi regime, they had a vibrant culture and long history in Europe prior to the Nazi era.... Similarly, students may know very little about Gypsies, except for the negative images and derogatory descriptions promulgated by the Nazis. Students would benefit from a broader viewpoint, learning something about Gypsy history and culture, and understanding the diverse ways of life among different Gypsy groups.

10. TRANSLATE STATISTICS INTO PEOPLE.

In any study of the Holocaust, the sheer number of victims challenges easy comprehension. Teachers need to show that individual people are behind the statistics, composed of families, of grandparents, parents and children. First-person accounts and memoir literature provide students with a way of making meaning out of collective numbers....

11. BE SENSITIVE TO APPROPRIATE WRITTEN AND AUDIO-VISUAL CONTENT.

One of the primary concerns of educators is how to introduce students to the horrors of the Holocaust. Graphic material should be used in a judicious manner and only to the extent necessary to achieve the objective of the lesson. Teachers should remind themselves that each student and each class is different, and that what seems appropriate for one may not be for all.

12. STRIVE FOR BALANCE IN ESTABLISHING WHOSE PERSPECTIVE INFORMS YOUR STUDY OF THE HOLOCAUST.

Often too great an emphasis is placed on the victims of Nazi aggression, rather than on the victimizers who forced people to make impossible choices or simply left them with no choice to make. Most students express empathy for victims of mass murder. But, it is not uncommon for students to assume that the victims may have done something to justify the actions against them, and thus to place inappropriate blame on the victims themselves....

13. SELECT APPROPRIATE LEARNING ACTIVITIES.

... Such activities as word scrambles, crossword puzzles and other gimmicky exercises tend not to encourage critical analysis, but lead instead to low level types of thinking and, in the case of Holocaust curricula, trivialize the importance of studying this history....

14. REINFORCE THE OBJECTIVES OF YOUR LESSON PLAN.

As in all teaching situations, the opening and closing lessons are critically important. A strong opening should serve to dispel misinformation students may have prior to studying the Holocaust.... A strong closing should emphasize synthesis by encouraging students to connect this history to other world events as well as the world they live in today....

These guidelines are intended to help educators in their teaching the history of the Holocaust and its implications for other issues. For example, one of the central issues in which the education system throughout the United States is engaged is "Who is a responsible citizen?" As students learn about the Holocaust and its lessons, they realize other things as well, as stated in the Introduction to the USHMM Guidelines:

- democratic institutions and values are not automatically sustained, but need to be appreciated, nurtured and protected.
- silence and indifference to the suffering of others, or to the infringement of civil rights can—however unintentionally—serve to perpetuate the problems; and
- the Holocaust was not an accident in history. It occurred because individuals, organizations, and government made choices which not only legalized discrimination, but which allowed prejudice, hatred, and ultimately, mass murder to occur.

Clearly defining the rationale of the teaching of the Holocaust can help educators choose the pedagogic approach most suitable to their students' interests. It is important to remember that young people's interest in any subject is related to its relevance to their day-to-day concerns, such as their self-identification, peer pressures, indifference, obedience and conformity. Therefore, the museum's guidelines advise the teachers to consider the following important questions:

- Why is it important that students learn about the Holocaust?
- What are the most significant lessons they can derive from learning this subject?
- Which particular reading materials, images, documents, etc. are most suitable for teaching each of the different aspects of the subject?

Teachers explained the rationale of their decisions as to how to teach the subject in different ways:

- The Holocaust is a watershed event, not only of the 20th century but in the entire history of humanity.
- Study of the Holocaust assists students in developing understanding of the ramifications of prejudice, racism, and stereotyping in any society. It helps students develop an awareness of the value of pluralism, and encourages tolerance of diversity in a pluralistic society.

- The Holocaust provides a context for exploring the dangers of remaining silent, apathetic, and indifferent in the face of others' oppression.
- Holocaust history demonstrates how a modern advanced nation can utilize its technological expertise and bureaucratic infrastructure to implement destructive policies ranging from social engineering to genocide.
- A study of the Holocaust helps students think about the use and abuse of power, and the role and responsibilities of individuals, organizations, and nations when confronted with civil rights violations and/or policies of genocide.
- As students gain a perspective that permits them to develop an historical outlook, they develop an awareness of the many historical, social, religious, political and economical factors which cumulatively resulted in the Holocaust. Thus, they acquire knowledge of the totality of factors that can contribute to the disintegration of civilized values. Part of one's responsibility as a citizen in a democracy is to learn to identify the danger signals, and to know how to react to them.

As the above quotations bring out, the USHMM gives prominence to the fact that the Jews were the main victims of the Nazi regime, and that they were murdered because they were Jews. However, non-Jewish victims of the Nazi regime are specifically dealt with because the USHMM's initiators and creators wanted the students, and other visitors to the museum, to examine the Holocaust from a universal perspective as well.

The teaching of the Holocaust has undoubtedly become increasingly widespread in the United States in the last few decades and the number of pupils and students exposed to the subject in various different frameworks is continually growing. Since most of these young people are, naturally, not Jewish, textbooks, curricula, and different projects offer a broad array of possibilities for raising awareness to the subject. It appears that the situation in the United States in regard to the teaching of the Holocaust has had, and continues to have, a strong influence on what is happening in other countries, where the general trend is to a broadening of the awareness, and the teaching, of this subject.

The Reaction to the Holocaust in Germany

The resumption of relations between Germany and Jews following World War II was astonishingly rapid and its "normalcy," at least on the surface, is no less surprising.[17] Nonetheless, even after the Holocaust, and in spite of the small number of Jews living in Germany, there are still manifestations of anti-Semitism. The number of Jews, approximately 35,000 before the 1990s, increased greatly in the following the collapse of the Soviet Union and the fall of the Berlin Wall and is presently assessed as about 100,000. During the 1990s, there was a noticeable increase in the number of anti-Semitic incidents, especially in the former East Germany, but elsewhere in the country as well.

Despite its thorough defeat in World War II, and the immense damage it suffered during the conflict, Germany was rapidly rehabilitated economically. At least during the first years after the Nazi downfall, Germany continued in many ways as if the Third Reich was still in existence. Irrespective of whether we view the era of the Third Reich—along with the events of the Holocaust that characterized it—as an historic anomaly in German history, or as the result of a process that occurred, not by chance, in the continuum of German history, it is obvious that present-day German society and German politics cannot be analyzed or understood without reference to the Holocaust.

Many Germans today prefer to look upon the year 1945 as an historical tabula rasa, a new era that began after the war, with the establishment of the Federal Republic. However, many others, both within and outside of Germany, fiercely oppose such an approach, pointing out a large number of lines of continuity between the Third Reich and the present Federal Republic, and criticize the unwillingness of many Germans to contend, honestly and openly, with the country's past. They believe that the democratic principles and economic success of the Republic rest upon guilt feelings and confusion created because of the Holocaust, rather than a firm foundation based on recognition and acceptance of the past. Today, it is still possible to claim that West Germany has failed to confront this past critically and honestly, and there is no doubt that most Germans have preferred to suppress the Holocaust, rather than come to terms with its full significance, and with its ramifications for their society and their culture. In addition, it should not be forgotten that the war—and the Holocaust—were ended through the actions and efforts of the Allied Powers, and that their parliamentary democracy was established by others and not by themselves. The demise of National Socialism was in every way imposed and artificial: the struggle against Nazism did not grow from within German society itself, in contrast to the situation in Italy, Spain, and Bolshevism in the former

Soviet Union, as well as in Eastern Europe. This has important implications not only for German society today, but for its future as well.

An interesting study of how the Nazi past is depicted, as reflected in the German public's historical discourse and, in particular, in texts written for children, was carried out by the Israeli researcher Zohar Shavit.[18] Shavit notes the existence of a clear-cut distinction in these texts and in the public discourse, in how wartime "ordinary" Germans, as opposed to Nazi Germans, are portrayed, as well as absurd similarities between Nazis and Jews, both implicit and explicit. She also found that in children's books written in Germany after the Holocaust there are no descriptions of the Nazi persecution of Jews and other minorities. There are also no prisoner of war camps, no unexplained murders of various citizens, no depictions of the brutal actions of the Gestapo and the S.S., or torture of helpless children, and no transports, extermination, camps or genocide. Children's literature in postwar Germany, according to Shavit, contributed to the distortion of history in which many other German elements were engaged, wittingly or unwittingly.

Be that as it may, in Germany in the years that followed the end of the Holocaust, many different, and sometimes contrasting, reactions to it can be discerned. These reactions can be broadly divided both chronologically and diagnostically into three periods: Gradual Transition, Reconciliation, and Changing Approaches.

The First Period (1945–1949): Gradual Transition

During these postwar years Germany went through a period of denazification initiated and directed by the Allied Powers. This trend was expressed mainly in the Nuremberg Trials, and was not manifested in daily life. While in other European countries during these years former Nazis and collaborators were physically attacked and even driven out of their communities, in Germany many of those who were identified as Nazis returned to their communities with no stigma or mark of shame.

A prominent characteristic of this period is the Germans' clinging to the Nazi ideology and to anti-Semitism. During the same years, there was also a gradual return of Jewish survivors of the Holocaust and those uprooted from their former abodes. It is estimated that out of a total population of 65 million then living in Germany, only about 150,000 were of Jewish descent. Most of these were housed in "displaced persons camps (DPs)" in Germany, and they gradually left the country during the years immediately following the war. Despite the destitution of the Jewish community in Germany after the war, it succeeded in creating a vibrant cultural life: new Jewish organizations were set up, newspapers were published, and various religious activities were initiated. In addition to these, organizations were established whose purpose was to bridge the gap between Jews and Christians. These organizations denounced the Holocaust and were the first to point out the need to investigate it scientifically. They also helped to care for the surviving victims, and suggested various ways of making restitution. Along with these, however, anti-Semitic acts continued to occur, such as desecration of graves in Jewish cemeteries, an act that was meant to symbolically erase even the country's Jewish past.

With the election of Konrad Adenauer as the first chancellor of the Federal Republic of Germany in 1949, the government of the country began to initiate plans, which constituted a modest beginning of compensation for the victims of the Holocaust. During this early period, the form of this restitution was monetary, and was termed "reparations," which in Israel had a negative connotation. It was claimed by not a few people that such restitution was a way to turn the moral dilemma of Germany's admission of the Holocaust, and its responsibility for it, into a purely monetary problem.

During most of these same years—that is, during 1945 and until 1948—the Nuremberg Trials of Nazis, imposed by the Allied Powers and adjudicated over by justices of the allied countries, were being held. (In the course of time the principles set down by this court became the basis of trials of other war criminals, and were then incorporated in important international treaties.) In the course of the Nuremberg Trials about three thousand Nazi war criminals were tried. In the main trial of twenty-two of the heads of the Nazi rule, twelve were sentenced to death by hanging, seven to life imprisonment, and three were acquitted.

The Second Period (1949–1967): Reconciliation (Versölung)

The Cold War. With the onset of the Cold War the Allies abandoned their attempt to force Germany to face its past, including the judgment of war criminals not yet brought to trial. In actuality, this attempt ended even before it began: the Soviet Union was perceived during this period as the "great enemy," and the need to deal with Germany's recent past was pushed to the sidelines. The goal of the United States government was to turn West Germany into an ally against the Soviet Union, and to do this they even encouraged its speedy rearmament. Compensation and reparations were a convenient way for both Germany and the Allies to allow it to be readmitted to the community of western nations. The Germans thus never had to come to terms directly with the deeds they had perpetrated during the war.

Reparations and diplomatic relations with Israel. The Reparations Agreement between Germany and Israel was undoubtedly reached because of moral motivations, but there is also no doubt that underlying these motivations there were practical considerations. For the Germans it was not only a way to regain legitimacy within the framework of a new world order, but it would also free them from the image of a nation of murderers by nature. Many Jews considered this no more than the "purchase" of forgiveness. A large number of Israelis were outraged at the very idea of direct negotiations with those who had tortured and murdered their loved ones, and awaited the Germans' genuine confrontation with the crimes they had committed. The controversy over the moral implications of the "reparations" cut through all strata of Israeli society and political alignments, and was a significant factor in the formation of the memory of the Holocaust in Israel. Germany's government, however, well aware of the fact that many of its citizens felt no need at all either for reconciliation with the Jews or with Israel, or to contend with feelings of guilt for the atrocities committed in the Holocaust, viewed the reparations mainly as an expedient political measure.

Immediately after the war, there was almost complete silence about atrocities committed by Germany during the war years, not only in Germany, but all over the world. Nevertheless, and despite the fact that some Germans felt true contrition, anti-Semitic acts continued to be carried out in Germany, at least during the first ten years following the end of the war. The restitution did not crack the German's wall of silence, nor lead them to face their denial and repressed feelings. In effect, the official process of compensation to the victims of the Holocaust had already begun in 1947, under the supervision of the Allies, and by the order of Law 59 that they promulgated in regard to the return of Jewish property. Although this law dealt only with some of the components of the victims' suffering, and was not a German law, most of the demands for compensation under this law were settled by the mid-fifties.

In 1951, when forty-seven nations officially declared the end of the state of war against Germany, Israel refused to participate in this declaration, claiming that the German leadership had not yet denounced Hitler's war against the Jews. Although in Germany this position intensified the trend of opposition to conciliation with Israel, and with the Jews, there were, even then, various factions within German society that called for such an initiative. In September of that year, Adenauer announced that a channel of communication should be opened with both Israel and world Jewry. The motivation for this was mainly moral, but it also expressed the need of at least some Germans to relieve themselves of the psychological distress the war events had caused them. Neither side was enthusiastic about negotiating directly with the other, but the very fact that some contact between Israel and Germany had been established made it possible for both to begin to come to terms with the past.

At the beginning of their discussions Israel demanded that Germany accept her stipulations for how they would be held, and would first declare that Germany was guilty of the Nazi atrocities and condemned them. In 1952 a treaty was signed in Luxembourg in which it was agreed that three-and a-half billion German marks would be paid by Germany to Israel, in addition to the sum paid to the Conference on Material Claims against Germany, which represented world Jewry. During the fifty years of its existence, this organization transferred over 100 billion marks to Holocaust survivors. In the course of time, and despite the multifaceted moral issues that the acceptance of compensation entailed, the issue of monetary restitution became a pragmatic one, a fact of *Realpolitik*: Israel was in desperate need of economic support, and the Germans needed the political approval of the countries of the West, especially that of the United States. Moreover, the reparations helped both sides to circumvent a psychological and traumatic confrontation with the past and, in addition, created the conditions for the gradual reestablishment of diplomatic relations between Germany and the Jews and Israel.

During the 1950s and early 1960s both countries refrained from taking any steps that would lead to full diplomatic relations: the recent past still weighed heavily on Israel, and Germany was wary of how the

Arabs would react. Yet, during these same years economic activity increased and, to a certain extent, cultural relations as well. Delegations of youth and students made mutual visits, and young Germans came to Israel to work as volunteers, in at least partial or symbolic atonement for their parents' crimes. Full diplomatic relations were established only in 1965.

Israel's victory in the Six Day War in 1967 led to an outburst of German sympathy towards Israel. This may have been, at least in part, due to a certain degree of relief in the guilt feelings that the Germans felt about the Jews, who could now be viewed as the victors and not perennial victims. Towards the end of the sixties, the relations between the two countries continued to improve when Germany supported Israel in various situations in the European sphere. It was during these years that Israeli educators and German educators realized that it was necessary to rectify how the Holocaust was taught in both countries.

The Auschwitz trials. Between the years 1963 and 1968, members of the S.S. who had run the Auschwitz concentration camp were tried in Frankfurt. The trials aroused great media interest and brought the subject to the public's attention both within and outside of Germany. It is important to emphasize that not one of the accused had violated the laws of the National Socialist state, and many Germans therefore opposed these trials, which they saw as "witch-hunts." The use of the excuse "following orders" in these trials was attractive to many Germans, as it erased their responsibility for the crimes that had been committed.

The question of guilt. Attempts to learn the lessons of the war began in the last years of the 1940s and continued for several decades after the end of the war. Many German intellectuals engaged critically with Germany's past during those years, and some are still doing so today. The American forces in Germany dealt with this issue within the framework of their policy of denazification, their initiatives for re-education, and through the propaganda distributed by the military government. The goals of the Allied occupation forces, along with the voices of German writers and intellectuals living in exile, among them Thomas Mann, who had experienced the collective trauma of the German people, led to a crack in the wall of literary silence. Writers and intellectuals who had remained by choice in Germany during the war, and had come to terms with their country's deeds, were now pressed to account for this choice.

In the years immediately following the end of the war, some young German intellectuals had expressed their revulsion for the Holocaust. They claimed that it had even de-legitimized the German language, for the associations it immediately awakened were of persecution and genocide. This difficulty, however, did not prevent them—as they sought the "truth" of the Nazi period—from continuing to express themselves through various stylistic means, sometimes surrealistic ones, that allowed them to separate themselves from the collective guilt and make personal, unfettered statements. Only a few German writers dealt with the Holocaust directly; most of them—Günther Grass, for example—focused on its universalistic aspects, on the hopelessness of the Second World War, and essentially of all wars, on the inescapable deaths in all wars, and on their total uselessness. Paradoxically, these German writers succeeded in writing about the atrocities committed by the Third Reich without explicitly mentioning the Jews. Even those who tried to learn and elucidate the lessons of the Holocaust ignored or disregarded the very real and great suffering of the Jews, which suggests that they, too, were as yet unable to face this past fully and openly.

The German historiography of the Holocaust. Like German literature, the German historiography of the Holocaust is still inadequate in many ways. It may be divided into two methodological categories: "intentionalist" and "functionalist-structuralist." The "intentionalist" school of thought claims that the Holocaust was a preconceived act, the logical extension of the anti-Semitism of the leaders of the Nazi Party even prior to its rise to power; the "functionalist-structuralist" school of thought claims that it was the result of the complex tensions that arose from interactions within the Nazi bureaucracy (its structures and institutions, and their functions) and its need to find a solution to "the Jewish problem" that arose in Germany in the areas it had conquered. Both of these schools of thought refrained from casting the blame on any individual: the former blamed an undefined political elite; the latter blamed even more vague administrative bodies.

The Holocaust in German textbooks. As can be expected, the way in which the Holocaust and the Second World War were presented in primary and secondary school textbooks in postwar Germany greatly influenced how its young generation perceived them. The challenge that faced the educators was how to avoid leaving an artificial and unexplained hiatus between the prewar past and the postwar present, and to teach about the events perpetrated in the course of the Second World War but, at the same time, to ensure a certain "disconnection" of the entire period from the natural flow of history. During the 1950s, the textbooks gave scant attention to the Holocaust, and many teachers preferred not to deal with it at all.

The first serious attempt to deal more deeply with this subject began in the early 1960s, after a wave of anti-Semitic graffiti appeared in Germany. This alerted some of the politicians, who demanded that learning materials that would contend with the increase in fascist ideology and anti-democratic sentiments be added to the social science curriculum. In 1961, the history of the Third Reich became mandatory in all schools, at all levels. Textbooks were rewritten, and history and political science teachers who were trained to deal with this subject were employed.

And yet, despite the official requirements, the teaching of the Holocaust in German schools is far from uniform: in the elite gymnasia the teaching is broader and more thorough than in the regular high schools. In addition, the way the subject is treated in the different states (Länder) of Germany, as reflected in their textbooks, is also far from uniform: the content of the history and social science textbooks is based on the directives of Germany's central education ministry—in which there are representatives of all of the states—but each state interprets and carries out these directives in its own way.

The Third Period (1967 to the Present): Changing Approaches

As already noted, the Six Day War in 1967 prompted a turnabout in relations between Germany and both Israel and the Jews in general. Somewhat unexpectedly, streams in the German political right, whose more radical elements had previously flaunted anti-Israeli posters bordering on anti-Semitism, were the ones that enthusiastically acclaimed the Israeli victory—for Israel could now be seen as victors and not as the perpetually subjugated sufferers, a distinction that helped to relieve German feelings of guilt. They continued, however, to differentiate between Jews and Israelis, and while extolling the Israelis, Jews remained the target of anti-Semitic characterizations. Groups on the German Left, on the other hand, and especially the New Left, which had previously supported Israel, now began to castigate it for its oppression of the Palestinians. Like circles on the Right, those on the Left also differentiated between Jews as a people in need of support, and Israelis, who now, in their view, personified evil.

The flip-flop in attitudes towards Jews and Israelis, and the deepening of this dichotomy, could not but have an effect on how groups on both the Right and the Left examined the past. The conservative Right's traditional animus towards Jews spawned a wave of Nazi literature that appeared in the mid-1970s, along with films, recordings, and stage plays that depicted Hitler and National Socialism in a heroic light. Some of these even alleged that the Holocaust had never occurred.

The considerable influence of this outpouring cannot be compared, however, with the even greater opposite effect on the German public of the American television docudrama *Holocaust*. Screened nightly in the course of one week in January 1979, *Holocaust* was raptly viewed by more than 40 percent of all of Germany's television viewers (i.e., about fifteen million people). It touched the consciences of a large number of them, and stirred up public debate as never before in Germany, accompanied by fierce controversy and even the opposition of various groups. Since each section of the series was followed by a two-hour-long panel discussion by academics and intellectuals, *Holocaust* served, in effect, as a popular and effective educational tool. Many Germans displayed a total lack of knowledge about the events depicted in it, and were shocked by what they saw. The question whose answer many Germans avoided was now answered unequivocally, and they knew that the Holocaust had indeed occurred. The subject was openly discussed in the street, in coffee shops, and all over, in the course of daily life. As the controversy went on, voices were heard calling for the documentation of the long history of the Jews in Germany, and especially of their contributions to culture. Another development that the series led to was a law extending the statute of limitations, which was about to expire, thus making it possible to continue to bring Nazi war criminals to justice. Since the screening of this series, the German public has been engaging critically with the Holocaust in various ways and in a much broader perspective than before, mainly through the cinema, television films and programs, books, exhibits, and museums.

The 1980s. During the 1980s several incidents occurred in Germany that again bore witness to ongoing friction between Jews and Germans. One of these was the "Auschwitz Denial Law," passed in 1985, which made it a criminal offense to deny the existence of Auschwitz. Conservatives circles, however, succeeded in passing another law along with it, making it a crime to deny the expulsion of Germans from Eastern countries, thus diminishing the import of denial of the Holocaust. Another example of friction, also in 1985, revolved around the program of an official trip to Germany of American president Ronald Reagan. The president was scheduled to visit and lay a wreath at the German military cemetery in Bitburg, where forty-nine members of the Nazi Waffen S.S. are also buried—a visit that led to heated debate not only in Germany, but even more so in the United States. During that same year, a play with anti-Semitic overtones by the playwright Rainer Fassbinder was produced by the Frankfurt Theater, and also led to fierce debate.

The general ambivalence in the 1980s of German attitudes to their Nazi past, and its form and content in the German collective memory, is reflected in how it was taught. A 1989 study of high school textbooks showed that although they present the dry facts about the events of the Holocaust, they fail to pay sufficient attention to its full scope and its significance. The events themselves are briefly described in a remote and generalized way, and the texts are comprised largely of tables and statistical data, and with no personalized accounts; almost all of them overemphasize various psychological characteristics of the personalities of Hitler and his cohorts in the National Socialist political elite, but explanations for the National Socialist party's rise to power, and of the factors that led to it, are both inadequate and superficial. Moreover, in most of the textbooks the persecution of Jews is not presented in the broader context of anti-Semitism, either in Europe in general, or in Germany specifically.

During that same year, two German educators, Birgit Wenzel and Dagmar Weber, suggested six ways in which the German high school curriculum for study of the Holocaust could be improved:

- A mere listing of facts and statistics [has] to be avoided.
- The victims of National Socialism should not be portrayed as faceless and anonymous; rather, the fate of individuals, with whom the students [can] empathize, should be an integral part of Holocaust education.

- The roles played by judges, bureaucrats, and leaders of industry and of the economy in the Nazi elite and the success (from their viewpoint) of the Nazi administration must be explained.
- Teachers must address the German people's passivity to and inaction in the face of the deeds of the Nazi regime during the war, as this is a central aspect of the German dilemma of coming to terms with the past.
- The Holocaust should not be depicted as inevitable.
- The Holocaust should be used to combat present-day anti-Semitism and hatred of foreigners and to teach the responsibilities of citizens in a democracy.
- Homework and class assignments should focus less on memorization of facts and more on analysis and interpretation. Pictures as well as interviews with survivors should also play a vital role in the study of the Holocaust.[19]

THE HISTORIANS' DEBATE. Towards the end of the 1980s, a trend developed in German historiography to regard the Holocaust as one of many events in the context of general history, and to thus invalidate or greatly minimize its unique character. Several noted German historians tried to rewrite painful chapters in their country's blemished history during the Third Reich, not by denying the destruction of the Jews by the Nazis but rather, by comparing it with what are ostensibly similar events, to banalize and relativize the Holocaust. To do this, parallels were drawn between the Holocaust and other events of the twentieth century, such as the atomic bombings of Hiroshima and Nagasaki by the United States, the massive bombing of Dresden, and the crimes committed by Stalin in the Soviet Union. This has been viewed by some as a way of denying the Holocaust through a clever, and therefore perhaps more dangerous, subterfuge.

One of the most prominent German historians, Ernst Nolte, claimed that the Holocaust was not a unique phenomenon at all. Like other German historians, he equated Auschwitz with Stalin's gulags, and asserted that many other parallels can be found in the twentieth century, from the massacre of the Armenians during the First World War, the genocide in Vietnam in the sixties and seventies, the murder of millions of Cambodians by Pol Pot's regime in the second half of the seventies, and including the massive murders in Afghanistan in the eighties. In his opinion, "the annihilation of several million European Jews, many Slavs, the mentally insane, and Gypsies is without precedent in its motivation and execution" but repeatedly suggests that it has so many parallels in other countries that it can be viewed as routine twentieth-century barbarity.

Furthermore, he claimed, the Nazi's policy of destruction was merely "a 'copy'—still more horrifying than the original, but a copy all the same" of genocidal policies perpetrated in the past by other peoples.[20] Andreas Hillgruber, one of the world authorities on the history of Europe in the twentieth century, using complex and convoluted reasoning, also tried to present the Holocaust as a phenomenon comparable to other events in history, and he, too, compared it with such genocides as Stalin's mass murders and Turkey's massacre of the Armenians in 1915.[21]

Other German historians and thinkers reacted to these ideas and came out against them, the most prominent of them being the social philosopher Jürgen Habermas. These intellectuals and historians underscored the unique characteristics of the Nazi crimes, and Germany's obligation to come to terms with the true significance of its past.[22]

More than being a disagreement about some undefined and esoteric methodology between academics and researchers, the historians' debate had—and has—ramifications beyond the walls of academe or the pages of learned journals. It affects political controversies in Germany at present and in the future, as well as the shape and content of Germany's national collective memory, and within it, the place of the Holocaust and the Third Reich.

The 1990s. The Berlin Wall fell on November 9, 1989—ironically, on the anniversary of Kristallnacht—and less than a year later, on October 3, 1990, East and West Germany were united. With this, another element in the state of affairs that resulted from Nazism and the Second World War was erased, and Germany became, again, what is perhaps the most important power in Europe. This, and the events associated with it, affected German-Jewish relations as well. East Germany's attitude to the Nazi period, which had been so different from that of West Germany, began to change as its inhabitants were increasingly exposed to a view of the past as it was articulated in West Germany.[23]

In the decade that followed, there was a tendency in Germany to draw closer to Jews, and this was accompanied by government efforts to commemorate the memory of the Holocaust. Throughout Germany memorial sites and monuments for the victims of the Nazi regime were erected. The Dachau concentration camp, declared a memorial site after postponements lasting twenty years, was opened to the broad public and is visited by a large number of people every year. In July

1999, after much argumentation and disagreement (that has not yet ended), a law was passed for the construction of a monument for the victims of the Holocaust. Also, after many years of planning and construction, and with the aid of the German government, a Jewish Museum was built in Berlin and opened to the public in 2001; the theme of this museum is "Two Thousand Years of German-Jewish History."

Nonetheless, because the past is a subject that remains difficult to grapple with, there are still attempts to repress it. One example of this is a permanent exhibit that opened, also with government backing, in 1971, and that documents Germany's history from the year 1800 to the present. The Holocaust is very poorly represented in this exhibit—by scanty statistical data and a few photographs from concentration camps—and with no background material on the long history of the Jews in Germany or about anti-Semitism in Germany: in the section allocated to the Third Reich, neither the word "Holocaust" nor the term "Final Solution" are mentioned, and the entire period of Hitler's rule is presented mainly as an aberration or a mishap in the smooth flow of Germany's history; the exhibit's catalogue, a thick volume, devotes only two pages and one un-captioned photograph to National Socialism, anti-Semitism, and the Holocaust; Kristallnacht is noted only in an appendix; and the Holocaust isn't mentioned in even one of the colorful tables that illustrate the political development of the Federal Republic of Germany.

A more recent event, the Gulf War in 1991, had a harmful, but apparently short-term, effect on relations between Germany and both the Jews and Israel: during the war the pacifist left-leaning groups (some from the Green Party) adopted an anti-American stance that was accompanied at times by an anti-Israeli one as well.

Nevertheless, the decade of the nineties as a whole was one in which the Germans were more open to Jews and to Israel. An important role in this was played by the cinema and television in shaping public opinion during this period. The film *Schindler's List*, in 1993, was noteworthy in this respect, and won the attention of both the public and the media. (It is highly likely that part of the attraction of this film was that its protagonist was a "righteous German.") More recently, a not negligible number of younger, post-Holocaust, Germans have begun to show an unprecedented interest in Jewish culture. Even more important in many ways is the fact that small groups of German academics have begun to study and research the history and culture of the Jewish people aside from and without any connection to the Holocaust.[24]

Summary

The incomparable uniqueness of the Holocaust has had a parallel unique effect on the multifaceted relationship between the Germans and the Jews and Israel that cannot be compared with that between any other two countries. The present state of this relationship is apparently based, at least to some degree, on an amalgam of imaginary fictions nourished by memories, acquired information (and sometimes disinformation), impressions from reading, and from watching films and television. Many Germans have never met face-to-face with a Jewish person, and thus construct a mental image of one from "meetings" with them in museums, films, the press, and books. For most Jewish people, on the other hand, it is still difficult to separate the "German" from the "Nazi." Efforts to normalize German-Jewish relations in general, and Germany-Israel relations in particular (not dealt with in this book), regardless of how vigorous and sincere, cannot but be affected by the dark cloud of the unprecedented crimes committed by the Nazis. To this must be added the shadow cast by the renewed appearance of neo-Nazi groups in both Germany and in other parts of Europe.

Even more worrisome are the figures obtained in comparative studies that gathered data about people's basic knowledge of the Holocaust and their opinions as to its importance (see below). The public opinion surveys, carried out by the American Jewish Committee in the last decade in thirteen countries, indicated a tendency towards the idea that the Nazi period has passed and should finally be put behind them. Moreover, the studies also showed that in Germany and Austria there is a clear tendency to view the Jews as those who are exploiting the Holocaust by their use of the memory of the destruction of their fellow Jews. The percentage of those holding this opinion increased from 28 percent in 1995 to 45 percent in 2001, according to a survey carried out in Austria in 2001. Particularly relevant were the answers to the question about the relevance of the Holocaust to life today, and how important it is that the citizens of the respondent's country know about and understand the history of the Holocaust: of all the countries in the survey, the Germans and Austrians had the lowest percentage of positive answers (in the 1990s). This attitude, and a tendency towards being "fed up with dealing with Auschwitz," has perhaps intensified on the backdrop of the second *intifadah*.

That societies or states have difficulty in facing and engaging critically with the dark chapters of their past, and sometimes go so far as to deny or attempt to erase them from their collective memory, is well known. In the case of Germany, however, such an attitude is unacceptable. Zohar Shavit offers an explanation of Germany's attempt to do so (which not all those dealing with the subject agree with):

> It appears that in the case of the narrative of the Third Reich and the Holocaust there is room to question the legitimacy of the very existence of a narrative that is so very perverted and distorted. Even if the invention of such a narrative was not intended, and perhaps not even expected, and also if it was not the "poet's intention," the result was a narrative that West Germany told to this generation and [will tell] to the generations to come about the Third Reich and the Holocaust, which is not only not a warped distortion, but also immoral.[25]

Knowledge and Remembrance of the Holocaust in Different Countries: Comparative Surveys

The teaching of the Holocaust varies greatly from one country to the next, as can also be seen from a comparison of how much is known about it, and attitudes about it, in different countries. Surveys sponsored by the American Jewish Committee provide not only the necessary data for such a comparison, but reveal facts relevant to the teaching of the Holocaust both in the present and in the future. Such surveys, which deal with knowledge about the Holocaust and with the memory of its history, have been conducted since 1992 in the United States, Great Britain, France, Germany, Australia, Austria, Poland, Russia, Slovakia, The Czech Republic, Sweden, Switzerland, and Argentina, and there are plans to conduct them in other countries as well. The data in the tables on the following pages have an important bearing on the teaching of the Holocaust. The influence, direct or indirect, of such teaching on the attitudes that were found in these public opinion surveys is difficult to assess, especially since surveys of other institutions have sometimes produced not only different, but even conflicting, data. The American Jewish Committee's surveys presented below have special importance because of their comparative dimension, an aspect that is usually lacking in the other surveys, most of which deal with the attitudes to the Holocaust in only one or another specific country.

In any case, the surveys show the following: that the higher the educational level, the greater the knowledge and awareness of the Holocaust; that knowledge and awareness are greater in France, Australia, and Great Britain than in the United States; and that in Germany there is a relatively greater knowledge of some of the aspects of the Holocaust than in other countries.

Especially interesting is the above-mentioned fact that the German and Austrian responses to the question about the relevance of the Holocaust to life today and the importance of a country's inhabitants knowing about and understanding its history (Table 5) resulted in the lowest percentage of positive answers (those who answered "essential" or "very important") of all the countries in the survey. Some of the results for this question were as follows: France 88 percent (1993); Australia 82 percent (1994); Great Britain 72 percent (1993); United States 72 percent (1992) and 76 percent (1994); Germany 68 percent (1994); Austria 62 percent (1995). Among those in Germany and Austria who answered positively, most did not choose the most affirmative answer, "essential," to the question. In a subsequent survey conducted in Austria in 2001, the number of positive answers to this question had increased to 76 percent. (Of all of the positive answers, 24 percent chose the more equivocal "very important" rather that the more affirmative "essential." However, there was also an increase in the number of those who thought that Jews now, as in the past, exert too much influence in world events, and that they exploit the memory of the Nazi destruction of the Jews for their own needs.)

The findings for seven of the questions in the surveys conducted by the American Jewish Committee are shown on the following pages. Each table presents the figures (in percentages) for the question noted above.[26]

We have already emphasized the fact that the past of each country affects its specific reaction to the Holocaust, as well as how it is taught there. But it is the differences in the answers of each of the countries that can lead us to ask questions relevant to the other countries as well.

TABLE 12.1
"As far as you know, what does the term 'the Holocaust' refer to?"*

Possible Answer, Country and Year	Extermination/Murder/ Persecution/Treatment of Jews by Hitler/Nazis/Germans	Extermination/Murder/ Persecution/Treatment of Jews	Other Relevant Responses	Other Answers	Don't know/ No answer
Australia (1994)	39	17	17	15	12
Austria (1995)	10	49	23	2	20
France (1993)	35	21	12	12	20
Germany (1994)	59	23	5	3	10
Gt. Britain (1993)	33	18	5	35	18
Poland (1995)	3	32	6	11	48
Russia (1996)	3	3	1	2	91
U.S.A. (1992)	24	30	7	10	28
U.S.A. (1994)	24	35	9	12	19
Czech Rep. (1999)	3	29	13	38	18
Slovakia (1999)	9	43	6	12	29
Sweden (1999)	9	43	6	12	29
Switzerland (2000)	5	27	18	35	15
Argentina (2000)	22	12	2	24	40
Austria (2001)	25	42	17	3	13

* In the French and American surveys, if an incorrect response was given, the respondents were told, "To be precise, the Holocaust was the Nazi extermination of Jews during the Second World War." In the Australian survey, all respondents were so informed. In the British survey, multiple answers were allowed.

"Other relevant responses" may include: concentration camps, German death camps, Hitler, Nazis, Germans, World War II, and the 1940s. "Others" may include: death/murder/slaughter, destruction/disaster/tragedy, war/nuclear war, cataclysm, the end of the world, starvation, or other answers.

The low figures in Poland and Russia for correct/partially correct responses reflect lack of usage of the English term "the Holocaust."

TABLE 12.2
"Approximately how many Jews were killed in the Holocaust?"*

Possible Answer, Country and Year	25,000	100,000	1 million	2 million	6 million	20 million	Don't know/ No answer
Australia (1994)	2	9	12	10	47	6	14
Austria (1995)	1	3	12	19	31	8	26
France (1993)	2	4	11	14	45	12	12
Germany (1994)	2	5	13	15	36	8	21
Gt. Britain (1993)	2	4	5	9	41	13	26
Poland (1995)	1	2	10	25	34	6	22
Russia (1996)	1	2	8	12	21	5	52
U.S.A. (1992)	1	4	7	13	35	10	30
U.S.A. (1994)	1	5	6	9	44	7	28
Czech Rep. (1999)	1	6	14	19	31	8	20
Slovakia (1999)	1	7	15	19	24	6	28
Sweden (1999)	1	2	5	9	49	4	31
Switzerland (2000)	1	4	8	11	45	8	22
Argentina (2000)	3	3	6	9	27	7	46
Austria (2001)	1	4	13	21	29	9	24

* Respondents in Poland were asked, "Approximately how many Jews were killed by the Nazis during the Second World War?"
Respondents in Russia were asked, "Approximately how many Jews in all of Europe were killed by the Nazis during the Second World War?"

TABLE 12.3
"From what you know, or have heard, what were Auschwitz, Dachau and Treblinka?"*

Possible Answer, Country and Year	Concentration Camps	Other Responses	Don't know/ No answer
Australia (1994)	85	4	13
Austria (1995)	91	4	6
France (1993)	90	4	6
Germany (1994)	92	3	5
Gt. Britain (1993)	75	4	20
Poland (1995)	91	8	2
Russia (1996)	50	2	49
U.S.A. (1992)	62	11	27
U.S.A. (1994)	67	4	28
Czech Rep. (1999)	92	3	5
Slovakia (1999)	81	6	12
Sweden (1999)	88	3	9
Switzerland (2000)	73	14	13
Argentina (2000)	22	3	75
Austria (2001)	93	1	6

* The question was closed-ended in the French, Australian, and American surveys, and open-ended with codes in the British, German, Polish, Austrian, and Russian surveys. Australian respondents were not given the option of answering "Other."

It appears that, in the countries surveyed, the presence of any amount of knowledge about the Holocaust is an indication that the education systems' objective in those countries is to relate that knowledge to the universal aspects of the Holocaust as well. Such an educational objective is lacking, as we have seen, in Israel's education system and, as we shall see in the last chapter, which deals with the teaching of genocide.

It is possible to claim, with all due caution, that the purpose of teaching about the Holocaust in a universalistic context—sometimes by obscuring its prominent and specifically Jewish significance—is gradually prevailing throughout the world. In different countries the Holocaust is learned more than other cases of genocide, which are learned only as an adjunct to it, and sometimes only mentioned.

In this connection it is worth mentioning the article "The Holocaust, Human Rights and Democratic Education," by David Shiman and

TABLE 12.4
"Many Jews in Europe were forced to wear a symbol on their clothes during the Second World War. What was it?"*

Possible Answer, Country and Year	Yellow star/ Jewish star/ Star of David**	Other Responses	Don't know/ No answer
Australia (1994)	72	17	12
Austria (1995)	84	1	17
France (1993)	88	9	3
Germany (1994)	91	1	8
Gt. Britain (1993)	56	9	34
Poland (1995)	74	8	18
Russia (1996)	34	7	59
U.S.A. (1992)	42	30	20
U.S.A. (1994)	42	24	33
Czech Rep. (1999)	67	24	9
Slovakia (1999)	78	4	19
Sweden (1999)	82	5	14
Switzerland (2000)	76	10	14
Argentina (2000)	20	17	64
Austria (2001)	89	0	12

* This question was closed-ended in the French, Australian, and American surveys, and open-ended with codes in all the other countries.
** The answer "Star of David" did not appear in the Australian, American, and French surveys.

William R. Fernekes, which deals with the relationship between Holocaust and genocide studies and basic concepts and themes regarding universal civil rights.[27] The authors attempt to show that the study of the Holocaust, genocide, and civil rights cannot be taught separately, and suggest directions that can aid in developing a vision of democratic citizenship. Although most of the examples given in their article are taken from the Holocaust, the authors suggest the possibility of relating to other events of genocide that occurred in the twentieth century, such as the genocide of the Armenians or the Cambodians, or even the genocides in Rwanda and the former Yugoslavia in the 1990s.

The claim that the dichotomies between "we" and "they" and between images of "ourselves" and "others," which lead to ethnocentric world-

TABLE 12.5
"In your view, how important is it for the people of your country to know about and understand the Holocaust—is it essential, very important, only somewhat important, or not important?"*

Possible Answer, Country and Year	Essential	Very Important	Only Somewhat Important	Not Important	Don't know/ No answer
Australia (1994)	29	43	23	3	2
Austria (1995)	20	42	17	5	16
France (1993)	45	43	11	1	0
Germany (1994)	18	50	19	7	7
Gt. Britain (1993)	33	39	20	4	4
Poland (1995)	17	69	11	1	3
Russia (1996)	31	31	22	8	8
U.S.A. (1992)	33	39	13	2	13
U.S.A. (1994)	39	37	12	2	11
Czech Rep. (1999)	22	45	23	4	5
Slovakia (1999)	22	33	26	12	7
Sweden (1999)	47	47	4	1	1
Switzerland (2000)	40	44	12	2	2
Argentina (2000)	12	50	21	10	7
Austria (2001)	24	52	11	4	9

* Respondents in Poland, Russia, the Czech Republic, Slovakia, and Sweden were asked, "In your view, how important is it for the people of your country to know about the Nazi extermination of the Jews during the Second World War?"

views, also have to be confronted. In their opinion, a critical approach must be cultivated, although not necessarily one hostile to authority. They also think that in all countries students should be encouraged to carefully consider Nazi Germany from the point of view of the Holocaust to ask moral questions about the policies and behavior of their own national institutions (schools, communities, and political organizations). It is also important, they assert, to discuss the question of the legitimacy of demands for obedience, and to begin to develop young people's personal criteria for setting limitations for agreeing to such demands, and the skills needed for understanding and taking an interest in what is happening in their surroundings as well as the need for accepting responsibility for both of these.

150   The Pain of Knowledge

TABLE 12.6
"Please tell me whether you strongly agree, mostly agree, mostly disagree, or strongly disagree: 'The Holocaust is not relevant today because it happened 50 years ago.'"

Possible Answer, Country and Year	Strongly Agree	Mostly Agree	Mostly Disagree	Strongly Disagree	Don't know/ No answer
United States (1992)	8	13	17	46	15
United States (1994)	8	13	17	48	14
Great Britain (1993)	5	13	20	53	9
France (1993)	8	12	15	64	1
Germany (1994)*	11	26	33	20	10
Australia (1994)	7	9	23	57	4
Austria (1995)	10	18	26	29	18

* In Germany there were significant differences in the responses from the former East and West parts of the country.

This question was asked in a different way in the surveys in other countries, and the results appear here in Table 12.7.

TABLE 12.7
"Some people say that 50 years after the end of World War II, it is time to put the memory of the Holocaust, Hitler's extermination of the Jews, behind us. Others say that we should keep the remembrance of the Holocaust strong even after the passage of time. Which opinion comes closer to your opinion?"

Possible Answer Country and Year	The Past Should Be Left Behind Us	The Past Should Not Be Forgotten	Don't know/ No answer
Argentina (2000)	19	71	10
Austria (2001)	29	59	12
Czechoslovakia (1991)	21	71	9
Czech Republic (1999)	17	74	9
Hungary (1991)	28	61	10
Poland (1991)	13	81	6
Poland (1995)	10	85	5
Russia (1996)	6	78	16
Slovakia (1999)	24	63	13
Sweden (1999)	4	94	2
Switzerland (2000)	21	72	7

Notes

1. Henry Rousso, *The Vichy Syndrome: History and Memory in France since 1944* (translated from the French by Arthur Goldhammer) (Cambridge, Mass.: Harvard University Press, 1991).
2. For a brief survey of this subject see: Yair Auron, *"Les Juifs d'Extreme Gauche en Mai 68"* (Paris: Albin Michel, 1998), pp. 145–148.
3. Emma Shnur, "Pédagogiser la Shoa?" *Débat*, 96, 1997, pp. 122–140, passim.
4. Jean-François Forges. "Pédagogie et morale," *Débat*, 96, 1997, pp. 145–151.
5. Philippe Joutard, "Une tache possible," *Débat*, 96, 1997, pp. 152–158.
6. Emma Shnur, "La morale et l'histoire," *Débat*, 96, pp. 159–165.
7. Bruce Carrington and Geoffrey Short, "Holocaust Education, Anti-racism and Citizenship," *Educational Review*, 49, 3, 1977, pp. 271–282.
8. Regarding the problematic relations between Raul Hilberg and Yad Vashem and the place of the ideological element in *The Destruction of the European Jews* as one of the reasons that this institution has not published this book, see Roni Stauber, *Lesson for this Generation: Holocaust and Heroism in Israeli Public Discourse in the 1950s* (Jerusalem: Yad Izhak Ben–Tzvi, 2000) (Hebrew), pp. 210–225.
9. Gerd Korman, "Silence in the American Textbooks," *Yad Vashem Studies*, 8, 1970, pp. 183–202; Alan Brinkley et al., *American History: A Survey*, 8th edition (New York, 1991), chap. 27.
10. Glenn S. Pate, "The Treatment of the Holocaust in Textbooks: The United States of America" in Randolph L. Braham (ed.), *The Treatment of the Holocaust in Textbooks* (New York: Social Science Monographs, Boulder and Institute for Holocaust Studies of the City University of New York, 1987), pp. 233–281, 307–310.
11. Peter Novick, "That is Past and We Must Deal with the Facts Today," *Holocaust in American Life* (Boston: Houghton Mifflin, 1999), pp. 85–102.
12. Margot Stern Strom and William S. Parsons, *Facing History and Ourselves: Holocaust and Human Behavior* (Watertown, Mass.: International Education, Inc., 1982), pp. 1–20, revised edition, 1994.
13. *Guidelines for Teaching about the Holocaust* (Washington, D.C.: USHMM), Third Revision Printing, 1994, pp. 1–8. For a comprehensive volume that encompasses the pedagogical issues confronting Holocaust studies, teaching curriculums, multi-disciplinary approaches, and moral dilemmas, see, Rochelle L. Miller (ed.), *New Perspectives on the Holocaust: A Guide for Teachers and Scholars* (New York: New York University Press, 1996).
14. Deborah E. Lipstadt, "Not Facing History: How Not to Teach the Holocaust," *The New Republic*, March 6, 1995, pp. 26–29.
15. Lucy S. Dawidowicz, "How They Teach the Holocaust", *Commentary*, 6, 1990, pp. 25–32.
16. The guidelines are quoted here verbatim, with some deletions, from the official USHMM publication. (See note 13.)
17. For relations between Germany and Israel, see Moshe Zimmerman and Oded Heilbronner (eds.), *"Normal" Relations: Israeli-German Relations* (Jerusalem: The Magnes Press, 1993) (Hebrew).
18. Zohar Shavit, *A Past Without Shadow: The Construction of the Past Image in the German "Story" for Children* (Tel Aviv: Am Oved, 1999) (Hebrew). Forthcoming in English by Routledge.

152   The Pain of Knowledge

19. Birgit Wenzel and Dagmar Weber, "'Auschwitz' in Geschichtsbuchern der Bundesrepublik Deutschland," in H. F. Rathenow and N. H. Weber (eds.), *Erziehung nach Auschwitz* (Pfallenweiler, 1989), pp. 421–422.
20. In: Richard J. Evans, *In Hitler's Shadow: West German Historians and the Attempt to Escape from the Nazi Past* (London: I. B. Tauris & Co., 1989), pp. 30–35.
21. Ibid., p. 52.
22. Ibid., pp. 112–113.
23. For East Germany's reaction to the Holocaust, see: Jeffrey M. Peck, "The World Reacts to the Holocaust: East Germany," in David S. Wyman (ed.), *The World Reacts to the Holocaust* (Baltimore and London: Johns Hopkins University Press, 1996), pp. 447–472.
24. See: Henry Wasserman (ed.), *The German-Jewish History We Have Inherited: Young Germans Write Jewish History* (Jerusalem: Magnes Press, 2004).
25. Shavit, A Past Without Shadow, p. 356.
26. David Singer, *Knowledge and Remembrance of the Holocaust in Different Countries: Data from American Jewish Committee-Sponsored Surveys* (New York: The American Jewish Committee, September 1999).
27. David Shiman and William R. Fernekes, "The Holocaust, Human Rights and Democratic Education," *The Social Studies*, Vol. 90, 1999, pp. 53–62.

13

On the Teaching of Genocide

The destruction of masses of people have occurred throughout the history of mankind. Most people agree, however, that the twentieth century saw more genocides than any another century, and some perceive and define it as the "century of the genocides," "the century of violence," or the "century of crime." For Jewish people, and for Israelis, this view—including the research and teaching aspects of genocide—should be of especially great interest. In Israel, there are two main approaches to the teaching of genocide. The first maintains that this subject should not be taught at all, and that only the Holocaust should be dealt with in the education system. The second approach subscribes to the teaching of genocide, but with a distinct division between it and the Holocaust. Our approach, however advocates the teaching of the Holocaust and genocide as one inclusive subject.

A Question of Terminology

As noted above, there is an ongoing and at times fiercely intense disagreement about the difference between the terms "Holocaust" and "genocide" among the researchers, a debate that encompasses many theoretical principles of fundamental importance. Some researchers make a clear-cut distinction between genocide and "the Holocaust," the latter being an unprecedented and unparalleled atrocity, a unique event in the entire history of mankind. According to this approach, the genocidal element is only one of the components of the Holocaust, which was a crime like no other, for it was all-inclusive, total, and broader in its scope than genocide. In contrast to those who emphasize the uniqueness and incomparability of the Holocaust, there are scholars who consider it to have been an event that falls within the overall category of acts of genocide, with some underscoring its uniqueness and others not. These researchers claim that all genocides are unique, each in its own way. (Some of these researchers are Jewish; a few are Israelis.) The words "Holocaust" and "genocide" are used here as distinctive though conjoined terms that sometimes overlap each other, and at other times are identical in certain aspects. The distinction in our presentation is a methodological one.

The word Holocaust has a connotative religious implication of which most people are not aware. The world holocaust, from the Greek "holokaustos," is a compound word consisting of the root "holos," meaning "whole," and "kaustos," meaning "burnt," hence meaning either "burning whole" or "total consummation by fire." Its original meaning is that of an offering the whole of which is burnt. The word appears originally in the Greek translation of the biblical sacrifice known as "olah," which was a wholly burnt offering. The word holocaust is also used as a translation of the biblical Hebrew "shoah" (which appears, for example, in Isaiah 47:11, Psalms 35:8, and Proverbs 3:25), as a word that describes "total destruction," and "overwhelming catastrophe."

Whether the term Holocaust (with a capital H) should be used only to define the destruction of the Jewish people or to also include the destruction of a variety of non-Jewish peoples, such as the Roma (Gypsies) (by the Nazis, in the same program of total destruction), is dependent on differing points of view. The word "holocaust" had actually been in use well before the World War II event for great catastrophes as well as for earlier instances of mass murder, including prior events of large-scale destruction of Jews; it was also used before World War II to describe the Armenian genocide. As noted, the original word for "Holocaust" in biblical Hebrew is "Shoah," and this term is sometimes used in other languages as well.

The term "genocide" was coined in 1944 by the Jewish-Polish legal scholar Raphael Lemkin, who combined the Greek word *genos*, meaning species or race, and the Latin suffix *-cide*, meaning murder of, or killing. Although its verbal meaning is the destruction or murder of a race, by convention it is used to mean the murder of a people. Lemkin, whose entire family was killed in the Holocaust, managed to escape from Poland to the United States and then devoted his life to the study of genocide, and to the struggle to include genocide as a crime in international criminal law. He first used the term in reference to the destruction of European Jewry by the Nazis, that is, with the meaning of murder of a people on the basis of their race. According to Lemkin's definition, however, the crime of genocide can encompass extermination on the basis of nationality, ethnicity, or religion. In the course of his research during and following the Second World War, he broadened the scope of his definition, and analyzed it in depth. Lemkin emphasized that the crime of genocide did not invariably entail the immediate and total annihilation of a group of victims, but could be perpetrated in the course of a series of planned actions whose purpose is to gradually destroy the basic components of a group's identity and way of life, among others by forcibly crushing or erasing its national, linguistic or cultural consciousness, by depriving the group's members of their personal freedoms, and by destroying its economic basis.

Lemkin's terminology has been adopted in international jurisprudence as the overarching definition of genocide and is used today in legal codes, international treaties, court judgments, scientific literature, and the media. It is used invariably with the connotation of the killing of human beings by reason of their membership in a national, ethnic, racial, or religious group, but in the opinion of many can also mean the murder of members of a political group in order to harm and eliminate the group, regardless of any individual blame.

Among historians, politicians, and jurists there is considerable controversy as to the applicability of the term genocide to various mass murders of the twentieth century, as well as of those occurring today, including cases of intra-national mass murders occurring against a political background, such as those perpetrated by Stalin in the former U.S.S.R. Thus, for example, at this writing a debate is taking place around the question of whether the events that occurred in the former Yugoslavia should be termed "genocide" or *only* "genocidal acts." Another example is the U.N. Security Council's refusal (under U.S. pressure), throughout the summer of 1994, to define what had happened in Rwanda earlier in that same year as genocide, despite the fact that hundreds of thousands were murdered and hundreds of millions of people throughout the world had seen these massacres happening, in real time, on their television screens. The United Nations recognized this as genocide only after most of the murder had ended.

This and similar controversies, as well as various other considerations, led to a suggestion to use the term "politicide" when speaking of genocide in a political context. According to this definition, politicide is the intentional killing, for ideological-political reasons, of people that the government of the country in which the victims live considers rivals or enemies. The terms genocide and politicide are not automatically or mutually exclusive, and an event may occur that includes acts that are at one and the same time both genocide and politicide. Thus, for example, the ruling governments of Stalin in the former Soviet Union, of Mao Tse-tung in China, and of Pol Pot in Cambodia carried out large-scale, intra-nation political killings, i.e., politicides, as well as killings of ethnic groups in order to annihilate them, i.e., genocides.

Another term that has been suggested for certain instances of mass murders is "ethnocide," usually defined as "cultural genocide" and meaning the intentional destruction of the culture of an ethnic, national, religious, or other type of a group of people, and not necessarily the taking of the peoples' lives. The multiplicity of names for various types of killing on a massive scale finally led to the proposal to use a broader and more inclusive term, "democide" (*demos*, is the Greek word for people), to encompass genocide, politicide, and ethnocide.

Estimates of the number of victims killed in the twentieth century in acts defined by the broad term suggested above, "democide," reach proportions that are beyond human comprehension. The American political scientist R.J. Rummel has estimated the number killed in events he defines as democide at 169,198,000 during the years 1900–1987, and estimates the total number of victims at the end of the twentieth century to be 174,000,000.[1] These figures do not include soldiers or civilians killed in warfare or unintentionally in war-related actions.

Above and beyond the semantic definitions and debates, it is clear that each and every act of genocide is an extreme crime in which human beings are killed by other human beings not due to any individual guilt or fault, but for one reason alone: they belong to a certain national, ethnic, racial, or religious group.

"The United Nations Convention on the Prevention and Punishment of the Crime of Genocide"

On December 9, 1948, against the background of Nazi crimes against humanity, first and foremost among them the destruction of the Jews of Europe, the United Nations Convention on the Prevention and Punishment of the Crime of Genocide (UNGC) was unanimously adopted by the general assembly of the United Nations. In this Convention genocide is defined as any of several acts "committed with intent to destroy, in whole or in part" a national, ethnic, racial, or religious group. According to Article II of the convention these acts are:

- Killing members of the group;
- Causing serious bodily or mental harm to members of the group;
- Deliberately inflicting on the group conditions of life calculated to bring about its physical destruction in whole or in part;
- Imposing measures intended to prevent births within the group;
- Forcibly transferring children of the group to another group.

The State of Israel signed the UNGC, and in 1950 adopted the "Knesset Law for the Prevention and Punishment of the Crime of Genocide (5710, 1950)." The Israeli legislation repeats the UNGC definition but is more decisive in one matter: that of punishment. The punishment for perpetrators of genocide, along with the procedure for bringing them for trial, is not defined in the UNGC. In this way the UNGC left breaches that allowed most of the perpetrators of genocide, after the convention was ratified, to escape punishment. The Knesset Law takes a far more categorical position as regards the punishment for such crimes and establishes that the punishment for one guilty of genocide is death, except under certain, unspecified, conditions. The Israeli legislators based the formulation of the "Law for the Punishment of Nazis and Nazi Collaborators" on this definition. This law was implemented in Israel for the first (and only) time in Israel in the Eichmann trial.

On Implementation of the United Nations Genocide Convention (UNGC)

Beyond the formulation and ratification of the UNGC, its importance lies in the question of what the U.N. and the international community are doing to prevent acts of genocide, many of which have continued to occur even after, and regardless of, the Convention's ratification. The actions taken as a result of the Convention are largely within the realm of extending assistance after the fact to those who were hurt by it, and less in prevention—despite the fact that the Convention specifies that under international law, genocide, whether committed in time of peace or in time or war is a crime. There are voices that call for the Convention to be amended to include specific ways of preventing genocide and not only for providing assistance to victims. The decision to establish the International Criminal Court (ICC), ratified in 1998 by more than sixty countries (Israel was not among them), may be an important step in this direction. This court has been functioning since 2002.

It is important to realize and to remember that acts of genocide can be committed only when the balance of power is such that the perpetrators have complete power over the victims. Such a state of affairs is dependent to no small degree on the behavior of the "third party"—those not involved directly—the side that always comprises almost the whole of human society.

When a genocide is being committed there is always a "third party," which can be divided schematically into three groups:

- Those who assist the murderers for various reasons, including the fact that since the murderers are the "strong ones" it is better to be "on good terms" with them.
- The comparatively few who, for moral, ethical, or compassionate reasons, come to the aid of the victims. (When these are non-Jews who aided Jews in the Holocaust, they are recognized in Israel as "Righteous Gentiles.")
- The by-standers, the vast majority that remains on the sidelines and does nothing.

A question, whose importance cannot be exaggerated, immediately comes to mind: Don't those who stand by and do nothing share some of the responsibility, and perhaps even some of the guilt, for the crimes committed, which they witnessed but did nothing to prevent?

The Teaching of Genocide throughout the World: An Overview

How genocide is taught in different places throughout the world is affected both by the controversies surrounding theoretical issues of terminology and those concerning the practical issue of the ways and the means available to the international community to prevent such large-scale crimes. One interesting aspect lies in the fact that where genocide is taught, there are the noticeable differences in the character of the courses that deal with the Holocaust and those that deal with genocide.

An important issue in any discussion on the teaching of genocide, especially in advanced academic courses, revolves around the arguments and debates surrounding semantic questions of terminology, especially those dealing with the broad and narrow definitions of the term "genocide" including—or perhaps mainly—the difference between "the Holocaust" and "acts of genocide."

While Holocaust studies have already secured a place in various educational frameworks in many countries in the world, the general field of genocide, as an independent subject, is still only at the beginning of its development. As such it is taught in high schools and universities, mainly in the United States and Canada, and to a lesser degree in Australia. In other countries genocide is, to the best of our knowledge, either taught minimally and superficially, or not taught at all. The variety of courses taught, mostly in universities, is indicative of great differences in approaches to the subject, in addition to which the courses are also taught using different methodologies, and in such diverse disciplines and departmental frameworks as history, political science, government, literature and language, multi-disciplinary studies, philosophy, psychology, theology, social work, and sociology. The differences between approaches can usually be discerned even in the names of the courses within which genocide is studied, such as the following typical course names:

- The Comparative Study of Genocide;
- The Politics of Genocide;
- Government Repression and Democide;
- Human Destructiveness and Politics;
- Genocide and "Constructive" Survival;
- Kindness and Cruelty: The Psychology of Good and Evil;
- Moral Consciousness and Social Action.

Even within the framework of these courses, which supposedly deal with different cases of genocide, the main topic dealt with in most of the curriculums is the Holocaust. In the textbook *Teaching about Genocide*,[2] details are provided about a survey, conducted in the United States in the early 1990s, which found that of twenty-nine university lecturers then teaching about genocide (and who answered the questionnaire) seventeen focus their teaching on the Holocaust, and of these, one-quarter include it in the name of their courses. This fact seems to indicate that Holocaust studies prompted genocide studies, and not the reverse. Throughout the world, in general, genocide is studied less—apparently much less—than the Holocaust. This subject is dealt with in two articles, one by Clive Foss,[3] the other by Helen Fein,[4] both of which appear in the above-mentioned textbook *Teaching about Genocide*. The authors of these articles both posit that the courses in which genocide is studied can be classified into three broad divisions:

- Courses in which the Holocaust is studied as the only or the main topic.
- Courses in which the Holocaust is studied in the general context of genocide.
- Courses in which, although genocide is the main subject, in some of them the Holocaust is the most prominent such occurrence.

The gap between the place of Holocaust studies compared to that of the study of genocide is especially great in high schools. Thus, in high schools in the United States, for example, other than the massive massacre of the Armenians in 1915–1919, the intentional starvation of the Ukrainians by the Soviet rulers in the early 1930s, or the internal genocide in Cambodia in the second half of the 1970s, almost nothing is studied about other incidents of genocide. For example, as of July 2004, as compared to twenty states that have "Holocaust Legislation," and twenty-six states (including the former twenty states) that have "Holocaust Academic Standards," only four states have "Armenian Genocide Academic Standards" (some other states "possibly" have Armenian Legislation or Armenian Academic Standards).[5] In those textbooks in which genocide is dealt with to some extent, the content is usually superficial, perfunctory, and simplistic, and sometimes inexact and even incorrect; often it seems that it is there only for appearance's sake.

To the best of our knowledge there are almost no surveys or studies of the effectiveness of the existing curriculum materials for teaching about genocide, and information about this matter is therefore lacking. In addition, since it is difficult to define exactly what "knowing about the Holocaust" or "knowing about genocide" means, there is a problem with evaluating how much knowledge either teachers or students have acquired. Nonetheless, even without such research, it is quite certain that knowledge about the Holocaust in most countries throughout the world is greater—even much greater—than that about other cases of genocide that occurred in the twentieth century. Claims have even been made that in many ways, except for the Holocaust, all of these genocides, and especially those that occurred in the more distant past, are "forgotten genocides," or even "hidden genocides." The well-known researcher of Holocaust and genocide education, Samuel Totten, maintains that despite indications of some progress during the last two decades, genocide studies in schools and universities in various countries constitute "what Elliot Eisner (1979), professor of education at Stanford University, has called the 'null curriculum,' or one of those subjects, events, or points of view that are not frequently taught."[6]

Questions about important philosophical and didactic aspects of genocide education, and several ways in which to contend with its complexity, can be found in the above-mentioned article by Samuel Totten and in another article he co-authored with William Parsons. Both Totten and Parsons are scholars and educators in the United States who have been dealing with research of genocide and genocide education for many years.[7]

Several trenchant questions about the teaching of the Holocaust that were posed by Elie Wiesel are applicable to the teaching of genocide as well:[8]

> How do you teach events that deny knowledge, experiences that go beyond imagination? How do you tell children, big and small, that society could lose its mind and start murdering its own soul and its own future? How do you unveil horrors without offering at the same time some measure of hope? Hope in what? In whom? In progress, in science and literature and God?

Teachers at all levels of learning have to ask themselves at least two questions before they begin to deal with the phenomenon of genocide, questions that seem at first to be self-understood:

- Why do we teach this subject?
- What should be our main goals when we teach this subject?

Many of those engaged in the teaching of this subject emphasize the unique characteristics that make genocide education difficult to deal with, among others, the fact that moral and ethical values comprise an inextricable facet of genocide, perhaps more so than in any other subject. Because of this it is important that the learner be brought into the educational process. We also have to emphasize the differences between learning, teaching, and education. There is a connection between our ability as individuals within our given social framework to engage critically with the profound questions that the subject of genocide elicits and the poor state of genocide teaching in general. There are many reasons for this, the main ones being:

- Genocide is a particularly complex and incomprehensible subject because both teachers and students are loath to deal with the horrific issues it entails, especially when teachers try to protect their young pupils from exposure to the details of such unbearable realities.
- The past or present policy of each country towards its minority groups, and at times the involvement of the country, or of people within it, in genocidal acts, or in acts with a genocidal character, or considerations of "realpolitik" that led or lead to indifference to past or present victims—any or all of these may create an ambivalent stand in that country to the teaching of the subject.
- Prejudices, racism, and anti-Semitism may sometimes affect, directly or indirectly, the decision about whether to teach this subject or not.

Above and beyond these problems there may be "technical" factors that either do not allow for teaching about genocide, or can serve as excuses for not doing so: most of the presently available textbooks do not deal with this subject suitably or at all; the curriculum is already overloaded in any case, and there is no "room" for it; the education system doesn't provide assistance to those interested in teaching it; the teachers have insufficient training and lack the background that will prepare them for coping with it, and so on.

As we have tried to show, this description about the teaching of genocide is characteristic of the situation for the teaching of the Holocaust prior to the early 1970s. In the decades that followed, many of the difficulties that led to that situation have been overcome and a significant number of the problems that we mentioned have been solved.

The progress made in the study of genocide has increased the recognition of its importance, and will hopefully also ensure that many of the difficulties and problems faced in teaching it as a school subject will also be solved. The way in which the subject is taught undoubtedly has to be different in accordance with each specific country, the level of learning, and the framework within which it is being taught. Clearly, too, teaching and learning about genocide will vary—at least in regard to some of the issues it entails—depending on which "side" the teachers and the pupils are related to: that of the victims or their relatives or descendants; that of the perpetrators and their families; or that of the bystanders and those connected with them.

An interesting and noteworthy example of this problem comes from the field of Holocaust education in Europe in the last few years. Along with the strengthening of European unification, the Council for Culture and Co-operation of the Council of Europe published a book for the use of teachers throughout Europe entitled *The Holocaust in the School Curriculum: A European Perspective*.[9] Published in French and English, the two official Council of Europe languages, this monograph attempts to examine the teaching of the Holocaust from a "European perspective," that is, from a perspective that encompasses the members of the group of the victims, of the murderers, and of the bystanders. It makes no attempt to evade the entanglements that a discussion dealing with these three groups necessitates. (That the book also includes a chapter dealing with the prevention of stereotyping Germans is also of interest.)

An important attempt to deal with the subject is the syllabus of a university course entitled "The Politics of Genocide," by Colin Tatz, a professor in Sydney, Australia, who has been engaged in the teaching of this subject for many years.[10] This syllabus tries to emphasize the central part played by governments in various genocidal incidents, including those that were part and parcel of colonization and resulted in the destruction of native populations. The United Nations Genocide Convention of 1948 is critically analyzed, and a suggestion is made to differentiate "between massacre, mass murder, gross colonial oppression, forced assimilation or religious conversion, and total (or attempted total) extermination of a whole genus," the last of which was the case, according to Tatz, in the destruction of the Armenians and the Jews in the twentieth century. Tatz also specifically deals with, and strongly advocates, the need for Australia to face and recognize the "genocide against the Aborigines," to which that country's government is not ready to fully admit to this day.

Another interesting suggestion for a study program, *Genocide and Human Rights: A Global Anthology*, was written by Jack Nusan Porter. The book's Introduction is dedicated to the memory of the author's parents, both Jewish partisans who fought in the forests of the Ukraine in the Second World War.[11] Porter suggests various clarifications for the topics he examines, and deals with the question of whether the subject should be taught at all. He concludes not only that there is much room for research in this field, for example, in the disciplines of sociology and anthropology, but that both research in and the teaching of genocide are of vital importance because the phenomenon of genocide is part of the reality of our lives today and has far-reaching implications for each individual and for modern societies as well.

In various countries in the world in the past few decades, and especially in the United States, efforts to expand the range of genocide studies and its teaching have been made in the public realm, and especially in academia. Two texts that deal with the Armenian genocide are worth mentioning in this context: the article "How and Why to Teach the Armenian Genocide: Seeking a Humanist Perspective," by Rouben Adalian,[12] and one among several courses, handbooks, and programs for teaching the Armenian genocide, "Everyone's Not Here: Families of the Armenian Genocide—A Study Guide," by William S. Parsons.[13]

Rouben Adalian dwells on several important problems that arise around the question of why we are enjoined to learn about (or to not learn about) the Armenian genocide. He asserts that the argument that it should be learned about only because it happened in the past is sorely lacking. The point of departure for the rationale of teaching about genocide—i.e., all genocides, including that of the Armenians—must be that it is not an event of the past but, rather, "a timeless event, to endure till the end of time." It must be taught in order "to prevent death's primacy in life, injustice's undeserving fruits, evil's superior post, mankind's unconscionable behavior and, above all, to restore life, vitality, rights and justice to an injured and still suffering people." In the case of the Armenians, this is highly pertinent because most of the countries in the world, including Turkey, do not recognize that what happened to the Armenians was genocide.

William Parsons' article outlines various modular courses, which include a videotape of interviews with survivors of the Armenian genocide and their grandchildren. Rather than presenting an overall historical analysis of the genocide and its ramifications, this program attempts to present a personal view of it through the life stories of several families. The surviving grandmothers and grandfathers repeatedly express the importance of dealing with this event for present-day needs, so that their grandchildren will learn from their forebears, as borne out by one of the grandchildren: "Trying to annihilate a whole race of people will never work . . . because as long as one survives . . . as my grandmother . . . that plan can never succeed."[14]

In the last twenty or thirty years significant progress has undoubtedly been made in the awareness of many countries in the world to the phenomenon of genocide, and to a certain, limited extent, in teaching about it (other than the teaching of the Holocaust as a separate subject). A closer look at the development of the teaching of genocide in those countries where it is taught indicates that in more than a few of them it is driven by the initiative and perseverance of "fighters for the cause," dedicated individuals who make it their life's work. Not surprisingly, not a few of those behind the initiative and the struggle are Jews who, besides studying and teaching the Holocaust, want to ensure that genocide is taught and learned due to their special identification with the suffering of other peoples.

A very useful and important tool for teachers, educators, and students who wish to deal with the subject is the *Encyclopedia of Genocide*, published in 1999. A special educational electronic edition has been available in Internet e-book form since 2003.[15]

On Teaching and Learning about Genocide in Israel: An Overview

Despite the progress in genocide education all over the world, it is surprising that it almost never appears in Israeli curriculums at any level. A study program entitled "Awareness of the World's Suffering—Genocide in the Twentieth Century" was prepared for—and at the request of—the Israeli Ministry of Education in 1994, but was subsequently not approved by the Ministry for teaching in high schools and colleges.[16] The program, or part of it, is nevertheless presently being taught in a few high schools, due to the initiative of individual teachers or school principals who thought it should be learned. In an article entitled "Was Hitler Defeated?" its author, Ilan Gur-Ze'ev, an Israeli scholar of the philosophy of education, deals with the controversy that this course touched off and criticizes the Ministry of Education for not approving it.[17] To the best of our knowledge, this is the only academic article that deals with the teaching of genocide in Israel.

Among young adults in Israel, the lack of knowledge or even an awareness of the genocides that befell other peoples or groups is deplorable. For example, in a 1996 survey, more than eight hundred BA students in seven universities and colleges were asked to assess their knowledge about genocide. The responses to the self-assessment question in which they were asked to evaluate their knowledge about the genocides of the Armenians and the Gypsies showed that such knowledge was close to zero.[18] An absolute majority of the respondents, 86 percent, answered that they had very little or no knowledge at all about the Armenian genocide (42 percent, "no knowledge at all"; 44 percent, "very little"); 13 percent answered that they had "some" knowledge; and only 1 percent claimed to be "well informed" about it.

In an earlier survey a similar group of students were asked about their knowledge of the Holocaust.[19] In this case, 59 percent claimed they had "very much knowledge"; 34 percent, "much knowledge"; 6 percent, "little knowledge"; and only 1 percent answered "no knowledge." The students in this survey were also asked whether they strongly agree, agree, disagree, or strongly disagree about whether "the Armenian genocide is irrelevant to us because it happened more than eighty years ago." The responses to this were: 58 percent, strongly disagree; 34 percent, mostly disagree. The student body in Israel also disagreed more unreservedly with the claim that the Armenian genocide is irrelevant than did adult populations in other countries in regard to the relevance of the Holocaust. In regard to the teaching of the Jewish Holocaust elsewhere in the world, 56 percent of the Israeli students answered that it is "essential" that all nations know about and "understand" the Holocaust, and 37 percent thought it is "very important." (For answers to similar questions in specific countries, see Tables 5 and 6 at the end of the previous chapter.)

We have to ask why an absolute majority of Israel students think that knowledge about the Armenian genocide is relevant today even though it happened over eighty years ago, and that it is important to learn about other genocidal events (and also that it is important that all nations know about the Holocaust)—although these students themselves neither know almost anything about these other genocides nor make any effort to do so.

In the first survey quoted above (see note 16), similar questions were also asked about the Nazis' mass murder of the Gypsies—a genocide that occurred at the same period of time as that in which the Jews were murdered, in the same places, at the hands of the same perpetrators, and in the name of the same racial ideology, although Nazi attitudes to the two groups was not identical. In the survey, 85 percent of the students answered that they had little or no knowledge at all about the genocide of the Gypsies (36 percent "no knowledge at all"; 49 percent, "very little knowledge"). Similar results about the Gypsy genocide were obtained in another survey among more than 100 fourth-year students at the Kibbutzim College of Education in Tel Aviv in 1997.[20] The answers to the self-assessment questions in this survey were on a scale of 1 to 4 (1 = no knowledge at all; 2 = little knowledge; 3 = some knowledge; 4 = much knowledge), and the average of the respondents' self-assessed general knowledge about the Gypsy genocide was 1.7. In the survey other questions were asked about the date of the genocide of the Gypsies, the identity of the perpetrators, and the number of victims. The answers to these questions indicated that among those who answered that they had some general knowledge about this event quite a few actually knew very little (these students usually tend to overestimate their knowledge in this matter). The average rating for the positive answers to the question "Is it important for us to know about the destruction of the Gypsies?" was a very high 3.13 (also on a scale of 1 to 4). However, the same respondents answered that they had actually not learned about this genocide in high school (average 1.11) or in college (average 1.14). The average results for other questions in the survey were as follows: for "How should we as Jews, victims of the Nazi regime, relate to the Gypsies, victims of the same regime?" were equivocal; for the question "Is it important that the genocide of the Gypsies should be memorialized in Yad Vashem [the Holocaust memorial museum in Jerusalem]? the rating was 2.41; for the question "Should the youth trips to [Jewish sites and the extermination camps in] Poland deal with the genocide of the Gypsies as well?" it was 2.12; and for the question "Should combined memorial ceremonies be held in Germany for the Jewish and the Gypsy victims of the Nazi regime?" it was 2.09.

In the Israeli reality, such questions are almost rhetorical throughout the education system. In high school textbooks dealing with modern world history or the history of the twentieth century, as well as in those dealing in depth with the Holocaust, there is only the briefest mention, if any, of the Gypsy genocide. Actually, all of the non-Jewish victims of the Nazi regime—Gypsies, homosexuals, political prisoners, the mentally ill, the physically disabled, Jehovah's Witnesses, Poles, and Russian prisoners of war—are similarly mentioned only in passing if at all. All of these are sometimes collectively labeled "Other victims," a term that is itself problematic: "Other" as compared to whom? "Other" in whose eyes? The findings of the surveys described above, rather than being surprising or unexpected, are a sign that much thought has to be given to the history curriculums of Israeli schools. Most of the students' answers indicate support, or at least readiness, albeit somewhat reserved, for changes in the content of the textbooks in use at present. Most of the students (average 1.25) thought that knowledge of the Gypsy genocide would not detract from the uniqueness of the Holocaust.

On the Universal Value of Human Life

In 1997 a book appeared in France with the title *La Concurrence de Victimes: Génocide, Identité, Reconnaissance* [Competition between the Victims: Genocide, Identity, Recognition] by the philosopher Jean-Michel Chaumont.[21] Consisting of three parts, "A Time of Shame" (1945–1967), "A Time of Pride" (1967 and on), and "Dilemmas of Recognition" (i.e., recognition of the crime and the disaster that befell a human being and those in his group), the book fomented much controversy and had strong reverberations throughout Europe. The author analyzes the place of the Holocaust in the definition of the self-identity of Jews in Europe, Israel, and the United States. In the Introduction, the author writes:[22]

> As to the victims of the Nazis, nothing is managed properly. Under an external veil of agreement such as "Never Again," the sacred obligation to remember or struggle against anti-Semitism and racial intolerance, strong differences divide the groups of victims of the Third Reich as to the nature of the memorial sites: Jewish deportees against underground fighters, Jews against Gypsies, homosexuals against political prisoners, antifascist Jews against Zionists. The list of confrontations and counter-arguments is long and goes beyond the crimes of the National-Socialists, especially in the United States where it involves a myriad of groups such as: Jews against Armenians, Jews against blacks, Jews against Native Americans, and even Jews against Tutsi, etc. . . .

These words also shed light on the fierce controversy about the genocides of other peoples that has been debated in Israel for more that a quarter of a century. At the heart of these arguments is the debated claim (or demand) regarding the absolute uniqueness of the Holocaust. This is at a time when the special importance of the Holocaust for Jews as Jews is, in our opinion, not linked to its uniqueness as a genocide, for in this case we are speaking of a "death industry," the fruit of an ideology and a theory that dictated destroying all members of a people as such. The Holocaust's singular importance is not a matter of its uniqueness, but rather its complicated entrenchment within Jewish history—for it cannot but remain an important component in the Jewish and the Israeli consciousness. In the same way, the non-recognition of an outrage perpetrated upon a person or a group is always a very important, and usually a central, factor in the consciousness of each individual victim or all of the victims of that outrage, and in their outlook. Sometimes such non-recognition of the crime can be a critical factor in the victims' process of coming to terms with the disaster and with their attempts to rehabilitate themselves, attempts that may go on for many years, and may never end. In this context it is suitable to remember the recurrent nightmares of the camp inmates described by Primo Levi, in which they return to their homes and their relatives do not believe their descriptions of the suffering they have gone through.

It is important that Israelis, and Jews in Israel and elsewhere, as members of one group of victims, ask themselves very difficult questions, such as how they should relate to the justified demands of other victims of genocide that the murderers of these victims, or their heirs, and the world, recognize the crimes perpetrated against them.

It is also important that we, as individual Jews and as Israelis, acknowledge the crimes perpetrated against other victims of genocide, and that we consider how the State of Israel should relate to their demands for recognition.

These questions are exemplified by the very real and actual situation that Israel faces today: Israel, directly or indirectly, supports Turkey's efforts in denying the fact that there was a genocide of the Armenians. This situation calls for a response by individuals and institutions, and by Jewish society both within Israel and elsewhere.[23]

It is inevitable that Israeli pupils' and young adults' knowledge about the genocide perpetrated upon the Jewish people ("The Holocaust happened to us") will be greater than that of similar disasters that befell other peoples. However, shouldn't this knowledge, and the fact that the

Jewish nation is a people that survived such a destruction, together with the fact that the Holocaust has such a central place in the Jewish national identity, be factors in making them more sensitive to the calamities of other peoples?

There are two approaches in Israel about exposing young Israelis to knowledge about the genocides of other peoples. One opposes it, arguing that it will detract from the uniqueness of the Holocaust and allow these young people to compare it with other genocides and to perceive it in relative terms—considering it as but one of many such atrocities would greatly diminish the historical value of the Holocaust. The other school of thought finds the Israeli education system almost entirely focused—exaggeratedly and inexactly—on the Jews as victims, while intentionally or unintentionally ignoring the mass murders of other peoples throughout history, especially in the twentieth century.

In order to overcome the problematic nature of both of these approaches, there have been suggestions to emphasize the unique characteristics of the Holocaust by comparing it with other genocides, and by doing this to prompt the pupils to deepen their knowledge about the Holocaust, while keeping in mind the historical importance and significance of other genocides. The supporters of this approach claim that such a comparative element can help Israeli pupils examine the Holocaust from a broader and more comprehensive perspective, one more universal in terms of both the Jewish experience and that of mankind as well.

* * *

One of the factors underlying the historical consciousness of a society is the question that has repeatedly arisen in this book: What *can* a society know, and what does it *want* to know about the historical truth of its own past and that of other societies? It appears that the glaring absence in the collective Israeli (and Jewish) consciousness of what has happened to "others," about "their genocide," is a moral issue that Israelis and Jews should deal with. What happened to "us" and what happened to "others" do not contradict each other but, rather, mutually complement one another. Learning about both can create the desirable synthesis between the unique and the general, and thus add moral and spiritual significance and universal import to the memory of the Holocaust, and to the just demand of the world to never forget it. We should not fear that such a synthesis may relativize the Holocaust or weaken its unique Jewish aspect: on the contrary—it will increase the universal awareness of the significance of the Holocaust.

The guiding principle of the course "The Pain of Knowledge," and the underlying approach of this book, is that the value of human life is universal, and that this is true for each and every human being, no matter what his or her race, religion, or nation.

Notes

1. R. J. Rummel, "The New Concept of Democide," in Israel W. Charny (ed.), *Encyclopedia of Genocide* (Santa Barbara, CA: ABC-CLIO, 1999), pp. 18–34.
2. Joyce Freedman-Apsel and Helen Fein (eds.), *Teaching about Genocide* (New York: The Institute for the Study of Genocide, 1992; new edition, 2002).
3. Clive Foss, "Introduction," in Joyce Freedman-Apsel and Helen Fein (eds.), *Teaching about Genocide* (New York: The Institute for the Study of Genocide, 1992), pp. 1–5.
4. Helen Fein, "Teaching about Genocide in an Age of Genocide," in ibid., pp. 9–12.
5. These figures are from the website of the USHMM: http://www.ushmm.org/education/foreducators/index.php?content=states.
6. Samuel Totten, "Educating about Genocide: Curricular and Inservice Training," in Israel W. Charny (ed.), *A Critical Bibliographic Review*, Vol. 2 (New York: Facts on File, 1991), pp. 194–200. And see also, Samuel Totten (ed.), *Teaching about Genocide: Issues, Approaches and Resources* (Greenwich: Information Age Publishing, 2004).
7. William S. Parsons and Samuel Totten, "Teaching and Learning about Genocide: Questions of Content, Rationale and Methodology," *Social Education*, 55:2, 1991, pp. 84–90.
8. Elie Wiesel, "Then and Now: The Experiences of a Teacher," *Social Education*, 42:4, 1978, p. 270.
9. Geoffrey Short, Carrie Supple, and Katherine Klinger, *The Holocaust in the School Curriculum: A European Perspective* (Strasbourg: Council of Europe, 1998).
10. Colin Tatz, "The Politics of Genocide" (Course Syllabus), in Joyce Freedman-Apsel and Helen Fein, *Teaching about Genocide*, pp. 72–77. See also Colin Tatz, *With Intent to Destroy: Reflecting on Genocide* (London and New York: Verso, 2003), pp. 171–184.
11. Jack Nusan Porter, *Genocide and Human Rights: A Global Anthology* (Lanhan: University Press of America, 1982), pp. 2–32.
12. Rouben Adalian, "How and Why to Teach the Armenian Genocide: Seeking a Humanist Perspective," *Armenian Review*, Vol. 40 (Spring 1987), pp. 69–77. About trends and curriculum developments in genocide studies, especially regarding the Armenian genocide, see Joyce Freedman-Apsel, "Looking Backward and Forward: Genocide Studies and Teaching about the Armenian Genocide," in Richard G. Hovannisian (ed.), *Looking Backward, Moving Forward* (New Brunswick, N.J.: Transaction Publishers, 2003), pp. 181–207. Apsel, who focuses

on trends and curriculum developments in genocide studies throughout the United States during the past several decades, promotes courses and curriculums that offer genocide studies and human rights as a framework, rather than those dominated by one particular genocide.
13. William S. Parsons (ed.), *Everyone's Not Here: Families of the Armenian Genocide—A Study Guide* (Washington, D.C.: Armenian Assembly of America, 1989), pp. 73-87. And see, for example: Simon Payaslian, *The Armenian Genocide: A Handbook for Students and Teachers* (Glendale: Armenian Cultural Foundation, 2001).
14. W. R. Ferenekes, "Everyone's Not Here: Families of the Armenian Genocide—A Study Guide," in Parsons, *Everyone's Not Here*, p. 40.
15. Israel W. Charny (Editor-in-Chief), *Encyclopedia of Genocide* (Santa Barbara: ABC-CLID, 1999).
16. Yair Auron, *Awareness of Suffering in the World: Genocide in the Twentieth Century* (Tel Aviv: Seminar Hakibbutzim, 1994) (Hebrew).
17. Ilan Gur-Ze'ev, "Hitler and Philosophy in the Israeli Curriculum," in *Destroying the Others' Collective Memory* (New York: Peter Lang, 2003), pp. 68–107.
18. Yair Auron, unpublished.
19. Yair Auron, *Israeli-Jewish Identity* (Tel Aviv: Sifriat Poalim, 1993), pp. 85–86.
20. Yair Auron, unpublished.
21. Jean-Michel Chaumont, *La Concurrence de Victimes: Génocide, Identité, Reconnaissance* (Paris: La Découverté, 1997).
22. Ibid., p. 9.
23. Yair Auron, *The Banality of Indifference: Zionism and the Armenian Genocide* (New Brunswick, N.J.: Transaction Publishers, 2000).

Afterword

The Pain of Knowledge is in many ways the first book, and the first academic course, of its kind in Israel, and in many ways in the entire world. Not only is it "academic" in the narrow meaning of the word, but it constitutes an attempt to encompass within one narrow but overarching framework the complicated and profound questions that arise in the teaching of the Holocaust and of genocide, both in Israel and in other places in the world. Our hope is that it will be helpful in developing this field further in the future.

This book certainly does not assume to address the full range of subjects and issues related to Holocaust and genocide education and their related problems, nor is it possible to include or even refer to the immense amount of material already written on these matters. It was obviously impossible to incorporate within this framework all of the subject's didactic and methodological problems, whose importance cannot be exaggerated. For example: At what age is it suitable to begin to teach this subject? How much of the details should the students be exposed to? Which learning aids are suitable for presenting the difficult content in such a way as to be effective educationally, but without causing mental or emotional anguish and, possibly, damage? And so on.

We were also constrained to refrain, in this book, from discussing such important topics as teaching through witnesses' testimonies, films, literature, works of art, etc. We have also not discussed various multimedia options and Internet sites, large amounts of which have appeared in the last few years in Israel and all over the world.

The memory of the Holocaust in Israeli society and its place in both Jewish and Israeli identity, as well as the genocides of other peoples—and thus the teaching of both in Israel and in other countries throughout the world—have both current and future ramifications for Israeli society and for the State of Israel.

Our purpose, and our hope, is that *The Pain of Knowledge* will motivate its readers both to think about the broad range of issues raised in it and to clarify and deepen their knowledge about them even further. Although our review of the study of the teaching of the Holocaust and genocide ends at this point, the subject has by no means been treated exhaustively, and although intrinsically part of the subject, many educational and ethical characteristics of the topics with which the book deals remain to be discussed elsewhere. We can only hope that the many issues that were not elucidated sufficiently within the present framework will receive the attention and the clarification they deserve.

Bibliography

Hebrew

Abramski, Irit (ed.), *Outlining the Holocaust for Arabic Speaking Students* (Jerusalem: Yad Vashem, Ghetto Fighters' House, 2000) (Hebrew and Arabic).

Auron, Yair, *Israeli-Jewish Identity* (Tel Aviv: Sifriat Poalim, 1993).

Auron, Yair, *Sensitivity to Suffering in the World: Genocide in the Twentieth Century* (Tel Aviv: Kibbutz Movement Teachers Seminary, 1994).

Auron, Yair, Zalikovitz, Gila and Keren, Nili, *Attitudes of Trainee Teachers to Anti-Semitism and Racism* (Tel Aviv: Seminar Hakibbutzim, 1996).

Barkay, Tamar and Levy, Gal, "Holocaust Remembrance Day in Progressive Eyes: Ethnicity, Class and Education in Israel," *Politika*, 1, 1999, pp. 27–46.

Bar-On, Dan and Selah, Oron, "The Vicious Circle of Israeli Youngsters' Attitudes towards their Actuality and towards the Holocaust," *Psychologia—Israeli Journal of Psychology*, Vol. 2, No. 1, September 1991, pp. 126–138.

Ben-Amos, Avner and Bet-El, Ilana, "Ceremonies, Education and History: Holocaust Day and Remembrance Day in Israeli Schools," in Rivka Feldhay and Immanuel Etkes (eds.), *Education and History: Cultural and Political Links* (Jerusalem: The Zalman Shazar Center for Jewish History, 1999), pp. 457–479.

Bishara, Azmi, "The Arabs and the Holocaust: Analyzing the Problems of a Preposition [sic]," *Zmanim*, Vol. 13, No. 53, Summer 1995, pp. 54–72.

Bishara, Azmi, "On Nationalism and on Universalism," *Zmanim*, Vol. 13, No. 55 (Responses Section), Winter 1995–1996, pp. 102–105.

Brug, Muli, "From the Top of Masada to the Heart of the Ghetto," in David Ohana and Robert Wistreich (eds.), *Myth and Memory: Transfigurations of Israeli Consciousness* (Tel Aviv: Hakibbutz Hameuchad, 1996), pp. 203–230.

Carmon, Arye, *The Holocaust: A Subject for the Upper Levels of the General School: Teacher's Guide* (Jerusalem: Ministry of Education and Culture, 1980).

Eldar, Yisrael, "The So-called Forgetting of the Holocaust," *Haaretz*, April 14, 1988.

Elkana, Yehuda, "On the Right to Forget," *Haaretz*, March 2, 1988.

Evron, Boaz, "Education towards Fascism and Escape," *Yedioth Ahronoth*, March 4, 1988.

Farago, Uri, "Attitudes toward the Holocaust among Israeli High School Students—1983," *Studies on the Holocaust Period*, Vol. III (Tel Aviv: Hakibbutz Hameuchad, 1984), pp. 159–178.

Feldman, Jackie, "Delegations of Israeli Youth to Poland in the Wake of the Holocaust and their Object," *Yalkut Moreshet*, 66, 1998, pp. 81–104.

Firer, Ruth, *The Agents of the Lesson* (Tel Aviv: Hakibbutz Hameuchad, 1989).

Funkenstein, Amos, "On Several Theological Interpretations of the Significance of the Holocaust," in *Image and Historical Consciousness in Judaism and in its Cultural Surroundings* (Tel Aviv: Am Oved, 1991), pp. 278–243.

Grossman, David, *Present Absentees* (Tel Aviv: Hakibbutz Hameuchad, 1992).

Gubran, Saalam, "The Arabs and the Holocaust: A Historical and Realistic Perspective," *Beshvil Hazikaron* [In Memory's Path], 17, 1996 (Jerusalem: Yad Vashem Education Department), pp. 15–18.

Guri-Rosenblit, Sarah and Ben-Yehoshua, Na'ama Tsabar, "An Evaluation of the Cognitive and Affective Changes about the Holocaust in Youth as a Result of Teaching the Holocaust through the Adopt-a-Community Method," *Theory and Practice in Planning Studies*, 3, 1980, pp. 113–132.

Gur-Ze'ev, Ilan and Pappe, Ilan "The Palestinian Control over the Memories of the Holocaust and the Naqba," in Ilan Gur-Ze'ev, *Philosophy, Politics and Education in Israel* (Haifa and Tel Aviv: Haifa University and Zmora Beitan, 2000), pp. 99–123.

Gur-Ze'ev, Ilan, "Has Hitler Really Been Killed?" in Ilan Gur-Ze'ev, *Philosophy, Politics and Education in Israel* (Haifa and Tel Aviv: Haifa University and Zmora Beitan, 2000), pp. 57–98.

Gutman, Yisrael and Schatzker, Haim, *The Holocaust and its Significance: Teacher's Guide* (Jerusalem: Zalman Shazar Center, 1983).

Gutman, Yisrael, *Shoah and Memory* (Jerusalem: The Zalman Shazar Center for Jewish History, 1999).

Gutwein, Daniel, "The Privatization of the Holocaust: Politics, Memory and Historiography," *Research Papers on the Period of the Holocaust*, 1998, pp. 7–52.

International School for Holocaust Studies, *Educational Program* (Jerusalem: Yad Vashem, 1998).

Keren, Nili, "Preserving Memory within Oblivion: The Struggle over Teaching the Holocaust in Israel," *Zmanim*, Vol. 16, No. 64, Autumn 1998, pp. 55–64.

Keren, Nili, *Shoah—A Journey to Memory* (Tel Aviv: Sifrei Tel Aviv, 1999), pp. 146–155.

Kovner, Abba, "From Generation to Generation," *Yalkut Moreshet* 50, April 1991, pp. 13–16.

Michman, Dan (ed.), *Post-Zionism and the Holocaust: The Role of the Holocaust in the Public Debate on Post-Zionism in Israel (1993–1996): A Collection of Clippings* (Ramat-Gan, Israel: Bar-Ilan University, 1997).

Michman, Dan, "Arabs, Zionists, Bishara and the Holocaust: A Political Campaign or an Academic Study?" *Zmanim*, Vol. 13 (Responses Section), Autumn 1995, pp. 117–119.

Michman, Dan, *In Days of Holocaust and Remembrance* (Tel Aviv: The Open University of Israel, 1983).

Nili Keren, "The Subject of the Holocaust in Israeli Society and in the Education System in the Years 1948–1981," *Yalkut Moreshet* 42, December 1986, pp. 193–202.

Ophir, Adi, "On Feelings that Cannot be Expressed in Words and on Lessons that Cannot be Questioned," *Beshvil Hazikaron* [In Memory's Path], 7, 1995, pp. 11–15

Popowski, Mikhal, *Testimony and Identity 1938–1946: The Holocaust as Reflected in Literature* (Tel Aviv: The Center for Educational Technology, 1994).

Schatzker, Haim, "Didactic Problems in the Teaching of the Holocaust," *Guidelines for Teachers of History*, 2, 1961, pp. 11–15.

Schatzker, Haim, "Problems in Contemporary Holocaust Teaching," in Rivka Feldhay and Immanuel Etkes (eds.), *Education and History* (Jerusalem: The Zalman Shazar Center for Jewish History, 1999), pp. 447–455.

Shamir, Moshe, *With His Own Hands: Pirkei Elik* (Tel Aviv: Am Oved, 1951).

Shavit, Zohar, *A Past Without Shadow: The Construction of the Past Image in the German "Story" for Children* (Tel Aviv: Am Oved, 1999). Forthcoming in English by Routledge.

Shiff, Ofer, Bar-Zohar, Ya'akov, K'fir, Drora, and Zeiger, Tali, "Training Students to Contend Educationally with the Subject of the Holocaust," *Dappim*, 23, 1996, pp. 7–26.

Sivan, Emmanuel, "Mourning, Bereavement and Memory," in *The 1948 Generation: Myth, Profile and Memory* (Tel Aviv: Ma'arakhot—Ministry of Defence, Israel) pp. 119–142.

Stauber, Roni, *Lesson for this Generation: Holocaust and Heroism in Israeli Public Discourse in the 1950s* (Jerusalem: Yad Izhak Ben-Tzvi, 2000).

Tzur, Tova, "The Trip to Poland as the High Point of an Educational Process," *Beshvil Hazikaron* [In Memory's Path], 7, 1995, pp. 5–7.

Zimmerman, Moshe and Heilbronner, Oded (eds.), *"Normal" Relations: Israeli-German Relations* (Jerusalem: The Magnes Press, 1993).

English and French

Adalian, Rouben, "How and Why to Teach the Armenian Genocide: Seeking a Humanist Perspective," *Armenian Review*, Vol. 40, Spring 1987, pp. 69–77.

Amichai, Yehuda, *Open Closed Open: Poems* (translated from the Hebrew by Chana Block and Chana Kronfeld) (New York, San Diego, London: Harcourt, 2000).

Anderson, Benedict, *Imagined Communities* (London and New York: Verso, 1983).
Auron, Yair, *Les Juifs d'Extreme Gauche en Mai 68* (Paris: Albin Michel, 1998).
Auron, Yair, *The Banality of Indifference: Zionism and the Armenian Genocide* (New Brunswick, NJ and London, England: Transaction Publishers, 2000).
Auron, Yair, *The Banality of Denial: Israel and the Armenian Genocide* (New Brunswick, NJ and London, England: Transaction Publishers, 2003).
Barkay, Tamar and Levy, Gal, "The Kedma School: An Alternative to the Ashkenazi, Classist and Ethnocentric State School System," *News from Within*, vol. XV, no. 6, June 1999, pp. 26–32.
Bar-On, Dan, "Between Fear and Hope: An Ongoing Dialogue with the Holocaust," in *Fear and Hope: Three Generations of the Holocaust* (Cambridge, MA and London, England: Harvard University Press, 1995).
Bar-On, Dan, *Legacy of Silence: Encounters with Children of the Third Reich* (Cambridge, MA and London, England: Harvard University Press, 1989).
Bauer, Yehudah, *The Holocaust in Historical Perspective* (Seattle: University of Washington Press, 1998).
Carmon, Arye, "Teaching the Holocaust as a Means of Fostering Values," *Curriculum Inquiry*, 9/3, 1979, pp. 209–228.
Carrington, Bruce, and Short, Geoffrey, "Holocaust Education, Anti-Racism and Citizenship," *Educational Review*, vol. 49, no. 3, 1997, pp. 271–282.
Chaumont, Jean-Michel, *La Concurrence de Victimes* (Paris: La Découverte, 1997).
Dawidowicz, Lucy S., "How They Teach the Holocaust," *Commentary*, 6, 1990, pp. 25–32.
Evans, Richard J., *In Hitler's Shadow: West German Historians and the Attempt to Escape from the Nazi Past* (London, I. B. Tauris & Co., 1989).
Ferenekes, William R., "Sample Course Which includes the videotape 'Everyone is Not here,'" in William S. Parsons (ed.), *Everyone is Not Here: Families of the Armenian Genocide: A Study Guide* (Washington: Armenian Assembly of America, 1989), pp. 73–87.
Forges, Jean-François, "Pédagogie et Morale," *Débat*, 96, 1997, pp. 145–151.
Freedman-Apsel, Joyce and Fein, Helen (eds.), *Teaching about Genocide* (New York: The Institute for the Study of Genocide, 1992; new edition, 2002).
Golub Jennifer, *Current German Attitudes Toward Jews And Other Minorities* (New York: American Jewish Committee, 1994).
Golub, Jennifer and Cohen, Renae, *What Do the Americans Know About the Holocaust?* (New York: American Jewish Committee, 1993).
Golub, Jennifer and Cohen, Renae, *What Do the Australians Know About the Holocaust?* (New York: American Jewish Committee, 1994).
Golub, Jennifer and Cohen, Renae, *What Do the British Know About the Holocaust?* (New York: American Jewish Committee, 1994).

Golub, Jennifer and Cohen, Renae, *What Do the French Know About the Holocaust?* (New York: American Jewish Committee, 1994).

Gorny, Yosef, *Between Auschwitz and Jerusalem* (London and Portland: Vallentine Mitchell, 2003).

Gur-Ze'ev, Ilan, *Destroying the Others' Collective Memory* (New York: Peter Lang, 2003).

Joutard, Philippe, "Une Tache Possible," *Débat*, 96, 1997, pp. 152–158.

Leibman, Charles, "Myth, Tradition and Values in Israeli Society [The Holocaust Myth]," *Midstream*, 24:1 January 1980, pp. 44–53.

Leibman, Charles and Don-Yehiya, Eliezer, *Civil Religion in Israel* (Berkeley: University of California Press, 1983).

Levi, Primo, *The Drowned and the Saved* (translated from the Italian by Raymond Rosenthal) (New York: Vintage International/Random House, 1989).

Lipstadt, Deborah, E. "Not Facing History—How Not to Teach the Holocaust," *The New Republic*, June 3, 1995, pp. 26–29.

Littell, Franklin H., "Inventing the Holocaust: A Christian's Retrospect," in Yisrael Gutman (ed.), *Major Changes Within the Jewish People in the Wake of the Holocaust: Proceedings of the Ninth Yad Vashem International Historical Conference (Jerusalem, June 1993)* (Jerusalem: Yad Vashem, 1996), pp. 613–634.

Markovits, Andre S. and Novek, Beth Simon, "The World Reacts to the Holocaust—West Germany," in: Wyman D. (ed.), *The World Reacts to the Holocaust* (Baltimore: Johns Hopkins University Press, 1996), pp. 391–446.

Michman, Dan, "The Impact of the Holocaust on Religious Jewry," in Yisrael Gutman (ed.), *Major Changes Within the Jewish People in the Wake of the Holocaust: Proceedings of the Ninth Yad Vashem International Historical Conference (Jerusalem, June 1993)* (Jerusalem: Yad Vashem, 1996), pp. 659–707.

Nora, Pierre, "Between Memory and History: Les Lieux de Mémoire," [The Sites of Memory], *Representations*, No. 26, Special Issue: Memory and Counter-Memory (Spring 1989), pp. 7–24.

Novick, Peter, "That is Past and We Must Deal with the Facts Today," in *Holocaust in American Life* (Boston: Houghton Mifflin, 1999), pp. 85–102.

Ofer Dalia, "The World Reacts to the Holocaust—Israel," in D. Wyman (ed.), *The World Reacts to the Holocaust* (Baltimore: Johns Hopkins University Press, 1996), pp. 836–923.

Parsons, William S. and Totten, Samuel, "Teaching and Learning about Genocide: Questions of Content, Rational and Methodology," *Social Education*, Vol. 55, No. 2, 1991, pp. 84–90.

Pate, Glenn S., "The Treatment of the Holocaust in Textbooks—The United States of America," in R. Braham (ed.), *The Treatment of the Holocaust in Textbooks* (New York: Boulder Institute for Holocaust Studies of the City University of New York, 1987), pp. 232–310.

Porter, Jack Nusan, *Genocide and Human Rights* (Lanhan: University Press of America, 1982).

Renn, Walter F., "The Treatment of the Holocaust in Textbooks—The Federal Republic of Germany: Germans, Jews and Genocide," in R. Braham (ed.), *The Treatment of the Holocaust in Textooks* (New York: Boulder Institute for Holocaust Studies of the City University of New York, 1987), pp. 3–15, 113–130.

Rousso, Henry, *The Vichy Syndrome: History and Memory in France since 1944* (translated from the French by Arthur Goldhammer) (Cambridge, MA and London, England: Harvard University Press, 1991).

Shavit, Zohar, *A Past Without Shadow: The Construction of the Past Image in the German "Story" for Children*. Forthcoming in English.

Shiman, David and Fernekes, Willam R., "The Holocaust, Human Rights and Democratic Citizenship Education," *The Social Studies*, vol. 90, 1999, pp. 53–62.

Shnur, Emma, "Pédagogiser la Shoa?" *Débat*, 96, 1997, pp. 122–140.

Shnur, Emma, "La morale et l'histoire," *Débat*, 96, 1997, pp. 159–165.

Short, Geoffery, Supple, Carrie, and Klinger, Katherine, *The Holocaust in the School Curriculum: A European Perspective* (Strasbourg: Council of Europe, 1998).

Smith, Tom W., *Holocaust Denial: What the Survey Data Reveal* (New York: The American Jewish Committee, 1995).

Strom, Stern Margot and Parsons, William S., *Facing History and Ourselves: Holocaust and Human Behavior* (Watertown, MA: International Education, Inc. 1982 and 1994; revised Edition).

Tatz, Colin, "The Politics of Genocide (Course Syllabus)," in Joyce Freedman-Apsel and Helen Fein (eds.), *Teaching About Genocide* (New York: The Institute for the Study of Genocide, 1992), pp. 72–77.

Totten, Samuel, "Educating about Genocide: Curricular and Inservice Training," in Israel Charny (ed.), *Genocide: A Critical Bibliographic Review*, Vol. 2 (New York: Facts on File, 1993), pp. 194–209.

United States Holocaust Memorial Museum, Washington, D.C., *Guidelines for Teaching About the Holocaust* (Third Revised Printing, 1994).

Weitz, Yechiam, "Shaping the Memory of the Holocaust in Israeli Society of the 1950s," in Yisrael Gutman (ed.), *Major Changes in the Jewish People in the Wake of the Holocaust: Proceedings of the Ninth Yad Vashem International Historical Conference (Jerusalem, June 1993)* (Jerusalem: Yad Vashem, 1996), pp. 497–518.

Wiesel, Elie, "Then and Now: The Experiences of a Teacher," *Social Education*, 42, 4, 1978, pp. 266–271.

Wyman, David S., "The World Reacts to the Holocaust—The United States," in D. Wyman (ed.), *The World Reacts to the Holocaust* (Baltimore: Johns Hopkins University Press, 1996), pp. 693–748.

Yerushalmi, Yosef Hayim, *Zakhor: Jewish History and Jewish Memory* (Seattle and London: University of Washington Press, 1982).

Young, James E., *The Texture of Memory: Holocaust Memorials and Meaning* (New Haven: Yale University Press, 1993).
Young, James E., *Writing and Rewriting the Holocaust* (Bloomington: Indiana University Press, 1998).
Zerubavel, Yael, "The Death of Memory and the Memory of Death," *Representations*, No. 45 (Winter, 1994), pp. 72–100.
Zrubavel Yael, "The Dynamics of Collective Remembering," in: *Recovered Roots* (*The Making of Israeli National Tradition*), Chicago: The University of Chicago Press, 1994, pp. 3–12.

Index

Aborigines, 163
Adalian, Rouben, 164, 171
Adenauer, Konrad, 131, 133
Afghanistan, 139
American Jewish Committee, x, xxi, 142-144, 152
Amichai, Yehuda, v, x, 2, 6, 59, 63
Anderson, Benedict, 13, 29
Anti-Semitism, xix, 106
App, Austin J., 113
Armenian/Armenians, 8, 100, 115, 117, 119, 123, 139, 140, 148, 154, 160, 163, 164, 166, 168, 169, 171, 172
Atomic bomb, 8, 119, 139
Auron, Yair, ix, xxiii, 77, 151, 172
Auschwitz, x, 1, 7, 9, 12, 57, 67, 68, 70, 87, 96-99, 134, 138-139, 143, 147, 152

Bar-On, Dan, 28-29, 30, 76, 77, 85, 90
Ben-Amos, Avner, 60, 61, 64
Benigni, Roberto, xv
Berlin
  Wall, The, xx, 129, 140
  central monument in memory of victims of the Holocaust in, xvi, 141
Bet-El, Ilana, 60, 61, 64
Biafra, 8
Bishara, Azmi, 82, 84
Blair, Tony, 99
Brug, Muli, 25, 29
Butz, Arthur, 113

Calley, Lt. William L., 123
Carmon, Arye, 39, 40, 46, 49, 53, 57
Carrington, Bruce, 100, 151
Carter, Jimmy, 109
Chaumont, Jean-Michel, 168, 172

Chetrit, Sammy Shalom, 62
Civil religion, 68, 69, 76, 77

Dachau, 57, 140, 157
Dawidowicz, Lucy S., 118, 120-123, 151
Democide, 156, 159, 171
Dialogue, Israeli-Palestinian, 80, 83,
Dialogue, Jewish-Christian, xix, 106
Diaspora, xvi, 8, 9, 16, 32, 33, 49, 65, 70, 73, 74
Diaspora Museum, 44, 49

Eastern Europe, xx, 48, 101, 102, 130
Eichmann, Adolph, xviii, 18, 20, 27, 33, 37, 38, 61, 105-108, 123, 157
Eldad, Yisrael, x, 88, 89, 90
Elkana, Yehuda, x, 87-89, 90, 95
England (*see* Great Britain)
Ethnocide, 156
Evron, Boaz, x, 88, 90
Exodus, 105
Expulsion, Spanish, xvii, 70

Facing History and Ourselves, 114-115, 117-120, 122-124, 151
Fascism, x, xx, 74, 88, 90, 91
Fackenheim, Emile, 11
Farago, Uri, 75-76, 77
Farantouri, Maria, 58
Farrakhan, Louis, 119
Fassbinder, Rainer Werner, 138
Federal Republic of Germany, 131, 141
Fein, Helen, 160, 171
Feldman, Jackie, x, 66-68, 71
Finkelstein, Norman, 86, 90
Firer, Ruth, 36, 40
Forges, Jean-François, 97, 151
Foss, Clive, 160, 171
France, xviii, xix, xxi, 4, 93

183

during Vichy Period, 92-93, 151
reactions to the Holocaust, 4, 93-94, 113, 168
teaching about the Holocaust in, 41, 92-99, 100, 113, 115, 143-148
Frank, Anna, 99, 105

Generation, The 1948, 22, 29
Genocide, ix, xi, xiv, xv, xvi, 5, 8, 10, 11, 12, 27, 36, 153, 154, 155, 156, 158, 159, 160, 161, 162, 163, 164, 165, 166, 167, 168, 169, 170, 171, 172, 174
"bystanders," 29, 55. 118, 125, 163
in Cambodia, 100, 117, 119, 139, 148, 156, 160
in comparative perspective of the Holocaust, 23, 109, 114, 118, 124, 130, 135, 148, 153, 154, 160, 165, 173
in former Yugoslavia, 100, 148, 155
of the Gypsies/Roma, 100, 118, 124, 126, 139, 154, 166-168
in Rwanda, 10, 100, 117, 119, 148, 155
teaching of in Israel, xxii, 36, 65-71
teaching of throughout the world, xxii-xxiii, 91-152, 173
UN Convention on the Prevention and Punishment of the Crime of Genocide (UNGC), 157, 163
Germany, xvi, xxi, 18, 19, 41, 46, 66, 86, 87, 101, 103, 106, 144, 151, 167
Denazification, 130, 134
East, xx, 129, 140, 152
Reactions to the Holocaust in, 128-143
teaching about the Holocaust in, 28, 53, 92, 115, 144-150
West, xxi, 18, 129, 132, 140, 143
Ghetto/ghettos, 6, 13, 15, 19, 21, 25, 26, 29, 33, 34, 60, 61, 68, 74, 83, 84, 94, 104, 105, 108
Gorny, Yosef, x, 7, 12
Grass, Günther, 135
Great Britain
reactions to the Holocaust in, xix, 99, 143, 144, 150

teaching about the Holocaust in, xix, xxi, 92, 99-101, 113, 115
Greenberg, Yitzchak, 62
Grossman, David, 81-82, 84
Gubran, Salaam, 79, 83
Guri, Rosenblit, Sarah 48, 49
Gur-Ze'ev, Ilan, ix, 80, 83, 165, 172
Gutman, Yisrael, x, 12, 29, 39, 40, 51, 55, 57, 58
Gutwein, Daniel, 26-27, 30
Gypsies (*see* Roma)

Habermas, Jürgen, 140
Halbwachs, Maurice, 3-5
Hersey, John, 105
Hilberg, Raul, 106, 151
Hillgruber, Andreas, 140
Hiroshima (atomic bombing of), 119, 139
Historians' Debate (in Germany), 139-140
Historical revisionism (also Historians' Debate), 94, 139-140
Historiography, xvi, 4, 25, 26, 29, 30, 119
German, of the Holocaust, 135, 139
History, xii, xiii, xix, xxiii, 3, 4, 5, 6, 8, 14, 23, 25, 26, 29, 32, 34, 39, 40, 43, 44, 45, 48, 49, 53, 54, 56, 59, 62, 63, 64, 74, 80, 81, 82, 85, 87, 88, 92, 96, 97, 98, 111, 114-130, 136, 139, 140, 141, 142, 143, 144, 151, 153, 159, 168, 170
general/world, xv, xvii, 36, 39, 41, 55, 112, 120, 139, 167
Jewish, xv, xvii, xxi, xxiii, 5, 10, 11, 12, 21, 31, 33, 36, 41, 49, 55, 58, 64, 74, 111, 121, 137, 141, 152, 169
Hochhuth, Rolf, 106
Holland, xviii, xix
Holocaust, The
Argentina (knowledge and attitudes), 143-150
attitude of the Yishuv in Palestine to (prior to establishment of Israel), 14, 19, 24-25, 86
attitudes of Israeli Arabs to, 79-84
Australia (knowledge and attitudes), 41, 143-150, 159

Index 185

Austria (knowledge and attitudes), 142-143-150
Czech Republic, Czechoslovakia (knowledge and attitudes), 65, 115, 143, 145-150
denial of, 94, 138
France, xix, xxi, 4, 41, 92-94, 99-100, 113, 115, 143-150
Germany, xvi, xx-xxi, 28, 53, 92, 128-150
Great Britain, 92, 99-101, 143-144, 150
and Heroism, 13-17, 20, 23-25, 35, 151
Israel (youth), x, 32, 36, 49, 70-71
Jewish lessons of, xii, 63
knowledge of, x, 33, 39, 48, 93, 113, 117-118, 142, 143-150, 160, 166, 170
lessons of, xi, 9, 11-13, 16, 24, 39, 52, 87, 88, 123, 135
particularistic lessons of, xii
Poland, xiv, 63, 74, 83, 112, 143, 145-150
"privatization," of 26-27, 30
and rebirth, 2, 14, 17, 20-21, 22-23, 60
Russia (knowledge and attitudes), 143, 145-150
survivors of, 14, 86, 130
Sweden (knowledge and attitudes), 143, 145-150
Switzerland (knowledge and attitudes), 143, 145-150
teaching of, xiii, xiv, xv, xxii, xxiii, 31-49
theological reactions to, 7
uniqueness of, 8, 23, 43, 62, 69, 142, 168-170
United States, 7-8, 41, 53, 62, 92, 101-103, 104-105, 107-110, 112, 114, 118, 120, 124, 127-128, 138, 143-150, 151, 154, 160, 161, 168
universal lessons of, xii, 52, 91
Zionist lessons of, xii, 16, 23, 24, 39

International Criminal Court (ICC), 154, 158

Israel
 journeys of youth to Poland, 36, 61, 63, 65-71, 74, 83, 88-90, 167
 Teaching in Israel, xiii, xxii, 31-40
 (*see also* Law)

Jehovah's Witnesses, 123, 124, 168
John Paul II (Pope), 106
Journeys of youth to Poland, 36, 61, 63, 65-71, 74, 83, 88-90, 167
Joutard, Philippe, 98, 151
Judenraat, 6

Kambanelis, Iakovos, x, 56, 58
Kapos, 6
Karissa, al- (disaster), 80
Kasztner, Israel (Rezso, Rudolf), 18-19
Kedma (high school), 61-63, 64
Keren, Nili, 36-37, 40, 55, 58, 77
Kishinev (pogrom), 102
Kovner, Abba, 37, 44, 49
Kramer, Stanley, 106
Kristallnacht, 103, 140, 141

Lanzmann, Claude, xv, 97, 98
Law
 Holocaust Martyrs' and Heroes' Remembrance Day Law, 16-17, 34
 Knesset Law for the Prevention and Punishment of the Crime of Genocide (5710/1950), 157
 Law for the Punishment of Nazis and Nazi Collaborators, 1950, 20, 157
 State Education, 1953, 13, 35
 State Education, Amended, 1980, 35
 Yad Vashem, 1953 (*see also* Yad Vashem, Law), 16-17, 23, 35, 37
Leibman, Charles, 76, 77
Lemkin, Raphael, 154-155
Levi, Primo, v, 1, 6, 97, 169
Life is Beautiful, xv
Lipstadt, Deborah, E., 118-120, 151
Littell, Franklin, 10-11, 12

Mann, Thomas, 134
March of the Living, The, 65
Masada, 5, 25-26, 29
Mauthausen, 56-57

Memorial, 2, 15, 16-17, 18, 33, 47, 51, 59, 60, 61, 67, 68, 83, 95, 99, 100, 108-111, 114, 124, 140, 167, 168
   ceremonial assemblies, 59, 60-61, 74, 111
   law for day of, 15-17, 59-60, 61
Memory
   agents of, xiv
   collective, xiii, xvii, xxii, 1-6, 20, 21, 22, 24-26, 29, 44, 61, 84, 87, 91, 93, 138, 140, 143, 172
   construction of, 1-6, 25-27, 51, 88, 110, 141, 151
   individual, 3
Mercy killing, 96
Michman, Dan, xxiii, 9, 12, 82, 84, 90
Moreshet, x, 40, 49, 71, 83
Mount Herzl, 16
Murders, mass, in, 139, 140, 155-156, 170
   Cambodia, 117, 119, 139, 156
   Laos, 117, 119
   Rwanda, 117, 119
   Tibet, 117, 119
Museum/Museums
   Diaspora, 44, 49
   Ghetto Fighters' House (in Israel), 34, 74, 83-84
   Hashoah Museum of Tolerance (in Los Angeles), 110
   Holocaust Memorial (in Washington, D.C.), x, xv, 114, 167
   Jewish (in Berlin), 141

Nagasaki, atomic bombing of, 119, 139
Naqba (Palestinian tragedy), 80, 83
Negation of the Golah (the Exile), 31
Nolte, Ernest, 139
Nora, Pierre, xii, xvi, xxiii, 4-6, 26
Novick, Peter, 85-86, 90, 114, 151

Ofer, Dalia, 32, 35-36, 40, 49
Ophir, Adi, 68-69, 71

Pappe, Ilan, 80, 83
Parsons, William S., 151, 161, 164, 171, 172
Pianist, The, xv

Pius XII (Pope), 106
Pol Pot, 139, 156
Polanski, Roman, xv
Poland
   Israeli youth visits to, x, 36, 65-71, 88, 90
Poles, 28, 60, 110, 124, 168
Politicide, 155-156
Popowski, Mikhal, 58
Porter, Jack Nusan, 163-164, 171
Post-Zionism, Post-Zionists, 27, 86-87, 90
Protocols of the Elders of Zion, 103

Reagan, Ronald, 138
Reich, The Third, 28, 30, 52, 54, 87, 129, 135-136, 139-140, 141, 143, 168
Remembrance days
   Holocaust Martyrs' and Heroes' Remembrance Day, xiv, 16-17, 34, 59-64, 74
   Memorial Day or the Fallen in Israel's Wars, 59, 60, 61
Reparations (from Germany), 18-19, 34, 65, 131-133
Resistance, xviii, 20, 24, 25, 26, 54, 93, 125
Roma (Gypsies), 100, 110, 118, 124, 126, 139, 154, 166-168
Roosevelt, Franklin Delano, 103
Rosenberg, Stuart, 106
Rousso, Henry, 93, 151
Rummel, R. J., 156, 171

S.S., 1, 28, 46, 130, 134, 138
Santayana, George, 121
Schatzker, Haim, 38-39, 40, 42, 45, 49, 51, 57
Schindler's List, xv, 109, 141
Selah, Oron, 76, 77
Shamir, Moshe, 32, 40
Shavit, Zohar, 130, 143, 151, 152
Shnur, Emma, 94-98, 151
Shoah, xv, 55-56, 58, 97, 110, 154
Short, Geoffrey 100, 151, 171
Sivan, Emmanuel, 22, 29
Slavs, Slavic Peoples, 124, 139
Spielberg, Steven, xv, 109, 110

St. Louis steamship, 106
Stalin, Joseph, 114, 117, 139, 140, 155-156
Stauber, Roni, 151
Strom, Margot Stern, 116-118, 151
Students' Revolt (France), 93

Tatz, Colin, 163, 171
Theodorakis, Mikis, 58
Totten, Samuel, 161, 171
Trial/Trials
   Auschwitz, 134
   Eichmann, xviii, 18, 20, 27, 33, 38, 61, 107, 108, 157
   Nuremberg, 19, 130-131
Tsabar Ben-Yehoushua, Na'ama, 48, 49
Turkey, 100, 140, 164, 169
Tzur, Tova, 66, 70

Ukrainians, starvation of, 160
United States of America
   destruction, genocide of Native Americans in, 117, 123
   reactions to the Holocaust in, 7, 41, 62, 85, 94, 101-111, 138, 143-150, 151
   teaching of the Holocaust in, 53, 92, 103, 111-128, 151, 159-161, 164, 172
Uris, Leon 105

Victims
   of genocide acts throughout the world, 99, 158
   Gypsies, Roma, 100, 118, 124, 126, 139, 154, 166-168
   Homosexuals, 96, 100, 110, 123, 124, 168
   Jehovah's Witnesses, 123, 124, 168
   Jews, 8, 12, 16, 18, 24, 62, 99, 106, 108, 124, 126, 128, 134, 163, 167-168, 170

mentally ill, 96, 168
of the Nazis, xvi, xx, 61-62, 99, 106, 109, 126, 128, 140, 167-168
physically disabled, 124, 168
Poles, 28, 60, 110, 124, 168
Political prisoners/opposes of the rule, 168
Slavs, Slavic Peoples, 124, 139
Soviet prisoners, 124
Vietnam, 123, 139

Wall, The, 105
War
   Algeria, 93
   Lebanon, 27
   Gulf, The, 141
   Six Day, 20-21, 27, 34, 36-38, 61, 86, 108, 134, 136
   World War I, 8, 22, 45, 100, 102, 139
   War of Independence, 2, 14, 22, 32, 80
   Yom Kippur, 34, 36-38, 61, 108, 110
Weber, Dagmar, 138, 152
Weimar, Republic of, 121
Weitz, Yechiam, xxiii, 23, 24, 29
Wenzel, Birgit, 138, 152
Wiesel, Elie, 106, 109, 111, 161, 171

Yad Vashem
   International School for Holocaust Studies, 42-43, 49, 74
   Yad Vashem Law, 16-17, 23, 35
Yerushalmi, Yosef Hayim, xv-xvii, xxiii, 10

Zerubavel, Yael, 5, 6, 25-26, 29
Zionism, xii, 12, 25, 32, 39, 69, 70, 74, 86
   ideology of, xiii, 80, 89